Mary Olivia Nutting

The Days of Prince Maurice

The Story of the Netherland War from the Death of William the Silent to its Close,

1584-1648

Mary Olivia Nutting

The Days of Prince Maurice
The Story of the Netherland War from the Death of William the Silent to its Close, 1584-1648

ISBN/EAN: 9783337169374

Printed in Europe, USA, Canada, Australia, Japan

Cover: Foto ©ninafisch / pixelio.de

More available books at **www.hansebooks.com**

The Days of Prince Maurice

THE STORY OF THE NETHERLAND WAR FROM
THE DEATH OF WILLIAM THE SILENT
TO ITS CLOSE
1584—1648

By MARY O. NUTTING
(MARY BARRETT)
Author of "William the Silent and the Netherland War"

BOSTON AND CHICAGO
Congregational Sunday-School and Publishing Society

COPYRIGHT, 1894,
BY CONGREGATIONAL SUNDAY-SCHOOL AND PUBLISHING SOCIETY

PREFACE

THE period during which Maurice of Nassau was the leader of the Netherland people is one which claims attention, not only on account of its exciting and memorable events, but even more because of its intimate connection with the subsequent history of England and of America. The writer has aimed to tell the story so that it shall be neither too long to be easily read, nor so condensed as to seem dry.

Among the works most consulted have been those of Motley, Davies, and Grattan, together with Rogers' "Story of Holland" and Markham's "The Fighting Veres." Some original authorities also have been used, particularly Meteren's "History of the Low Countries," and "Les Lauriers de Nassau," by Orlers and Haestens, a very rare book published at Leyden in 1612, which narrates the victories won while Prince Maurice was commander-in-chief. It is illustrated with many careful representations of battles and sieges, and gives an excellent portrait of the prince, which is reproduced here.

M. O. N.

MOUNT HOLYOKE COLLEGE,
   SOUTH HADLEY, MASS.

CONTENTS.

I.
HOW MATTERS STOOD IN 1584.
The two sections of the seventeen provinces. — How the republic was governed. — A republic unwillingly. — Area of the provinces. — Population 13

II.
ANTWERP BESIEGED.
Importance of Antwerp. — Philip's commander-in-chief. — Location of the city. — Parma's first steps. — How Antwerp was governed. — Quarrels and follies. — Parma prepares to bridge the Scheldt 19

III.
PARMA'S BRIDGE AND THE FIRE SHIPS.
Pile-driving. — The floating bridge. — The river closed. — Fall of Brussels. — Gianibelli and his "hell burners." — The great explosion. — "Koppen-Loppen" forgets the rocket. — The bridge repaired 31

IV.
THE FIGHT ON THE KOWENSTYN DIKE.
Gianibelli's new fire ship. — Strength of the Kowenstyn dike. — The assault. — The dike broken. — Desperate fighting. — Strange apparition. — Premature rejoicing at Antwerp. — Defeat and despair. — The capitulation. — Parma's triumphal entry. — Citadel rebuilt. — Consequences to the city 42

V.

MATTERS BETWEEN THE NETHERLANDERS AND THEIR NEIGHBORS.

Protection of France desired. — Reasons for seeking that of England. — Sovereignty of the Netherlands declined by Henry III. — Secret reasons. — Sovereignty offered to Elizabeth. — The queen's speech to the Dutch envoys. — Aid furnished 58

VI.

THE EARL OF LEICESTER IN THE NETHERLANDS.

The queen sends Leicester to the Low Countries. — His reception. — He accepts the position of governor-general. — Delays to inform the queen. — Her displeasure. — Davison intercedes for the earl 70

VII.

MILITARY MOVEMENTS OF PARMA AND LEICESTER.

Unpaid soldiers. — Parma besieges Grave. — Hard fighting. — Treachery of the commander. — Neusz stormed. — First exploit of the young prince. — Zutphen invested by Leicester. — Desperate struggle near Warnsfield church 79

VIII.

SIR PHILIP SIDNEY.

Sidney's ancestry. — Letter of his father. — His youth and travels. — Dissuades the queen from marrying Anjou. — Literary works. — At Flushing. — Wounded at Zutphen. — The cup of water. — Days of suffering. — The chaplain's account of his death. — General mourning. — Spenser's poem 91

IX.

TREASONS AND TROUBLES.

Leicester goes to England. — Is graciously received by the queen. — Treachery of Stanley and York. — Elizabeth's ill temper. — Barneveld's letter to her. — Prince Maurice made the provisional head of the government. — Firmness of the States-General. — The queen sends over Lord Buckhurst 100

X.

LOSS OF SLUYS, AND DRAKE'S BUCCANEERING.

A seaport needful. — Sluys besieged by Parma. — Situation of the city. — The women build a redoubt. — Maurice appointed captain-general. — Return of Leicester. — Surrender of Sluys. — Drake's exploit at Cadiz. — Insincere diplomacy 114

XI.

THE STORY OF THE ARMADA.

The great fleet. — Plans of Philip. — Disasters off Cape Finisterre. — England aroused. — Macaulay's poem. — First skirmishing. — Engagement of August 3. — In Calais Roads. — The fire ships and the panic. — The battle and the pursuit. — Destruction of the Spanish fleet. — England's deliverance. — The Spanish story 124

XII.

HOW BREDA WAS TAKEN.

Treachery at Gertruydenberg. — Unsuccessful naval expedition. — The situation in France. — The League. — Philip's private motives. — Scheme for surprising Breda. — The turf boat towed within the town. — The midnight assault. — Breda won 140

XIII.

PARMA IN FRANCE, AND MAURICE AT HOME.

Paris besieged by Henry of Navarre. — Parma relieves it. — Great military improvements made by Maurice and Lewis William. — Zutphen and Deventer taken. — Verdugo's opinion of Maurice 150

XIV.

THE CLOSE OF PARMA'S CAREER.

Philip's ill treatment of Parma. — Insincerity of the king. — Parma sent to relieve Rouen. — Prepares for a third French campaign. — His death. — Archduke Ernest in the Netherlands. — Assassinations plotted. — Henry IV declares war against Spain. — Death of Archduke Ernest . . . 161

XV.

THE FIRST YEAR OF ARCHDUKE ALBERT.

Albert's character. — Calais besieged. — Elizabeth's proposition. — Calais taken by the Spaniards. — The Dutch and English fleets take Cadiz. — Treaty between Henry IV and Elizabeth. — The Netherland Republic joins the alliance. — Insincerity of the two monarchs. — Second armada sent out by Philip. — Its fate. — Arctic voyages of the Dutch . 172

XVI.

A VICTORY AND A MARTYRDOM.

Battle of Turnhout. — Moral effect of Maurice's victory. — Philip's repudiation of his debts. — The German emperor offers to mediate. — The Polish ambassador's orations. — Elizabeth's ready reply. — Anna van den Hove buried alive 186

XVII.

NEGOTIATING WITH ELIZABETH.

Henry's dealings with Spain. — Elizabeth's attitude. — Dutch envoys at Henry's court. — Stormy interviews with Elizabeth. — Treaty of Vervins 195

XVIII.

LAST DAYS OF PHILIP II.

Philip deeds the Netherlands to his daughter. — He leaves Madrid. — Painful journey. — The Escorial. — The king's sufferings. — His three days' confession. — His directions for his funeral. — His last hours. — Mystery of such a death. — An accomplished pupil of Machiavelli. — A deceiver finally himself deceived 202

XIX.

CAMPAIGNING IN FLANDERS.

Maurice on the defensive. — Voluntary taxation. — The "archdukes" in Brussels. — Their proposition to Elizabeth. — The States-General plan an invasion of Flanders. — Maurice and Lewis William disapprove. — The fleet delayed. — March toward Nieuport. — Albert raises an army . . 212

XX.

THE BRIDGE AT LEFFINGEN.

Sudden council of war. — Count Ernest sent to Leffingen. — Fight with the archdukes' army. — The panic and flight. — The archdukes' council of war. — Anxiety and prayer at Ostend 224

XXI.

THE BATTLE OF NIEUPORT.

News of Count Ernest's defeat. — The fleet ordered to sea. — Arrangements for the battle. — What the prince said to his men. — The first onset. — Lewis Gunther's cavalry charge. — The infantry fight. — Lewis Gunther's repulse. — Maurice rallies the troops. — Victory. — Narrow escape of the archduke. — Thanksgivings. — The admiral bantered. — The news in England. — Coldness between Maurice and Barneveld 231

XXII.

BEGINNING OF THE SIEGE OF OSTEND.

Situation and importance of Ostend. — The garrison. — The archduke begins the siege. — Efforts to blockade the town. — Artillery. — Maurice takes Rheinberg. — Progress of matters at Ostend 248

XXIII.

THE CHRISTMAS PARLEY.

Vere asks a conference. — Hostages and commissioners sent. — Vere maneuvers to gain time. — Second arrival of the Spanish commissioners. — Their evening with Sir Francis

Vere. — The archdukes confidently awaiting the surrender. — Vere reinforced. — Dismisses the commissioners. — His letter to the States-General. — Philip Fleming and his diary. — Preparing for the expected assault. — The storming party fails 257

XXIV.

THE INDIA TRADE, AND THE PROGRESS OF THE WAR.

The English and Dutch East India Companies. — Dutch acquisitions in the East. — Maurice invades Flanders, and afterward captures Grave. — Mutineers of Albert's army. — Death of Elizabeth, and accession of James. — His cool reception of the Netherland envoys 270

XXV.

SIEGE OF OSTEND, Continued.

The external forts lost. — Ambrose Spinola takes command of the Spanish army. — Successive governors of Ostend. — New fortifications built within the old. — "Little Troy" planned 277

XXVI.

SLUYS TAKEN AND OSTEND LOST.

Maurice approaches Sluys. — The Swint held by the enemy. — A circuit made. — More troops sent into the town. — Unsuccessful attempt to send supplies. — Famine severe. — Spinola attempts to relieve the town. — He is repulsed. — Surrender. — A better seaport than Ostend. — Ostend capitulates. — Results of the siege 285

XXVII.

SPINOLA'S INVASION OF THE PROVINCES.

Treaty between James and the archdukes. — Spinola made commander of the archdukes' army. — Reforms introduced. — Invades the United Provinces. — Maurice alert. — Battle of Mülheim, and panic of Maurice's cavalry. —

Progress in the East Indies. — Spinola's second invasion. — Takes Groenlo and Rheinberg. — Complaining. — A naval battle. — Vice-Admiral Klaaszoon 296

XXVIII.
HOW THE TWELVE YEARS' TRUCE WAS MADE.

The peace party and their opposers. — First move made by the archdukes. — Difficulty of opening negotiations. — Armistice of eight months proposed. — Attempt to bribe Aerssens. — The king's ratification. — Victory of Heemskirk's fleet at Gibraltar. — Arrival of the ambassadors at The Hague. — The Provinces refuse to give up the India trade, or to permit public Roman Catholic worship. — Negotiations broken off. — The English and French ambassadors offer to mediate. — Conferences resumed at Antwerp. — The three indispensable points are yielded by Spain. — The truce proclaimed 306

XXIX.
WHAT HAPPENED DURING THE TRUCE.

English Puritans settle at Leyden. — Draining of the Beemster Lake. — Jeannin proposes amendments to the Dutch constitution. — The Bank of Amsterdam. — Beginning of the Arminian controversy. — Remonstrants and Contra-remonstrants. — The five points of Arminianism. — Politics and theology mixed. — The Synod of Dort. — Treatment of the Remonstrants. — Canons of Dort. — Sentence of the Arminian clergy. — The Heidelberg catechism. — Estimates of the synod 323

XXX.
BARNEVELD'S TRIAL AND EXECUTION.

Alienation of the prince. — Barneveld arrested by his order. — Intercession of Louis XIII in behalf of Barneveld. — Unfairness of the trial. — The prisoner's last evening. — Sentence pronounced. — The execution. — Excitement against the Remonstrants. — Banishment of their ministers 336

XXXI.

AFTER THE TRUCE.

The English Puritans in Leyden. — Reasons for emigration to America. — Consequences of their going. — Louvestein. — Grotius and his wife. — She plans his escape. — The maid's care of the chest. — Grotius welcomed at the French court. — State of the Provinces at the close of the truce. — Spinola besieges Bergen-op-Zoom. — Conspiracy of Barneveld's sons. — New alliances with France and England. — Spinola lays siege to Breda. — Maurice unable to relieve it. — His failing health and death. — His character 346

XXXII.

THE CONCLUSION.

Frederic Henry becomes commander-in-chief. — Treaty of Westphalia. — Growth of the Provinces during the war. — Manufactures. — Agriculture and horticulture. — Learning and art. — The example of the Netherlands a benefit to the world. — Its great influence on the history of England and America 358

THE DAYS OF PRINCE MAURICE.

CHAPTER I.

HOW MATTERS STOOD.

ON the tenth of July, 1584, the great and good Prince of Orange, William the Silent, was shot in his own house at Delft. The assassin, Balthasar Gérard, had been hired by Philip II. The Netherland people were in the thickest of their long conflict with Spain, and the loss of their great leader was overwhelming. There was no one who could fill his place. A medal commemorating those dark days bears the emblem of a storm-tossed bark, and the inscription, *Incerta quo fata ferent.*[1] But a divine hand was upon the helm; the vessel was not destined to go down. The young son of the martyred prince, in his studious seclusion, was being prepared to become their commander, and at length to accomplish the nation's deliverance.

The struggle of the Netherland provinces to throw off the intolerable yoke of the Inquisition and of

---

[1] "Not knowing whither the fates may lead."

Spain had now been going on for sixteen years; and although it was much to be no longer living under the cruel "edicts," to have seen the last of Alva and the "Council of Blood," to have won — whether in defeat or victory — records so glorious as those of Harlem and of Leyden, not many then alive would see the end of the war. It was to outlast two generations more.

Seldom, if ever, has the world witnessed a contest so remarkable. The succession of events which led to it, the immense odds against which the Netherlanders fought, their splendid daring and wonderful persistency, as well as the far-reaching consequences of their victory, all combine to render it memorable forever. "It was a war," says an eminent professor of history,[1] "in which the highest principles were vindicated, and vindicated irreversibly. In those principles lies the very life of modern liberty. The debt which rational and just government owes to the seven provinces is incalculable. Holland is the Holy Land of modern Europe."

For the first ten years all the provinces were united in carrying on the war; but later the ten forming the southern portion of the low countries and nearly identical with the modern Belgium were beguiled again into allegiance to Spain. Thenceforth they were called

[1] Thorold Rogers, in the preface of The Story of Holland.

the Spanish Netherlands, or the "obedient" provinces; and were governed by a viceroy of the Spanish king. No Protestants were allowed to reside there, though some remained in cities not yet subdued.

After the ten southern provinces had deserted the patriotic cause, the remaining seven, led by William and his brother, Count John of Nassau, had formed, in January, 1579, what was called the Union of Utrecht. This confederation served a good purpose for a long time, though it was not all that could have been desired. The seven provinces bound themselves to stand shoulder to shoulder in carrying on the war, but each retained control of its internal matters as before. Public affairs were administered by the Estates-General, a body composed of deputies from each province. It was often called simply "The States." We must bear in mind, however, that this term referred to the members constituting the assembly, not to the provinces sending them. Each province also had its own "states" to manage its internal affairs; and each chose its own stadtholder, or governor. It often happened, however, that the same person was stadtholder of more than one province. William was stadtholder of both Holland and Zealand, which were the leading members of the confederation, as the two provinces together furnished about seven tenths of the entire revenue.

The United Provinces had no thought of becoming a republic until long after this. It had not occurred to them that a nation could be its own ruler; they expected either to make Philip of Spain concede the liberties for which they were fighting, in which case they would remain his subjects, or, which was more likely, they would get some better monarch to take them under his protection. They had begun to make efforts in that direction, inasmuch as their beloved Prince of Orange would not consent to become their sovereign. Indeed, the duke of Anjou, a brother of the king of France, had been formally installed as ruler of the five smaller provinces in 1582. His position was not one of great power, but somewhat like that of the president of a republic, except that it was to descend to his children, should he have any. But Anjou proved to be so bad a man that it was a deliverance, rather than a loss, to the provinces when he died in June, 1584.

In reading of such a war, it is difficult to realize that the territory of the young nation that carried it on was not quite as large as the state of Massachusetts and half the state of Vermont. What is now called Holland, which is very nearly the same as the seven provinces, contains only 12,630 square miles. The area of the ten obedient provinces was then nearly the same; but the modern Belgium has lost something on the side next to France, so that it contains about a thousand square miles less. Nor should it be forgotten that what land the little republic had was very liable to be under water. Yet this inconvenient circumstance had its advantages. In their never-ending struggle with the encroaching sea its people got no small part of the discipline which enabled them to hold out in a war of eighty years, and to conquer at last. The slenderness of their country's natural resources made them not only a hard-working and thrifty people, in an extraordinary degree, but it sent them abroad on the seas to explore, and to establish an extensive commerce with distant lands. Their foreign dominions in time became much larger than their native country.

The population of the United Provinces was far greater in proportion to their territory than is the present population of the section of New England already mentioned; indeed it was absolutely greater. In 1888 the inhabitants of Massachusetts were estimated to number 2,044,504; half the population of Vermont was 166,500; in all, 2,211,004. At the beginning of the war, in 1568, the population of all the seventeen provinces was about three millions; but in 1609 that of the seven United Provinces is stated by Motley to have been 3,500,000. The northern provinces had greatly increased in population in spite of the war; while the southern, or obedient provinces, had dwindled. A table is given in the work, "Les Lauriers de Nassau," from which it appears that in 1610 there were in the seven provinces of the republic — namely, Holland, Zealand, Utrecht, Gelderland, Overyssel, Groningen, and Friesland — one hundred and five cities and towns, and four hundred and sixty-two villages. This slight *résumé* of the situation will make it easy to go on with the story.

CHAPTER II.

ANTWERP BESIEGED.

THE siege of Antwerp was the next great event of the war. It had been foreseen by William of Orange months before Parma had begun any visible preparation for it; and early in June, 1584, he had taken occasion to warn several of the leading personages of that city, who were at Delft to attend the christening of the infant Frederic Henry. He had not only told them in what manner Parma would attempt to reduce Antwerp, but also how his schemes might be completely foiled. It was not long before they had sorrowful occasion to remember his words.

There were weighty reasons why the Spaniards wanted to get Antwerp just then. Some of them were perfectly obvious. It was a city of immense wealth, and at this period was the commercial metropolis of the Low Countries, if not of all Europe. Five thousand merchants daily assembled in its magnificent Exchange. Meteren asserts that "as many as seven or eight hundred ships and boats have been seen arriving from various quarters at once." He adds: "We have seen a calculation from which it appears that the city of Antwerp the year before the war, and even during the siege, had 1,726,000 florins of annual revenue." Then its position, in the very heart of the region which was now the scene of the war, with the republic of the United Netherlands on the north and the " reconciled " provinces on the south, gave it great strategic importance. The Spanish soldiers used to say to the people: " If we get Antwerp, you shall all go to mass with us ; if you save Antwerp, we will all go to conventicle with you." But there was another reason, not less weighty though not yet so obvious : Philip's great project for conquering England, which had long been secretly simmering, would make it indispensable for him to have the best port in the Netherlands in which to marshal his invincible fleet. And there was no harbor like that of Antwerp. In the broad and deep Scheldt all the fleets of Europe might safely lie at anchor. Once mustered there, his Armada could sail across some fine morning and conquer England with no trouble at all. So it was determined that Antwerp should be taken.

It was just before the siege began that William the Silent was assassinated. The death of this great leader was like losing the pilot in the midst of the storm. The Spaniards, on the contrary, never had a better commander than now. Alexander Farnese, prince of Parma, was one of the ablest generals of

ALEXANDER FARNESE, PRINCE OF PARMA.
From Bor's History of the Netherlands, 1621.

this hard-fighting age. He was the nephew of Philip II and grandson of Charles V on the mother's side; while on the father's, he was great-grandson of Pope Paul III. He had already had much experience in war, and had won distinguished success, although only thirty-eight years of age. His fine, imposing figure, his bold, handsome countenance, his alert, decided air, all combined to make men stand in awe of him. Though quick and keen in his perceptions, he was cool and sagacious in conduct. His energy was untiring, his perseverance endless.

But what he had now to do was likely to prove no easy task, even for so consummate a general as Alexander of Parma. Like his predecessors, he had learned that it was a serious business to attack a Netherland city, even when, as at Maestricht, he had as many troops outside the walls as there were citizens within, and nobody to interfere. Over and above all the ordinary and respectable methods of defense, these unscrupulous Netherlanders had a way of welcoming their assailants with kettles of boiling oil, molten lead, or blazing pitch. Moreover, his present forces were not adequate to storming the city. If Antwerp could be taken at all, it would have to be done by a blockade. To accomplish this it would be necessary to bridge the river — a piece of work evidently not to be done in a hurry.

Antwerp lies upon the right bank of the Scheldt, which at this point is nearly half a mile wide and sixty feet deep. The rise and fall of the tide is usually about eleven feet. For a long way above the city the general direction of the river is northeasterly, but as it reaches Antwerp it takes a turn and runs northwesterly thence to the sea. Twelve or fifteen English miles below the city it divides into broad estuaries embracing the islands of South Beveland and Walcheren. The fertile lowlands on either side of the river are preserved from constant inundation only by a vast system of dikes stretching along its sides in parallel lines and occasionally meeting other dikes running at right angles with them. By breaking down certain of these bulwarks, and thus inundating the whole of the lowland, the citizens could have made it impossible for Parma to blockade Antwerp by bridging the Scheldt, or indeed in any other manner. It was this step which William had strongly urged upon them only a few weeks before his death. But most of the inhabitants did not yet see the necessity for a measure so extreme.

During the early part of the summer Parma was busy in building detached forts along the river, and it presently became apparent what they were for. Brussels, Ghent, and Antwerp form the angles of a nearly equilateral triangle, measuring about thirty miles on each side. Halfway between Ghent and Antwerp, upon the Scheldt, is Dendermonde; while between Brussels and Antwerp, upon branches of the Scheldt, are Vilvoorden and Mechlin. By means of these new forts these neighboring cities were to be prevented from helping either Antwerp or each other. Meanwhile, since bribery could never come amiss, and might save much hard fighting, Parma was doing his best to win everybody whom it was thought safe to approach in that way. "The ducats of Spain, Madame," wrote the French envoy to the queen-dowager, Catherine de Médicis, "are trotting about in such fashion that they have already vanquished a great quantity of courages. Your majesties too must employ money, if you wish to advance one step." For the people of the Netherlands, in order to secure aid, were at this time disposed to offer the sovereignty of their country either to England or to France; and the French king wished to have the pleasure of refusing it.

The Antwerpers were quite easy for a long time, flattering themselves that they could get assistance from Henry of Valois, if by chance they should need it, which seemed not at all likely. "The preparations went on before our very noses," said one of them, "and every one was ridiculing the Spanish commander's folly." The river was too broad, too deep, its ocean tides too powerful to be bridled by human hands. It was absurd to dream of such a thing.

The city authorities had indeed been so much influenced by what their prince had urged as to pass an order for piercing the great Blaw-garen dike. Had they actually done it then, Antwerp would have become for the time virtually a seaport, and might have laughed at all that Parma could do. But unfortunately the municipal government was one which afforded opportunity for a vast deal of disputing and interference. The burgomaster, in whom the chief executive authority was of course supposed to reside, had really but little power. In the board of magistrates he had merely a single vote; and his duties elsewhere compelled him to be often absent. He was the nominal head of the board of militia colonels, which claimed a good deal of power; but he could be voted down even there. There were sixteen captains who had the right to come into the meetings of the colonels if they liked, and urge their own views; and eighty other captains to back them if necessary, not to mention boards of ward masters, of selectmen, of fortification, of shipbuilding. All these were claiming equal authority and all wrangling among themselves; so it may easily be imagined how matters went on at the weekly sessions of the general council. As Meteren remarks: "This great number of commanders was the reason why there was no authority."

The burgomaster of this turbulent and imperiled city was Philip de Marnix, lord of Sainte-Aldegonde. It was at the request of the great leader whom the nation had with unspeakable sorrow just buried at Delft that he had accepted the difficult and unenviable office. For twenty years he had been prominent among the patriots of the Netherlands. It was believed to have been he who in 1565 drew up the celebrated document called the Compromise — the league of the Netherland nobles against the Inquisition. Since that day he had fought on many a bloody field, and suffered a long imprisonment for his country's sake. His splendid and versatile talents made him eminent among scholars, poets, and orators, as well as among soldiers and diplomatists. It was he who wrote the national hymn, "Wilhelmus van Nassouwe," which "for three hundred years has rung like a clarion wherever the Netherland tongue is spoken." He was a devout Christian as well as a devoted patriot, and it seemed that the government of Antwerp at this crisis had been committed to a truly good man.

But the task of saving the city was almost too much for mortal patience and wisdom. No sooner was it known that the magistrates had voted to break down the Blaw-garen dike and to open the sluices far down the river than all the Antwerp butchers were furious. To flood the broad meadows defended by the Blaw-garen dike, which extended along the right bank of the river, below the fort of Lillo, would be the undoing of their business. What was to become of the twelve thousand oxen whose rich pastures would thus be abandoned to the sea? How would the Antwerpers get their beef, and how were the butchers to get even their bread?

So the whole guild of the butchers was quickly convened, and they sent a committee of sixteen to protest against this needless and ruinous measure. These were followed by sixteen militia colonels, who went so far as to declare that if the magistrates should persist, the militia would by force prevent the scheme from being carried out. After much time had been wasted in disputes it was decided to let the Blaw-garen dike alone and open the sluices on the other side of the river, near Saftingen. Accordingly the Flemish side was soon flooded nearly to the gates of Antwerp, with the very serious exception of certain highlands at Beveren, Kalloo, and the Doel. But before winter the butchers and the militia colonels discovered to their sorrow that this did not answer the same purpose.

Meanwhile there was much difficulty about laying in the supplies requisite for a siege. The States-General, fully aware that the fate of the nation might hang on that of Antwerp, had voted a large sum for this purpose, Holland and Zealand alone having furnished two hundred thousand florins; and Antwerp was herself to do a good deal besides. It only remained to carry out the order.

The matter was entrusted to Treslong, the admiral of Holland and Zealand, a gallant sailor and a hard fighter, but not possessed of much business talent. Moreover, his crooked and obstinate temper hindered his doing his best. Just then he was sulky because Sainte-Aldegonde favored a French alliance, and also on account of a private quarrel with President Meetkirk. So instead of bestirring himself to provision Antwerp he lingered week after week at Ostend drinking to the health of Queen Elizabeth, who was much more to his taste than Henry of Valois. And Parma, hearing that Treslong was out of humor with his government, improved the opportunity to offer him tempting bribes. The admiral listened and lingered, though he did not yield. Finding that the States-General were growing impatient, — especially after they had brought from Holland thirty *krom-stevens*, which he said were the only kind of vessels he could use in victualling Antwerp, — he stormed and threatened till they sent him to prison.

Much time had thus been wasted and the work was still to be begun. A good deal of grain was brought in by private adventurers, however, as the prospect of a siege made the citizens willing to pay three or four times as much as usual. The swift little boats, convoyed by armed vessels, made nothing of running by Parma's batteries, which by this time were thickly sprinkled along both banks. Sometimes they were captured to be sure, when the Spaniards would coolly cut off the arms and legs of all the crew and send them in the boat drifting up to the city with the rise of the tide. Yet the trade went briskly on until the magistrates of Antwerp took it into their sagacious heads that the skippers were making too profitable a business out of these exciting voyages. Accordingly they decreed that no one should take more than a certain fixed price for grain, and that all consumers should purchase directly from the ships. Of course this put an end to the grain business; it was no longer worth while to run such terrible risks. The ninety thousand persons in Antwerp had to be content with what provisions they had, for there was no prospect of getting any more.

Nine miles below Antwerp there were two fortresses belonging to the States: Lillo was on the Brabant side of the river, and Liefkenshock just opposite, in Flanders. On the tenth of July — the very day when the Prince of Orange was assassinated at Delft — the latter fortress, not yet finished, was surprised and taken. Four hundred of the garrison were butchered, and as many more driven into the river. Fort Lillo sustained a siege of three weeks, during which the Spanish commander Mondragon lost two thousand men. Its defenses proved so strong that at length the besiegers gave up.

After Parma had established as many batteries as he liked all along the river, he set about building his bridge. He had not a large force at his command, — only ten thousand foot and about seventeen hundred horse, — but he did his best with it. He had his headquarters at Kalloo, and half the army was under his personal command; the other half was with the veteran Count Mansfeld, near Stabrock, ten miles down the river on the other side.

At Kalloo quite a little army of mechanics and laborers of all sorts were now toiling incessantly at the grand enterprise, while a multitude of bakers, brewers, and butchers were busy in supplying the commissariat. An immense amount of preliminary work was required in order to provide for the transportation of supplies, as well as the construction of the needful machinery. One item was the digging of a canal from Kalloo to Steeken, a place twelve miles southwest, through which floats of timber, munitions of war, and whatever else was needed might be easily brought.

Before the end of September, Ghent, Dendermonde, and Vilvoorden all capitulated; and the resources of the two former, which were upon the Scheldt, were thus conveniently at the disposal of Parma. The fall of Vilvoorden, within ten miles of Brussels, cut off the chance of communication by water between Brussels and Antwerp; and Mechlin also was closely invested. So the Antwerpers found themselves shut off from all the neighboring cities which might have helped them. The Zealand vessels could not approach to their relief, for though they had effected a shallow inundation by opening sluices far down the river on the Brabant side, the great Blaw-garen and Kowenstyn dikes were still high and dry. The flooding of the lowlands on the Flemish side had even aided their foe, who had thus been enabled to bring a fleet of thirty sail from Ghent by a short cut across the submerged country from Borght to Kalloo. This had saved the risk of running by the guns of Antwerp.

CHAPTER III.

PARMA'S BRIDGE AND THE FIRE SHIPS.

WHILE the citizens were still assuring each other that the Scheldt could never be closed, and the States-General were contriving a plan for taking Zutphen, and the Netherland people generally were expecting an army from France to come to their aid, Parma was industriously driving piles for the ends of his bridge.

A little below Kalloo he had discovered a sand bar stretching across the bed of the river, and this favorable point was accordingly selected. The Scheldt is here twenty-four hundred feet broad and sixty feet deep. The first step was to build a strong fort on each bank. The one on the Flemish side was named Saint Mary, while the other bore the name of Philip, in honor of the king. Next, a host of laborers were set to driving immense piles fifty feet deep into the river bed. Day by day the two parties toiling on either side approached a little nearer each other until they were only thirteen hundred feet apart. Upon the piles were laid huge timbers strongly framed together, which when planked formed a massive roadway twelve feet wide. This was fortified by blockhouses of great thickness all along.

It was now winter, and the severest part of the undertaking still remained to be done. Great blocks of ice, swept in by the tides, came thundering with tremendous violence against the palisade, but it did not give way. The channel was too deep for driving any more piles, and Parma built a floating bridge across the remaining space. It was made of thirty-two barges, each sixty-two feet long and twelve feet wide. These were anchored at stem and stern with loose cables — each boat being twenty-two feet from the next — and all were firmly bound together with quadruple hawsers and chains. Upon the boats rested a framework of heavy timbers, with a plank pathway above and strong parapets at the sides. At each end of each boat was a piece of heavy artillery, well manned. This made a kind of floating battery, with thirty-two guns pointing up the river and the same number pointing down. The bridge was still further protected from assault by two heavy rafts armed with sharp iron prongs and hooks; one of these was anchored a little distance above and the other below the floating portion of the bridge.

On the twenty-fifth of February, 1585, the whole structure was completed, and Parma celebrated the event by a grand military pageant. He had good reason to exult, for an immense work had been done in the face of great obstacles. Some of these anybody could see; others, far more serious, were never known till recent historians deciphered his secret letters to

VICINITY OF ANTWERP

the king. Just then Philip II was so much absorbed with wire-pulling in France and elsewhere that Netherland affairs were rather neglected, and Alexander was often at his wits' end for want of funds. "The million promised me," he wrote, January 15, 1585, "has arrived in bits and morsels, and with so many ceremonies that I have n't ten crowns at my disposal. How I am to maintain even this handful of soldiers — for the army is diminished to such a mere handful that it would astonish your majesty — I am unable to imagine. It would move you to witness their condition. They have suffered as much as is humanly possible." And just after the triumphant completion of the bridge he wrote again of the miserable condition of his army. After describing the forlorn state of those who garrisoned the captured cities he added: "As for the rest of the troops, they are stationed where they have nothing to subsist upon save salt water and the dikes. . . . And I have no money at all, nor do I see where to get a single florin." Fortunately for him, however, the Netherlanders did not know it. One cannot help admiring the indomitable courage and persistency of the prince of Parma, notwithstanding he was on the wrong side.

And now at length the citizens of Antwerp awoke. A massive structure, bristling with artillery, spanned the broad and turbulent river. The impossible had been achieved: the Scheldt was actually closed.

A fortnight after the triumphant inauguration of the fatal bridge there came tidings of the fall of Brussels. During the long siege of that city many persons had literally starved to death. It is related by Strada that there were mothers who poisoned their children and themselves to escape the more horrible and no less certain doom of starvation. The terms of the surrender required the burghers either to leave Brussels forever within two years, or to become Catholics. The liberties of the city were surrendered to the disposal of the king.

In the fate of Brussels Antwerp foresaw her own possible doom, and roused herself to meet the crisis. The bridge must be destroyed, or the city must fall. Sainte-Aldegonde had been doing his utmost; but the dissensions of the various parties and the fatal delusion of looking to France for help had defeated all his attempts thus far.

There was then living in Antwerp an Italian named Gianibelli, who was wonderfully expert in engineering of all kinds, and had once journeyed from Italy to Spain on purpose to offer his services to Philip II. Not receiving much attention, he had returned in high dudgeon, vowing that the Spaniards should yet rue the day when they turned their backs upon him. Naturally, he was more than willing to undertake the destruction of Parma's bridge.

He wanted for this congenial enterprise three small vessels which he had selected from the city fleet, the three together having a capacity of about a thousand tons. But the economical magistrates bade him be content with two, one of seventy, and the other of eighty, tons. One was called the Fortune, the other, the Hope. Smothering his vexation, Gianibelli set to work to convert his little vessels into floating volcanoes, whose explosion should annihilate the bridge. Seven thousand pounds of gunpowder were placed in the hold of each vessel, enclosed in walls of marble masonry five or six feet thick. Above and around each mine were packed immense quantities of cannon balls, chain-shot, iron hooks, tombstones, paving stones, and all sorts of dangerous things. The whole was smoothly covered over with a light flooring of planks and brickwork, upon which lay a pile of ordinary combustibles, as if the vessels were simple fire ships. On the Fortune the mine was to be exploded by a slowmatch; while on the Hope a piece of clockwork was so arranged as to strike fire from a flint at the appointed time.

Just before this grand attempt, the Zealand vessels under command of Justinus of Nassau, assisted by troops from Lillo under Count Hohenlo, made a sudden attack upon their lost fort at Liefkenshock and carried it at a blow. They also seized the fort of Saint Anthony farther down the river. Then they hastened to a point near Fort Saint Mary, hoping to entrench themselves on the end of the broken dike, and thus be able to cannonade the bridge. But

Parma's men were on the spot before them, and they were obliged to give it up.

This took place upon the fourth of April. The bridge was to be blown up on the evening of the fifth. The two "hell-burners" were to be preceded by a fleet of thirty-two small craft, which were simple fire ships, covered with tar and turpentine, and filled with combustibles. These were to be sent down with the ebb tide, eight every half-hour. It was hoped that they would set fire to the raft, and keep the Spaniards busy till the grand explosion should take place.

Unluckily, the management of the affair had been entrusted to Admiral Jacob Jacobzoon, an officer who was commonly called "Runaway Jacob," or "Koppen-Loppen." Like the blunderer he was, he began by dispatching the whole fleet of fire ships, helter-skelter, as fast as he could; and then he sent down the Fortune and the Hope close behind.

It was five or six miles from the city to the bridge, and although the evening was dark, the approaching vessels were discovered silently gliding down the river, before the fires were lighted. Instantly the drums beat to arms, for the Spaniards expected there would be a concerted attack on the bridge, the Zealanders below aiding the Antwerpers above. The bridge, the palisades, the neighboring forts were quickly alive with troops. Parma was now here, now there, crossing and recrossing to give directions, until all was ready. Then he took his position in the blockhouse where the floating bridge joined the palisades, on the side toward Kalloo.

The shadowy forms of the mysterious fleet came nearer and nearer, and the Spaniards strained their eyes with gazing, their ears with striving to catch some sound. Suddenly each vessel flamed up with a fearful glare. The broad river, the troops crowded upon the bridge, and even the very clouds were lighted up with the lurid blaze. The Spaniards stood watching in silence till the little fire ships drifted one after another upon the well-armed raft or grounded on the banks.

Then the two fatal vessels prepared by the cunning Italian came drifting toward the bridge. The pilots, after arranging everything for the explosion, had made their escape unseen. Instead of flaming like the others, these had only a little fire upon the deck. Neither of them was caught by the raft. The Fortune staggered just inside of it, and then went aground near Kalloo. The slowmatch burned out, there was a slight explosion, and nothing more.

A few daring volunteers boarded the vessel to explore while the troops gazing from the bridge made merry over the supposed failure of the whole scheme.

But the Hope had now got between the end of the raft and the shore, and presently she struck with violence against the bridge, close to the blockhouse where the prince of Parma was standing with some of his principal officers around him. While several bold fellows sprang on board to extinguish the little fire that was smoldering there, a young ensign, seized with an overpowering apprehension for his general's safety, fell on his knees before the prince of Parma and vehemently conjured him to leave that spot. At first Alexander refused, but finally yielded to the ensign's passionate entreaties and walked toward Fort Saint Mary. Just as he reached it the explosion took place. In an instant vessel, blockhouse, and two hundred feet of the bridge, with all the soldiers standing upon it, were blown into the air.

"The Scheldt yawned to its lowest depths," says Motley, "and then cast its waters across the dikes, deep into the forts, and far over the land. The earth shook as with the throb of a volcano. A wild glare lighted up the scene for one moment, and was succeeded by pitchy darkness. Houses were toppled down miles away, and not a living thing, even in remote places, could keep its feet. The air was filled with a rain of plowshares, gravestones, and marble balls, intermixed with the heads, limbs, and bodies of what had been human beings. . . . A thousand soldiers were destroyed in a second of time, many of them being torn to shreds beyond even the semblance of humanity."

Several of Parma's most eminent officers perished in the catastrophe. Alexander himself was struck senseless by a flying stake; and as he was known to have been upon the fatal spot but a moment before, the horrified survivors at once inferred that their leader was no more. All was consternation and despair. The fleet that lay waiting at Lillo needed only to make its way through the breach and convey to Antwerp the expected relief.

It had been agreed that if the bridge should be so effectually shattered as to make it practicable for the Zealand fleet to come up, the admiral should send up a rocket. In order to ascertain the result he was to dispatch a swift barge down the river immediately after the explosion. But the luckless " Koppen-Loppen " was so nearly distracted by the appalling noise that after sending off the barge to reconnoiter he took to his heels without waiting for tidings. The boatman himself dared not come near the fatal spot; and after a little rowing hither and thither came back and reported that the whole thing had failed.

Meanwhile everybody in Antwerp was eagerly watching for the signal rocket. Sainte-Aldegonde and Gianibelli were standing together in one of the forts close to the city walls, expecting the joyful token of their complete success. But it never came. The triumph they had fairly won was thus snatched from them in the moment when their hand almost grasped it, by the incompetency and cowardice of those on whom they depended.

Parma had soon recovered from the shock of the explosion; and though every moment expecting that the shattered bridge would be assailed on both sides, he had labored with such courage and energy that the ruined portion was quickly repaired. Three days passed before the Antwerp people found out that the bridge had actually been broken; and by that time it was apparently as strong as ever.

CHAPTER IV.

THE FIGHT ON THE KOWENSTYN DIKE.

IN spite of this terrible disappointment the Antwerpers kept up their courage, and worried the Spaniards night and day with contrivances of all sorts. "They are never idle in the city," wrote Parma to the king a month or two after the explosion at the bridge. "Every day we are expecting some new invention. . . . We are always upon the alert, with arms in our hands. Every one must mount guard, myself as well as the rest, almost every night and the better part of every day." The daring cruisers of Zealand darted hither and thither in their swift vessels all over the submerged territory, threatening a fort here or seizing an outpost there with provoking audacity, and vanishing as suddenly as they came. Every night signals gleamed from Antwerp to Lillo and back again; so that the troops at the bridge were constantly expecting a combined attack with all kinds of infernal contrivances.

Meteren relates that Gianibelli was allowed to make a second attempt. At first he had the promise of three large ships; but the authorities, having heard meanwhile that once somebody broke a bridge somewhere else by using one ship, decided that one must do for Gianibelli. This penny-wise policy was exhibited repeatedly in the course of the siege. One feature of the present scheme was to send vessels heavily armed with iron, in order to break the bridge by dashing against it under full sail. "But nobody would adventure himself in these ships willingly," adds Meteren, "and such as had deserved to die, they dared not trust." So this part of the plan was dropped. On the new "hell-burner" Gianibelli put four thousands pounds of powder, and to prevent any one coming to extinguish the fire he hung all around the sides of the vessel casks lined with masonry and filled with powder, which were to explode one after another, according to the length of the slowmatch connected with each. Ten little fire ships were to accompany this. But when all was nearly ready, it was decided to try to break the Kowenstyn dike instead; and after the siege was over Parma had an opportunity to inspect Gianibelli's unused contrivances at his leisure.

The great Kowenstyn dike, whose preservation had appeared to the Antwerp butchers so vital, and whose destruction was now the city's last hope, extended from a point not far above Lillo on the right bank of the Scheldt to Stabroek, a village of Brabant. Its whole length was three miles. At the top it was scarcely six paces across. Parma had fortified it with everything that the engineering of those days could contrive. Besides strengthening it with timberwork and piles, he had bordered its slippery sides with stakes driven close together all along each side of its broad base. There were five forts upon it: one at each end, and the three others at intervals of about a mile. The low spongy meadows crossed by this dike had once been the bed of the Scheldt; and if only a broad breach could be made, the river might return to its ancient channel, leaving Parma and his bridge to themselves. The Brabant side was already overflowed to the very gates of Antwerp, so that the Zealand flatboats might have conveyed thither abundant supplies could they only have had a passage through the dike. But on the Flemish side there was so much of the surface still above water at the Doel, Kalloo, and Beveren, and these spots were so strongly held by Parma's troops that it was out of the question to reach the city that way.

Various feigned assaults were made upon the bridge as well as the dike while the great scheme was maturing. On the seventh of May something was attempted in earnest. The fleet from Lillo surprised the sentinels on that part of the dike between Fort Saint George and the Fort of the Palisades, and five hundred bold Zealanders gained a footing there. But owing to a misunderstanding of signals the Antwerp fleet failed to come to their support and the Zealanders could not hold the position. About two hundred of them perished on the dike, or were drowned in the flight.

The grand assault took place on the twenty-sixth of May. Two hundred vessels had been fitted out, some bearing cargoes of provisions from Zealand, some laden with sacks of sand or wool and other materials for erecting hasty breastworks upon the dike. Count Hohenlo and Admiral Justinus of Nassau had charge of the expedition coming from Zealand, while the Antwerp vessels were commanded by Sainte-Aldegonde.

About two o'clock in the morning of that day the sentinels on the Kowenstyn were startled to see four flaming ships approaching from the direction of Lillo. The drums beat to arms, and the Spaniards, not without shuddering, mustered upon the dike, for aught they knew to be blown into the clouds. The glare of these fiery apparitions revealed a host of gunboats behind them, and presently a party of Zealanders landed on the same portion of the dike from which they had been repulsed not quite three weeks before. There was another desperate struggle, and the Zealanders were on the point of being driven off once more, when they heard the cheery shouts of the Antwerp men on the other side of the dike. The Spaniards, being thus attacked both in front and rear, were obliged to give way; and the whole Netherland force, amounting to three thousand, effected a landing. Without losing a moment, some of them began to dig away at the dike; while on either side of the intended breach the rest hastily fortified themselves by means of the materials they had brought with them. But in the midst of their digging and delving a strong detachment from Fort Saint George fell upon them. Hand to hand they struggled and bled and fell. It was one of the most desperate actions in the whole war. At last the patriots drove the Spaniards back and held the entire line between Saint George and the Palisades, which was a full mile.

For three hours they remained unmolested and triumphant. The guns of Saint George had ceased to play upon them, and the Palisades had almost fallen into their hands. The sappers and miners dug furiously at the dike, and at last it yielded. There rose a great shout of triumph as the sea began to sweep through the gap they had made, for they were now sure that Antwerp was saved. One of the Zealand barges, laden with bread and beef, at once pushed its way through toward the city. Hohenlo and Sainte-Aldegonde beside themselves with joy, sprang on board, resolved to be the bearers of the glorious news without a moment's delay.

While they were hurrying up to the city to bid the people ring their bells and light their bonfires, and while the gallant fellows on the dike were swinging their hats and shouting for joy, old Count Mansfeld was holding a very grave council of war down at Stabroek. Something must be done forthwith, or the rebel victory would be as complete as they fancied it. Their chief was at Beveren, a dozen miles away, and there was no reaching him, with three thousand desperadoes entrenched on the dike between, and a hundred and sixty Zealand vessels hanging along its sides. Some of the Spanish officers advised to wait till night before making an assault. Possibly Alexander might meanwhile get news of their situation, and come to their relief.

Here the colonel of the Italian legion, Camilla Capizucca by name, made a pointed little speech on the other side. "If we wait either for night or for Parma," said he in substance, "it is all over with us. Before the coming of either the dike will be broken past all hope of mending, and nothing will remain but to raise the siege. Let me lead my own men to the attack this very hour."

This aroused the rest, and the veteran Count Mansfeld was not the man to hold them back. Just at this moment there came in from the most remote portion of the Stabrock encampment about two hundred men of the Spanish legion, with several eminent officers. These, joining the three hundred chosen veterans of the Italians who were already drawn up in marching order, dropped upon their knees and repeated a short prayer to the Virgin, who was believed to be especially interested for the capture of Antwerp. Having finished their devotions, they marched cheerily along the dike to the Fort of the Palisades, which was sorely beset by the patriot forces. At this unexpected reinforcement, the besieged took heart and made a bold sortie. The besiegers fell back to their own entrenchments and the fort was rescued, henceforth to be called Fort Victory. Just as the royalists were about to move upon the rebel works, in the midst of which the sappers and miners were still digging, a joyful outcry reached them from their comrades on the other side. Parma was coming!

He had gone early that morning to Beveren, to snatch a little sleep, when the sound of a distant cannonade reached his ear. Hurrying back to the bridge, where the young Count Mansfeld was in command of a part of the Italian legion, he found that the Dutch vessels had come down from Antwerp in order to divert the attention of those troops from the principal scene of action. The young count had received a quaint and pointed message from his father at Stabroek just before the patriots got possession of the dike. "Charles, my boy," said the old warrior, "to-day we must either beat them or burst." Alexander paused only long enough to drive off the Antwerp vessels with his boat artillery, and then, bidding Count Charles heed well his father's words, he pressed on at the head of all the troops that could possibly be spared. Under the fire of patriot gunboats they fought their way along the slippery dike to Fort Saint George, the general himself marching on foot at the head of his men. On arriving he ordered an outer breastwork of woolsacks and sandbags to be instantly thrown up, and planted a battery to play on the entrenchments of the rebels.

And now, on this mere thread of land a mile long, five thousand men fought hand to hand in mortal strife. The patriots had solemnly vowed that day to save Antwerp or die. The soldiers of Parma, inspired by their general's presence, and comprehending what the issue must involve, were no less determined than they. Four times they charged the patriot entrenchments, on both sides at once, in vain. The slaughter was fearful. Captain Heraugière had only thirteen men left out of two hundred. On the fifth assault, it is related that the troops of Parma distinctly beheld the well-known figure of the dead commander of the

Spanish legion charging at the head of his own men. Everybody knew that Don Pedro Pacchi had fallen at the siege of Dendermonde, several months before; yet all through the ranks they saw him, wearing the very same coat of mail, making the very same gestures which they remembered so well. The mysterious apparition was never accounted for, but it served the purpose. Animated by what they believed to be a divine interposition, the Spaniards charged with such fury that the works were carried at last. Meanwhile the hot firing from the forts had disabled many of the patriot vessels; and now the ebbing of the tide forced the others to move away from the dike. This change of position, being taken for a retreat, caused a fatal panic, in which there were slain or drowned not less than two thousand men. The Spaniards even swam after the fugitives who were trying to reach the ships; and having carried their swords in their teeth, they butchered their foes in the midst of the waves.

The day was lost. "We had cut the dike in three places," wrote Captain James, an English officer who shared in the fight, "but left it most shamefully, for want of commandment." There was nobody to give orders; for Hohenlo and Sainte-Aldegonde were in Antwerp, already celebrating their supposed triumph.

"Our loss — a thousand men," — wrote Parma that

night to the king, — "is greater than I wish it was. It was a very close thing, and I have never been more anxious in my life. The whole fate of the battle was hanging all the time by a thread. The fight lasted from seven to eight hours, with the most brave obstinacy on both sides that has been seen for many a long day."

Meanwhile, only a few miles away, Antwerp was holding a perfect carnival over her imagined deliverance. Down there at the dike Parma was hastily filling up the gaps with the bodies of the slain; while in the city bonfires were blazing, bells ringing, cannon pealing, and all was too little to express the public rejoicing. Wharves and storehouses were made ready for the bountiful supplies soon to come pouring in. A splendid banquet was spread in the town hall; the choicest wines graced the festive board, and the fairest ladies honored it with their presence. Count Hohenlo presided, and his handsome, aristocratic face, his long fair curling hair, his princely bearing suited the position well. In the midst of the feasting and drinking came the fatal tidings. A few mangled and bleeding forms were brought into the town hall, and in the presence of the gay assembly they were laid down to die. All was consternation. Rushing from the banquet, Hohenlo hid himself from the curses and threats of the enraged citizens, whose too hasty exultation had so suddenly given place to utter despair.

It was all over with Antwerp. She had no longer any heart to keep up the struggle. Twice her deliverance had been really won, and twice the incompetence and folly of some of her own leaders had thrown the victory away. The disappointment was most bitter. There seemed to be no one on whose leadership they could rely, as they had done while William lived. Prince Maurice, who was one day to achieve so much for his people, was still a mere youth; and the promised aid of Queen Elizabeth was too doubtful and dilatory to be waited for. The Zealand cruisers were growing discouraged and inactive, and the lucrative commerce of Antwerp was sure to be ruined by long continuance of the siege. It only remained to make the best terms they could.

Within a few days after this great defeat it began to be whispered in the city that Sainte-Aldegonde was to hold a secret conference with the prince of Parma. Instantly that numerous class of persons who take it upon them to find fault with whatever is done, or left undone, by the government, raised a cry of bribery. Yet in the course of a month negotiations were openly begun, the broad council sending three deputies with the burgomaster to Parma's camp.

There were three conditions on which the commissioners were instructed to insist, namely: that religious liberty should be allowed; that the citadel should not be rebuilt; and that there should be no foreign garrison. Accordingly they did insist; but the courteous prince of Parma stood no less stiffly on his own platform than they did upon theirs. Religious toleration and constitutional rights were the two things of all others which Philip II would never grant, under any possible circumstances.

The citizens were dissatisfied and unreasonable — as hungry people are apt to be. The city magistrates wrangled much among themselves. August arrived, and still the negotiations lingered. Famine was now at the door. Almost every day, fierce mobs gathered in the streets, clamoring for bread. At last the commissioners accepted Parma's terms, abandoning the religious stipulation altogether. Alexander made some trifling concessions as to the garrison, promising to bring into the city only German and Walloon soldiers in numbers sufficient for a bodyguard. The city was to submit to the royal authority, to practice no religion but the Roman Catholic, and to pay a fine of five hundred thousand florins. Any persons who would not return to the ancient Church must wind up their affairs and leave the country within two years, keeping their heresy very close in the mean time. The treaty was signed August 17, 1585.

Ten days later the prince of Parma entered Antwerp in triumph. According to the custom of those days the citizens prepared a vast amount of allegorical pageantry for the great occasion. The military procession entered at the Keyser gate, where it encountered a magnificent triumphal chariot. In it, surrounded by lovely maidens, sat a beautiful woman, personifying the city. This queenly "Antwerpia," greeting Alexander with a kiss, recited a laudatory poem and presented him with the keys of the city, one of them being made of gold. The conqueror fastened the golden key to his chain as a trophy no less prized than the insignia of the Golden Fleece, with which he had lately been invested. He found upon the public square, called the Mere, a colossal statue of himself, set up as a fitting companion to that of Alexander of Macedon. Then there arose before him an enormous phœnix, elephants, dragons, ships of war, and many other astounding objects, all supposed to have some impressive allegorical significance appropriate to the occasion. At last the long procession arrived at the cathedral. Much incense and holy water had been required to disinfect the sacred edifice of its recent Protestantism. After the performance of a grand Te Deum, and much more of street parade, Parma was at last permitted to reach the palace prepared for him.

As soon as three days of these festivities were over Parma made certain changes in the board of magistrates which brought matters under his own control. The citadel had always been hateful to the people, as its obvious purpose was to overawe the city, not to protect it. A few years before they had leveled two of its five sides to the ground. But now it was adroitly managed to have the magistrates themselves propose to rebuild this precious monument of Alva's tyranny. "The erection of the castle has thus been determined upon," wrote Parma, "and I am supposed to know nothing at all of the resolution." Six weeks later he mentioned that the people were "working away most furiously at the citadel, and within a month it will be stronger than ever before."

Had Alexander been fully aware of the state to which the city was reduced at the time the treaty was signed, he would doubtless have exacted severer terms. Three days afterward it was found that there was not a loaf of bread left in Antwerp. On the other hand, had the citizens been aware of Parma's straits, they might have taken heart to hold out a little longer. Doubtless it is harder to starve for one's country than to fight for it; yet not a few Netherland cities had already nobly endured this sharpest ordeal of patriotism. Harlem had for six weeks subsisted on flaxseed and turnip seed, had eaten dogs and cats, horsehides and shoe leather; and Leyden had done the same till in many a house, from famine and from pestilence, whole families lay dead. Had Antwerp likewise faced starvation and kept her gates locked a month or two longer, it would have been no more than Brussels had lately done; no more than Roman Catholic Paris soon afterwards did when besieged by Henry of Navarre; no more than was done by the gay and luxurious Paris of 1871. Nor would it inevitably have been in vain. The fleets of Holland and Zealand were even then planning another expedition equipped with fire machines and what not to attack the palisades; and the following winter proved so tempestuous that the bridge could not have outlasted it.

But Antwerp had not the heroism of Leyden. The opulent city had grown pusillanimous through her devotion to gain. She did not stay for downright starvation; it was only a question of being longer shut up from the lucrative commerce which she loved. Certainly she was sorry to sell her birthright; but after all the pottage was more practical. She would have enjoyed freedom of conscience had it been perfectly convenient, but, since she must choose between the two, she cared more about gold.

However, there were many in Antwerp who made a different choice. They would not put up with the Inquisition, they could not let the Bible go on any terms. Hastily disposing of their possessions, they went forth to other lands. With these liberty-loving heretics departed the prosperity of Antwerp. Less than three months after the surrender Parma wrote to the king: "Certainly the poor city is most forlorn, the heretics having all left it." The historian Meteren, after describing the previous condition of Antwerp, remarks: "But all this traffic, all this power and glory, is since the capture gone into decay, and still diminishes daily, being transported to other towns, with no appearance of amendment so long as the war shall last; for the garrison, the castle, the restraint in religion are wholly contrary to free traffic and commerce." Since that day Antwerp has never regained its former position. One can hardly repress a certain severe satisfaction in recollecting that during a large portion of these three centuries the Scheldt has been practically closed to commerce, as if some phantom host were maintaining an invisible blockade.

CHAPTER V.

MATTERS BETWEEN THE NETHERLANDERS AND THEIR NEIGHBORS.

THE people of the Netherlands, stout-hearted and self-reliant as they were, had long desired the protection and assistance of some neighboring power in their unequal contest with Spain. And notwithstanding their disastrous experience under the duke of Anjou, a strong party was still in favor of seeking an alliance with France, though many preferred to ask the protection of Queen Elizabeth. Of course France would be able to aid them far more than could England, provided she were as much disposed, which was not very certain. At this time France was more populous and powerful than any other kingdom in Europe except Spain. Her people numbered ten or twelve millions, while England had only three or four. Paris contained at least three hundred and twenty thousand inhabitants, while London had hardly half as many. Moreover, between France and Spain it was quite a matter of course to have a war on hand, and these two nations might as well be fighting about the Netherlands as anything else. And though it must be admitted that the French king and the majority of his subjects were Roman Catholics as much as the Spaniards; though only a dozen years before Paris had witnessed the massacre of Saint Bartholomew, whose horrors Protestants could never forget; still religious toleration was at present enjoyed throughout the kingdom. And the same boon would doubtless be cheerfully conceded to the Netherlands. Besides, the heir apparent, Henry of Navarre, was a Protestant.

On the other hand it was urged that although England might have a smaller territory and fewer people than France, she certainly had a much more able sovereign. "The Netherlanders were too shrewd a people," remarks Motley, "not to recognize the difference between the king of a great realm who painted his face and wore satin petticoats, and the woman who entertained ambassadors, each in his own language, on great affairs of state; who matched in her wit and wisdom the deepest or the most sparkling intellects of her council; who made extemporaneous Latin orations to her universities; and who rode on horseback among her generals along the lines of her troops in battle array; and yet was only the unmarried queen of a petty and turbulent state." Besides, Elizabeth was sincerely and irrevocably a Protestant, thanks to her father's quarrel with the

Pope; and though not of the Netherland type of Protestantism, she could not help feeling a real sympathy for all who had renounced Rome.

However, the Netherlands offered themselves first to France. Soon after the death of Anjou two envoys were sent to propose to King Henry III the same position which Anjou was to have had, that is, a limited sovereignty over all the provinces embraced in the Union of Utrecht, except Holland and Zealand. But the envoys were very coldly received; indeed they did not obtain an audience at all. After waiting a month or two at Rouen — for they were not permitted to come to Paris — the king sent a secretary to tell them that he was much obliged to the States for their proposals; but it would not be convenient at present for him to undertake a war with Spain, though he would be happy to do almost anything else in the world to oblige them.

Des Pruneaux, the French envoy to the States, had accompanied the two deputies on this bootless errand; and professed himself so much mortified at the result that he wished he were dead. He knew enough of their country to consider it a prize worth having; and finally prevailed on the French king to let him conduct the deputies again to France, in hope that something might still be done. It was evident that Henry wished the sovereignty offered to him without conditions, or at least without written ones. Moreover, Holland and Zealand must join the other states in their proposals. There was a warm discussion of the matter in the Provinces; but finally the French party carried the day. Early in 1585, while Brussels and Antwerp were besieged, a solemn embassy was despatched to offer the sovereignty of all the states to King Henry, "on conditions to be afterwards settled."

The embassy, which consisted of sixteen members, proceeded at once to the French capital, for this time the king was " at home."

At Paris the envoys were sumptuously entertained at the royal expense, and in the course of six weeks they were received at court with great pomp. After being conducted through several ante-chambers, crowded with lords and ladies, they reached the royal presence. They found his majesty attired in white satin doublet and hose, with well-starched ruff, a short cloak on his shoulders, and a little velvet cap on the side of his head. His long hair was carefully curled and perfumed; and suspended from his neck by a broad ribbon was a little basket full of puppies. Although he smiled good-humoredly as the ambassadors advanced, he held himself stiff and motionless. There was a great deal of ceremonious speech-making and banqueting before the parties came to an understanding. The envoys tried to secure a provision that the reformed religion only should be permitted in their states; but they were forced to give it up and to offer the sovereignty without any conditions whatever. And after having come to this, they had the extreme mortification of finding their proposals decidedly declined. The king politely sent to each of the sixteen envoys a parting present of a gold chain weighing just twenty-one ounces and ten grains; and let them return as they came.

All this trifling was very mysterious to most people, then, but it appears from the researches of modern historians among the state papers and private correspondence of those days that there were secret reasons for the unaccountable conduct of the French court. The truth was that the queen-mother, Catherine de Médicis, desired to make something handsome for her own pocket out of the Netherland proposals. Philip II had lately conquered Portugal, to the throne of which kingdom Catherine pretended to have some title. The claim was at least three hundred years old; but such as it was, she could now turn it to good account. "The ambassador of Spain," wrote the queen-mother, January 16, 1585, "has made the most beautiful remonstrances he could think of about the deputies from the Netherlands. All his talk, however, only increases my desire to have reparation for the wrong done me in regard to my claims upon Portugal, which I am determined to pursue by every means in my power." If the king of Spain did not wish aid and comfort given to his rebels in the Low Countries, he must satisfy her without delay.

So here lay the secret of the delays by which eight months of precious time had been wasted. Henry III and his mother were almost equal to Philip himself at lying. While they were carrying on this elaborate trifling they were professing great affection for Philip's faithful servant, the prince of Parma. And while they were directing the eyes of the anxious Netherlanders to Queen Elizabeth as their best dependence, and promising soon to join her in affording aid, they were likewise proposing to help Philip in an invasion of England. Meanwhile his majesty of Spain was secretly expending all the money he could well scrape together in kindling a civil war in France.

By the time the Netherland envoys were finally dismissed Parma had closed the Scheldt, and fortified the Kowenstyn dike, so that the doom of Antwerp was virtually sealed. Queen Elizabeth now intimated to the States that although France had refused her aid, they should not be left without any ally. Though it would be a difficult matter for England to help these distressed neighbors, it would be most perilous to herself if they were overpowered by Spain. As the sagacious Lord Burleigh had put it, "Upon comparison made betwixt the perils on the one part and the difficulties on the other, it was concluded to advise her majesty rather to seek the avoiding and directing of the great perils, than in respect of any difficulties to suffer the king of Spain to grow to the full height of his designs and conquests."

After some preliminary consultations a solemn embassy was sent in July, 1585, to offer the sovereignty of the Netherlands to the queen of England. This was precisely what Elizabeth did not want. The honor would cost more than it would be worth. She was willing to give her protection and assistance; indeed, her own interest required that; but she positively refused to become their queen. The envoys urged and implored, but this time Elizabeth really meant No, and they had to give it up. She was willing to furnish money and troops, provided she were assured of being fully repaid after the close of the war. In order to this, four cities, including the important ports of Flushing and Brill, were to be given up to her as security.

Now the Dutch were rather sharp in bargaining, as well as the thrifty queen; and it took some time to get these matters settled. The States wanted at least five thousand foot and one thousand horse, besides the garrisons for the four cities, to serve at the queen's expense during the war. The queen wished to provide only four thousand foot and four hundred horse, out of which the garrisons were to be deducted. However, in order to relieve Antwerp, Elizabeth offered four thousand additional men, to serve until the siege should be raised; but they were to be paid for by the States within three months afterward. Sluys and Ostend were meanwhile to be held by her as security for this very prompt repayment. If this seemed rather hard terms, there was at least the comfort of knowing that however close bargains the queen might exact, she meant to perform what she promised.

In the royal archives at The Hague there may still be seen, in the original manuscripts, full records of the speeches made on both sides during this important negotiation. Those of the queen, though in the French language, and extemporaneous, are so dignified and spirited that they are well worth reading. Elizabeth belongs to us Anglo-Americans, no less than to those who are British subjects now; for we were all equally English three hundred years ago.

It was now the fifth of August, and the spokesman of the Netherland envoys had just been arguing his case before her majesty at the palace of Nonesuch.

No sooner had he finished than the queen replied as follows [1] : —

"Gentlemen, I will answer you upon the first point, because it touches my honor. You say that I promised you, both by letters and through my agent Davison, and also by my own lips, to assist you and never to abandon you, and that this had moved you to come to me at present. Very well, masters; do you not think I am assisting you when I am sending you four thousand foot and four hundred horse to serve during the war? Certainly, I think yes; and I say frankly that I have never been wanting to my word. No man shall ever say with truth that the queen of England had at any time and ever so slightly failed in her promises, whether to the mightiest monarch, to republics, to gentlemen, or even to private persons of the humblest condition. Am I, then, in your opinion, forsaking you when I send you English blood, which I love, and which is my own blood, and which I am bound to defend? It seems to me, no. For my part, I tell you again that I will never forsake you.

"*Sed de modo?* That is matter for agreement. You are aware, gentlemen, that I have storms to fear from many quarters — from France, Scotland, Ireland, and within my own kingdom. What would be said if I looked only on one side, and if on that

[1] As quoted by Motley.

side I employed all my resources? No; I will give my subjects no cause for murmuring. I know that my counselors desire to manage matters with prudence; *sed aetatem habeo*,[1] and you are to believe that of my own motion I have resolved not to extend my offer of assistance, at present, beyond the amount already stated. But I don't say that at another time I may not be able to do more for you. For my intention is never to abandon your cause, always to assist you, and never more to suffer any foreign nation to have dominion over you.

"It is true that you present me with two places in each of your provinces. I thank you for them infinitely, and certainly it is a great offer. But it will be said instantly, The queen of England wishes to embrace and devour everything; while, on the contrary, I only wish to render you assistance. I believe, in truth, that if other monarchs should have this offer, they would not allow such an opportunity to escape. I do not let it slip because of fears that I entertain for any prince whatever. For to think that I am not aware — doing what I am doing — that I am embarking in a war against the king of Spain, is a great mistake. I know very well that the succor which I am affording you will offend him as much as if I should do a great deal more. But what care I?

[1] "But I am of age."

Let him begin, I will answer him. For my part, I say again, that never did fear enter my heart. We must all die once. I know very well that many princes are my enemies, and are seeking my ruin; and that where malice is joined with force, malice often arrives at its ends. But I am not so feeble a princess that I have not the means and the will to defend myself against them all. They are seeking to take my life, but it troubles me not. He who is on high has defended me till this hour, and will keep me still, for in Him do I trust."

Then the queen alluded to the demurring of the envoys to accept her proposal on the ground that their powers were not extensive enough. She did not think they needed to hesitate on that account. "Nevertheless," she continued, "I don't wish to contest these points with you. For very often *dum Romae disputatur, Saguntum perit.*"[1] It was precisely so in the present case. Antwerp was perishing while they were higgling over the bargain at London.

A week later the envoys had another audience, in which the terms were definitely settled, subject to the approval of the government of the States; and again Elizabeth made a spirited extemporaneous reply. The ambassadors remarked among themselves that her majesty's tongue was wonderfully well hung. She

[1] "While they are disputing at Rome, Saguntum falls."

concluded by saying, "For myself, I promise you in truth that so long as I live, and even to my last sigh, I will never forsake you. Go home and tell this boldly to those who sent you hither."

While they were gone there came news of the surrender of Antwerp. This made the outlook decidedly darker, but Elizabeth did not flinch. On the contrary, she now took up the cause of the Provinces with more determination than ever. In fighting for them she knew that she was fighting for England too, and that it was better to meet the enemy on Netherland soil than on her own. As the fall of Antwerp had made useless the force she had offered for the purpose of relieving it, she now granted what she had before refused, and sent the five thousand foot and one thousand horse, besides garrisons for Flushing and Brill. The delay of the States to ratify the engagements between England and themselves put her in a very bad humor, it is true; but having scolded the deputies to her heart's content, she finally recovered her temper, and in a formal manifesto published in Dutch, French, English, and Italian, declared herself on their side before the world.

CHAPTER VI.

THE EARL OF LEICESTER IN THE NETHERLANDS.

"TOUCHING the last point of your demand," said her majesty in the address from which some passages have already been quoted, "according to which you desire a personage of quality — I know, gentlemen, that you do not always agree very well among yourselves, and that it would be good for you to have some one to effect such agreement. For this reason I have always intended, so soon as we should have made our treaty, to send a lord of name and authority to reside with you, to assist you in governing, and to aid with his advice in the direction of your affairs."

The personage of quality selected for this mission was no other than the queen's favorite, Robert Dudley, Earl of Leicester. He was not only of exalted rank, but of splendid and fascinating presence and princely wealth. He was ambitious, skilled in political intrigue, and conscience never stood in his way. At this time he was fifty-four years of age, being just two years older than the queen. Though in person he

ROBERT DUDLEY, EARL OF LEICESTER.
From Bor's History of the Netherlands, 1621.

was now growing somewhat stout, florid, and bald, he was no less stately in bearing, magnificent in attire, and dear to his queen than he had been in the flower of his youth. She had named him to the ambassadors as "one whom I love as if he were my own brother." Yet the favorite was at times soundly berated by the imperious queen, as we shall see.

The position which he was expected to hold was a very indefinite and anomalous one. He was to be nominal commander-in-chief of the English troops — whose real general was Sir John Norris — and the representative of her majesty's authority, which in the present state of affairs was no better defined than his own. He was to keep up a very magnificent style of living, in order to support the dignity of his mission; but he was to have no salary whatever. The doting queen was parsimonious even with him. "Whether Elizabeth loved Leicester as a brother, or better than a brother, may be an historical question," says Motley; "but it is no question at all that she loved money better than she did Leicester."

However, the appointment was an honor, and he did not hesitate to spend some thousands of pounds in preliminary equipments. One important item of these was the levy of a choice body of lancers. He arrived in the Low Countries December 19, 1585, attended by a fleet of fifty sail, and many of the great nobles of England. The young Count Maurice of Nassau, and other Netherland nobles, as well as his nephew, Sir Philip Sidney, governor of Flushing, waited to meet him at his landing. For several weeks he was occupied with a sort of triumphal progress through the country. The Netherland people always liked imposing spectacles; and upon this grand occasion they seemed even to outdo themselves in processions, banquets, and carousals. Allegorical performances, half classic, half Christian, were much in vogue at that time, as well as Latin orations of grandiloquent style and appalling length. At The Hague, as Leicester approached, "a fleet of barges was sent to escort him. Peter, James, and John met him upon the shore, while the Saviour appeared walking upon the waves, and ordered his disciples to cast their nets and to present the fish to his excellency. Farther on, he was confronted by Mars and Bellona, who recited Latin odes in his honor. Seven beautiful damsels, representing the seven states of the United Netherlands, offered him golden keys; seven others equally beautiful, embodying the seven sciences, presented him with garlands; while an enthusiastic barber adorned his shop with sevenscore of copper basins, with a wax light in each together with a rose and a Latin posy in praise of Queen Elizabeth. Then there were tiltings in the water between champions mounted upon whales and other monsters of the deep — representations of siege, famine, pestilence, and murder — the whole interspersed with fireworks, poetry, charades, and harangues."

Amid all these astonishing spectacles, however, Lord Leicester managed to keep an eye upon whatever would tell him the real condition and resources of this very peculiar country. He was not long in discovering that, though nature had seemingly given the Netherlanders little except hindrances, the very obstacles had proved wonderful helps. In their neverending warfare with the hungry sea always lying in wait to devour their meager little territory at a mouthful; in their toilsome efforts to extort harvests from an unpromising soil, beneath a sky where the sun shines scarcely once a week, — the people had grown into real athletes, dauntless and invincible, patient in toil and hardship and tenacious to the uttermost of what had been so dearly won. And now both country and people seemed to him well worth having. "Great pity it were," he wrote to Lord Burleigh during his first fortnight among them, "that so noble provinces and goodly havens, with such infinite ships and mariners, should not always be as they may now, easily, at the assured devotion of England." Lord North also wrote home glowing accounts, setting forth "what multitudes of people they be, what stately cities and buildings they have, how notably fortified by art, how strong by nature, how fertile the whole country and how wealthy;" and lamented that he "lacked wit to dilate this matter."

The more Leicester and his countrymen became acquainted with the Netherlands, the more anxious they grew lest Spain should recover them, and thus readily conquer England. A hundred times over they wished that Elizabeth would but accept the sovereignty which the Netherlanders so ardently longed to bestow upon her, either in person or by proxy; and thus secure to her own realm the best possible bulwark against the designs of Spain. But the great queen was exceedingly set in her way; and on this point she was inexorable. She had even forbidden Leicester to accept any office or title inconsistent with her previous refusal of the sovereignty.

In truth, Leicester inwardly hankered after this forbidden fruit. The States wanted a political leader and the earl wanted power. It was not long before their deputies, unaware of the prohibition, — which Leicester had carefully concealed even from his own colleagues, — waited upon him, and made a formal offer of the position of governor-general.

Leicester thought best to conceal his eagerness under the cloak of a decent modesty, and therefore asked a few days to consider. But he was not long in signifying his willingness to accept; and within a fortnight it was all arranged, without even saying "by your leave" to the queen. On the fourth of February, 1586, the new governor-general was inaugurated with great pomp at The Hague.

The States, at least, were entirely loyal and sincere in this. They honestly supposed that in bestowing so much authority upon her representative they were doing what would best please the queen. The official advisers of the earl and all the Englishmen there considered the measure almost indispensable to the security of both countries. But Leicester, who alone knew the queen's express prohibition, was well aware that he must expect a storm the moment his disobedience should be known.

As if to make the matter worse, some weeks were allowed to pass after the proposition had been made and accepted before her majesty was informed of it at all. And then the news reached her in some roundabout way — of all ways the most irritating — instead of coming from the favorite himself, whose adroit and graceful pen ought to have been prompt to own the offense and sue for the royal pardon. In truth, the gallant earl seems to have been afraid to face the consequences of his act, and so arranged it that Mr. Davison should go to her majesty and state the case.

Meanwhile, he wrote to Lord Burleigh, begging his friendly offices with the offended queen; and protesting his entire devotion to her majesty's service in this as well as all other acts, even to his parting breath. Davison was delayed by adverse winds, and before he arrived in England the whole story was out.

The queen was furious. She fairly blazed with passion. She stormed and swore so fearfully that nobody dared say a word. Even the white-bearded Lord Burleigh was told with an oath to hold his tongue; and finding it useless to brave the storm, he prudently went to bed and waited for fair weather. Lord Walsingham stayed, but the queen would not listen to anybody, except the mischief-making ladies of her court; they told her the most exasperating stories about the Countess of Leicester getting ready to join her husband abroad, with such a retinue of lords and ladies, all so magnificent, and finer carriages and side-saddles than even her majesty's own. So when Davison at last arrived with his explanations and apologies, he found that the indignant queen had already commissioned Sir Thomas Heneage to proceed at once to the States and make them undo all they had done. What provoked her more than anything else was the contempt with which she conceived that she had been treated by the undutiful earl in his venturing to accept the government at all, his omitting to write, and his delay in sending Davison. Furthermore, since this step would disgrace her in the eyes of the world by its inconsistency with her recent manifesto, — in which she had disavowed any desire to increase her own power by taking up the cause of the Provinces, — she directed that Leicester should at once publicly resign his new office in the very place where he had received it.

Davison heard of the state the queen was in as soon as he arrived; but he manfully presented himself at court. The queen began by swearing and storming tremendously, but the messenger did not quail. When she stopped to take breath, he took the opportunity to begin the defense. Though often interrupted, he succeeded in telling her several things which she ought to have been informed of long before. But she would not even look at the penitent and devoted letter which her favorite had sent, until a second interview had in some degree soothed her exasperated feelings. At last she was prevailed upon not to require Leicester's public and immediate disgrace. The earl professed to be broken-hearted, no less on account of Elizabeth's displeasure than on account of his mortifying position before the world. She at last consented that he should retain the office; but the confidence of the Netherland people, both in Leicester and in herself, was seriously damaged. There began to be suspicious that she was secretly negotiating with Spain, and they were not wholly unfounded. Not that she meant to make peace for England without including the Provinces; she had no disposition to do that, had it been in her power.

CHAPTER VII.

MILITARY MOVEMENTS OF PARMA AND LEICESTER.

PARMA had now nearly all the cities of Flanders and Brabant in his possession; but there was much work yet to be done, and little means with which to do it. Philip did not send money to pay his troops; they were few, sickly, and starving. Parma had borrowed of the Flemish merchants till they would lend no more; and the territory of the "obedient" provinces was bare of subsistence, even for its own population, who were almost desperate with famine.

In the midst of his own embarrassments there was doubtless some small comfort for Parma in perceiving that some of his enemies were no better off. Queen Elizabeth's troops in the United Provinces were evidently already in a shabby and forlorn condition, for she was not prompt in furnishing their pay. To do her justice, she was not in easy circumstances. It has been estimated by Motley that the entire revenue of her government was perhaps equal to one sixtieth of the annual interest on the present national debt of

England. It was doubtless difficult to make ends meet, however anxious she was to do so.

The first move which Alexander planned for the campaign of 1586 was to capture those cities which the patriots still held, upon the river Meuse, and particularly Grave. If this were accomplished, Brabant would be altogether clear of the rebels, and on its most exposed side it would be considerably protected by the encircling Meuse.

Grave was not a very large city, but it was strong and had a commanding position upon the river Meuse, nearly a hundred English miles northeast of Brussels. It was amply fortified on the landward side, while, as for the rest, the deep and rapid river served as a defense. Early in the year, Count Mansfeld had been sent to lay siege to it. He had accordingly proceeded to enclose it with a line of forts, five of which lay upon the Brabant side of the river, some above and some below the town. A floating bridge led to a well-fortified camp upon the opposite shore.

The city had a garrison of eight hundred troops, besides about a thousand burghers able to bear arms. The commander was a young nobleman called Baron Hemart. There was some slight skirmishing outside, but no strenuous effort was made to relieve the city until spring. By this time it was hard pressed, for all supplies were cut off; and the Netherlanders felt that something must be done at once.

Leicester sent a force of three thousand men, commanded by Count Hohenlo and Sir John Norris, early in April. They were ordered to throw into the place reinforcements and supplies, at whatever risk. They advanced along the right bank of the Meuse, on the way taking the castles of Batenburg and Ravenstein. During the night of April 15 four or five hundred English soldiers were sent to entrench themselves upon the dike that guarded the river bank, almost exactly opposite the city.

The next morning Count Mansfeld observed his new neighbors on the other side of the river, and ordered out three thousand Spaniards to attend to them. One thousand of these were selected and sent across the bridge to make the assault, while the rest were to be held in reserve. It had been raining hard for some time, and the river was rising rapidly. The floating bridge swayed back and forth as the men marched slowly and cautiously across. It was less than an English mile from the end of the bridge to the entrenchments they were to assault. The Spaniards charged upon the run, without waiting for the reserve to arrive, and being tired and out of breath, were at first repulsed. But fresh troops soon appeared, and at the third onset they carried the works. The few hundreds of Englishmen took to flight, directing their steps along the river dike, in hopes to meet their comrades who had encamped six miles below, and were expected to advance at dawn. The Spaniards pursued them in hot haste along the slippery dike for two miles, when they suddenly came in sight of the main body of the States' troops, under Hohenlo and Norris. The English rallied, and, facing about, drove the Spaniards back in their turn. But before they reached the bridge another turn was given to the fortunes of the day by the appearance of more Spaniards just crossing from the Brabant side.

The frail bridge trembled and wavered under the hurrying tread of the Spanish troops, but presently both armies, each now numbering about three thousand, stood facing each other upon the right bank. It was raining hard, the wind blew a gale, and the swollen river foamed and raged almost at their feet. For a moment both armies stood still upon the slippery causeway, and looked each other in the face; then they plunged into the deadly strife, fighting hand to hand and foot to foot. For an hour and a half the battle raged. Every inch of the narrow dike which was the scene of this furious struggle was trampled by the densely-crowded thousands wrestling there; every footprint was red with blood. The Netherland leaders were in the thickest of the fight, braver than the bravest. But at last the fury of the still-increasing storm became too much for mortal strength to endure. The Spaniards dreaded every moment to see their frail bridge give way, and at length retreated.

The lowlands around Grave were so extensively submerged by the flood that boats could sail almost anywhere. In spite of the besiegers, the city was reinforced within a few days by five hundred men and provisions for a whole year. To the Netherlanders it now seemed out of the question for it to be reduced; and so long as the States held it they were sure to control the river. Leicester was excessively proud of this success, though he had little enough to do with it, and he seemed to regard it as almost the winding up of the war. There was much banqueting and speech-making in Amsterdam and Utrecht; and the governor-general indulged in the most sanguine hopes of recovering Antwerp and extinguishing Parma altogether.

But Alexander was not to be extinguished so easily. Instead of ordering Mansfeld to raise the siege, he came in person to his camp before Grave and began to "batter it like a prince," as Lord North admiringly observed in writing to Burleigh. On the seventh of June Parma marched into Grave. Strong and well supplied as it was, the young commander had basely surrendered it to please a woman. Megen and Batenburg gave up the same day, and Venlo, an important place thirty miles above, was taken shortly after. Parma had now got control of every town upon the Meuse, and there was nothing to prevent his beginning a similar campaign along the Rhine.

Leicester's brilliant anticipations of soon clearing out the Spaniards were not likely to be realized at once. He had taken the field with a considerable force, but before he had done anything of any consequence he heard of the surrender of Grave. He indignantly declared that even women might have held out in a town like that, and straightway summoned a court-martial. The young Baron Hemart was tried and sentenced to death. The culprit represented that it was through the tears and entreaties of the terrified women of Grave that he had been induced to surrender — which was of course the best face that could be put upon the act. Had the statement been true, it would have showed that Grave was inhabited by women very unlike those of Maestricht and Harlem. But the blame belonged to one woman only. She was of good family, but inclined to the Spanish side; and so the States lost this important post and the young Baron Hemart lost his head.

Parma next proceeded to besiege Neusz, upon the Rhine. It was a very strong city, twenty miles below

Cologne, and was not only well provisioned but was commanded by a young officer of "extraordinary capacity and valor though but a boy," to quote Parma's own words. Within a month, after much desperate fighting, the town was stormed. The wounded commander was dragged from his couch and from the arms of his lovely and devoted wife, to be hanged at his own window. A Calvinist clergyman and his deacons, together with "fifty other rascals" — as Parma put it — were hanged at the same time. Most of the town was burned, and four thousand of the citizens were put to the sword. "My little soldiers were not to be restrained," wrote Parma to the king. To do him justice, he was not in the habit of allowing them to commit such atrocities, as some of his predecessors had made a point of doing.

Leicester had twice mustered a force of four thousand troops to raise this siege, but both times he had been forced to abandon the attempt for want of funds, which the queen was always slow to furnish and the States were now too distrustful to place in his hands. He had freely lavished his private resources till neither ready money nor plate remained.

Parma now proceeded to Rheinberg, twenty-five miles below. In order to divert Parma from Rheinberg, as well as to recover a position of much importance, Leicester now resolved to lay siege to Zutphen.

There had been one encouraging success to the patriots during the siege of Nuesz. Sir Philip Sidney and the young Prince Maurice of Nassau had surprised and captured Axel, a strongly fortified and important town on the border of the great tide inlet connected with the West Scheldt. The scheme was of Prince Maurice's own contriving, but the hearty coöperation of the gallant Sidney did much to ensure its success. Having placed a garrison in the town, the victors broke the dikes and thus laid under salt water a vast amount of standing grain and other property belonging to the obedient provinces. This was the first military exploit of the studious, hard-working youth who was soon to be ranked as the greatest general of his time. Young Cecil wrote to his father: "It hath made us somewhat to lift up our heads."

Early in September, having taken the neighboring town of Doesburg, Leicester proceeded to invest Zutphen itself. This city stands upon the right bank of the Yssel, which here flows nearly north. The surrounding country is level and low, so that parts of it are usually inundated in winter, though in summer it is a well-tilled and productive region. Zutphen had been in the hands of the Spaniards ever since the memorable siege and massacre of 1572, when, to save time and trouble, they tied five hundred of the burghers in pairs, back to back, and drowned them like dogs. To recover it would be to secure entire control of that river, since Deventer and Kampen were theirs already. This was doubly important since Parma had driven them from the Meuse and was likely to drive them also from the Rhine. The city had a good wall and moat on the landward side, as well as an external fortress, and the river protected it on the west. There was an island opposite which was well fortified, and on the farther shore, in what was called the Bad Meadows, were three Spanish forts.

Leicester established his own quarters on the left bank of the river over which he had laid a bridge of boats; he stationed Sir John Norris on Gibbet Hill, a rising ground near the city. His forces amounted to something like six or seven thousand foot and two thousand horse. Of the infantry, about five thousand were Englishmen; and numbers of brave knights and nobles who had come over in Lord Leicester's train were now with him in camp as volunteers.

No sooner did Parma get news of what was going on at Zutphen than he broke up his camp at Rheinberg, just as Leicester had expected. But he still maintained a partial blockade of that city by building a bridge over the Rhine at Wesel, a few miles below, and leaving a small force there to keep the river closed. With the remainder of his troops he went on toward Zutphen, which is some fifty or sixty miles from Rheinberg to the northwest.

Zutphen was not yet so closely invested but that Alexander was able to give it a sufficient garrison. He even entered the city himself, one night, in order to encourage his forces there, as well as to learn more of the situation. There was urgent need of supplies in order to be able to sustain a long siege; and Parma at once arranged to send enough to feed four thousand for three months. These were to be dispatched from his headquarters, a dozen miles east of Zutphen, on the night of Thursday, October 2. It was intended that the convoy should arrive at a certain point a mile or two from the city just before light; and then word was to be sent to Verdugo, commander of the garrison, who would come out with a strong force and bring the convoy safely through the enemy's lines.

Doubtless this was very well planned; but it did not turn out just as Parma wished. He had sent a trooper to tell Verdugo that the provision train was coming; but the trooper had fallen into the enemy's hands, and Leicester had found out the whole plan in time to make a few arrangements of his own.

On the road by which the convoy was to approach, about an English mile from the eastern gate, there was a little country church with a cluster of cottages around it called Warnsfield. Before five in the morning Sir John Norris with two hundred horsemen silently placed themselves in ambuscade near Warnsfield church. Three hundred pikemen were with them, and a large force was in reserve, should it be needed, which, however, they did not expect. A heavy fog covered the lowlands that morning. So dense was it that one could scarcely see any object beyond reach. Already they could faintly hear at a distance the sound of the slowly-approaching convoy, when Leicester himself rode up with a little band of his young noblemen and their attendants — some fifty in all — who would not be left behind.

The slow creaking wheels of the wagons came nearer and nearer, the tramp of the soldiers was now distinctly heard, but the men lying in wait could as yet see nothing. At this moment the fog suddenly lifted, and in the broad daylight the five hundred Englishmen suddenly found they had three thousand to fight. The long line of wagons was guarded on each side by dense columns of pikemen and musketeers. It was headed by a strong force of arquebusiers and cavalry under famous leaders. And furthermore Verdugo was presently coming out from the city to help them in.

The young earl of Essex, at the head of a hundred troopers, dashed into the enemy's cavalry and drove them back upon the musketeers and pikemen. Then adroitly wheeling, while a volley of balls whistled around them, they formed and charged the second time. Many horses and some of the gallant riders rolled in the dust, but the little troop would not give way. The more unequal the strife, the more the Englishmen held on.

The fight lasted an hour and a half, the Englishmen, from highest to lowest, behaving like heroes. Again and again they seized the horses of the convoy but could not get possession of the train. Foot by foot it made its way toward the town; and presently two thousand Spaniards sallied from the eastern gate. The patriot forces, whose reserve had failed to arrive, were compelled to give way. In the course of that day and days following the city was fully supplied. For many years both Netherlanders and Spaniards had no stronger expression to use in describing any desperate action than to say that it was as hot as the fight at Zutphen.

CHAPTER VIII.

SIR PHILIP SIDNEY.

ON that fatal morning at Zutphen the brave young Sidney fell. His name, already illustrious and beloved in England, has ever since been dear in all lands that have heard it. That noble and beautiful life, crowned as it was by a heroic and Christian death, thrills one like some rare old poem, perfect, though all too brief.

Among the gallant knights of Henry VIII there had been one Sir William de Sidney who distinguished himself on the field of Flodden and afterwards became the tutor and chamberlain of the young Edward VI. During the brief reign of the boy king he gave Sidney the castle of Penshurst, an ancient baronial mansion in the county of Kent. Henry Sidney, the son of Sir William, was the intimate friend of Edward VI and was a noted statesman in the succeeding reign. He married Lady Mary Dudley, daughter of that earl of Northumberland who attempted to place Lady Jane Grey, his daughter-in-law, upon the throne. Sir Philip, the eldest son, was born at Penshurst in 1554. Queen Mary gave him the name of her royal consort, Philip of Spain, whom, fortunately, he resembled in nothing else. The beautiful boy, "wise of heart beyond his childish years," yet gladsome and loving, frank and true, grew up in the stately old halls of Penshurst, carefully and tenderly reared by his excellent parents. There still remains a letter written by his father when this cherished son was about twelve years of age, from which the following passages are quoted: —

I have received two letters from you — one in Latin, the other in French — which I take in good part, and will you to exercise that practice of learning often. . . . And since this is the first letter that ever I did write to you, I will not that it be empty of all advices. . . . Let your first action of the day be the lifting up of your mind to Almighty God by hearty prayer, with continual thinking of Him to whom you pray, and of the matter for which you pray. . . . Apply your study to such hours as your discreet master doth assign you, earnestly; and the time I know he will so limit as shall be both sufficient for your learning and safe for your health. Be humble and obedient to your master, for unless you frame yourself to obey others, yea, and feel in yourself what obedience is, you shall never be able to teach others how to obey you. Be courteous of gesture, and affable to all men, with diversity of reverence, according to the dignity of the person. There is nothing that winneth so much with so little cost. . . . Let your mirth be ever void of all scurrility, and biting words to any man; for a wound given by a word is oftentimes harder to be cured than that given by the sword. . . . Above all things, tell no untruth, even in trifles; . . . there cannot be a greater reproach to a gentleman than to be accounted a liar. Study and endeavor yourself to be virtuously occupied. So shall you make such an habit of well-doing in you, that you shall not know how to do evil.

All that the fond father hoped was fulfilled in the manhood of the noble son. After some time spent in the university, he was for three years on the continent, visiting what was best worthy to be seen, and meanwhile devoting himself with ardor to his studies. On his return, his uncle the earl of Leicester presented him at the English court. He was tall and stately in figure, with handsome features, rich auburn hair, and deep blue eyes full of feeling and thought. The queen at once recognized his superior abilities, as well as the charm of his presence; and in token of her regard, she appointed him her cupbearer. He bore a part in the stately ceremonies of the queen's visit to Kenilworth; but she was reluctant to give him the arduous and responsible duties abroad for which he longed, because "she feared to lose the jewel of her times."

In 1576, however, he was sent on a special embassy to Vienna, ostensibly to felicitate Rodolph II on his accession to the imperial throne; but in reality to bring about an alliance between England and the various Protestant states of Germany against the Catholic powers. He made many friends, and his able and acceptable services won the highest praise. Returning in 1577, through the Netherlands, he met the great William of Orange, who pronounced him "one of the ripest and greatest counselors of the day, in Europe"; and for years corresponded with him on public affairs.

It was when Sidney had been only three years at court that the queen desired his opinion as to the proposed marriage with the duke of Anjou. This high compliment to his judgment did not beguile him into giving the approval which he knew she would like to receive. He had the courage and sincerity to tell her majesty what he really thought and why — a thing which her council had not ventured to do. A remonstrance so daring might have been the ruin of all his future prospects, as Sidney well knew. But the queen's judgment was too deeply impressed by his arguments to permit her to go on.

It was while residing with his sister, the countess of Pembroke, that Sidney wrote his famous romance, the Arcadia. His poetical gifts were already known, and in 1581 he published his Apologie for Poesie. This work has been pronounced the most finished prose production of that period, and the earliest critical work of merit in the English language.

As the governor of Flushing he was most efficient and self-sacrificing. He was quick to discern abuses and fearless in telling the truth to the government at home. "If the queen pay not her soldiers," he wrote to Secretary Walsingham, "she must lose her garrisons; there is no doubt thereof; but no man living shall be able to say the fault is in me. What relief I can do them, I will. I will spare no danger if occasion serve. I am sure no creature shall be able to lay injustice to my charge; and for further doubts, truly, I stand not upon them."

Sidney plunged into the thickest of the fight at Zutphen, and two horses having been shot under him, he had mounted a third, when the fatal moment came. As he was dashing forward to rescue Lord Willoughby, then surrounded by the enemy, he received a musket ball a little above the left knee. The thigh bone was shattered and the flesh torn far up the leg. Faint with loss of blood, he was borne from the field. They brought water — doubtless with no small risk and in scanty supply — to allay his burning thirst. Just as he was about to drink he saw the longing eyes of a dying soldier fixed on the precious cup. "Thy necessity is greater than mine," said the noble sufferer, at once sending to him the untasted draught. This sweet and beautiful act was just like himself. Its memory will be fragrant and dear as long as Sidney's name is known.

"This young man," wrote Leicester, "was my

greatest comfort, next her majesty, of all the world; and if I could buy his life with all I have, I would give it. How God will dispose of him I know not, but I must needs fear greatly the worst, the blow being in so dangerous a place and so great; yet never did I hear of any man that did abide the dressing and setting of his bones better than he did. And he was carried afterwards in my barge to Arnheim, and I hear this day that he is still of good heart and comforteth all about him as much as may be. God of his mercy grant me his life!"

Lady Sidney and other friends gave him the most devoted care, and all that the imperfect surgery of those days knew how to do was done. In the Low Countries, as well as in England, the most intense and affectionate anxiety was felt. Through all the sixteen days of anguish the sufferer was patient and serene. Fully aware of his condition, he dictated his will with minute remembrance of all his friends and servants, wrote a long letter in pure and elegant Latin to an eminent divine, and spoke much and with power upon the immortality of the soul.

There is still extant in the British Museum a touching little sketch of those last days, written by his chaplain, from which we quote a few passages. "The night before he died," wrote the chaplain, "I said: 'I trust you are well and thoroughly prepared for death, if God shall call you.' At this he made a little pause and then he answered : ' I have a doubt ; pray resolve me in it. I have not slept this night ; I have very earnestly and humbly besought the Lord to give me some sleep ; he hath denied it ; this causeth me to doubt that God doth not regard me nor hear any of my prayers — this doth trouble me.' Answer was made that for matters touching salvation or pardon of our sins through Christ he gave an absolute promise, but for things concerning this life God hath promised them but with caution ; that which he hath absolutely promised we may assuredly look to receive, craving it in faith. ' I am fully satisfied,' said he. ' No doubt it is even so ; then I will submit myself to his will in these outward things.' . . . Within a few hours after I told him that I thought that his death did approach, which indeed he well perceived, and for which he prepared himself. . . . Not long after, he lifted up his eyes and hands, uttering these words : ' I would not change my joy for the empire of the world ! ' For the nearer he saw death to approach the more his comfort seemed to increase. His former virtues seemed to be nothing, for he wholly condemned his former life. ' All things in it,' said he, ' have been vain, vain, vain ! '

"It now seemed as if all heat and life were gone out of him, that his understanding had failed, and that it was to no purpose to speak any more unto him. But it was far otherwise. I spake thus unto him: 'Sir, if you hear what I say, let us by some means know it, and if you have still your inward joy and consolation in God, hold up your hand.' With that he did lift up his hand and stretched it forth on high, which we thought he could scarce have moved. After this, that we might see his heart still prayed, he raised both his hands and set them together on his breast, after the manner of those who make humble petitions, and so his hands did remain, and even so stiff that they would have continued standing but that we took them the one from the other."

So, amid the loving ministries and tender tears of friends, while inwardly praying, and soothed by the soft music which he loved, the trusting and heroic soul departed, on the seventeenth of October, 1586.

The United Provinces mourned with a profound and tender sorrow. They entreated the privilege of burying the young hero in the land which he had given his life to save. They promised to raise for him " as fair a monument as had any prince in Europe." But England could not permit the dust of her favorite son to sleep on a foreign shore, and the queen herself assumed the expense of a magnificent funeral. The body, after long lying in state at Aldgate, was entombed with royal pomp in Saint Paul's. The nobility all went into mourning — the first time this honor had been paid to any private individual. Du Plessis said to Lord Walsingham: " I bewail his loss, not for England only, but for all Christendom." Even Philip II remarked: " England has lost in one moment what she may not produce in an age."

The poet Spenser commemorated his friend in a poem from which the following lines are quoted: —

> A king gave thee thy name; a kingly mind
> That God thee gave, who found it now too dear
> For this base world, and hath resumed it near
> To sit in skies, and sort with powers divine.
> Kent thy birthdays, and Oxford held thy youth.
> The heavens made haste, nor stayed nor years nor time;
> The fruits of age grew ripe in thy first prime,
> Thy will, thy words; thy words the seals of truth.
> Great gifts and wisdom rare employed thee thence
> To treat from kings with those more great than kings;
> Such hope men had to lay the highest things
> On thy wise youth, to be transported thence !
> . . . .
> What hath he lost that such great grace hath won?
> Young years for endless years, and hope unsure
> Of fortune's gifts, for wealth that still shall dure;
> O happy race with so great praises run!

CHAPTER IX.

TREASONS AND TROUBLES.

A FEW weeks after the fight at Zutphen, Leicester informed the State Council that he intended soon to go to England, in order to attend the session of parliament. Though this was altogether unexpected, the Council took it calmly, and did not go upon their knees to beg the earl to reconsider a resolution so alarming. Councilor Wilkes, one of the two English members, noted that "the States used but slender entreaty to his excellency for his stay and countenance there among them, whereat his excellency, and we that were of the council for her majesty, did not a little marvel."

Perhaps it was rather surprising, considering that not a year before Lord Leicester had been hailed almost "as a Messiah." But for several months it had been evident that he was growing more unpopular every day. What began it was the queen's excessive displeasure at his having been appointed governorgeneral. The States wanted to resume, so far as they could, the authority so mistakenly bestowed; partly from fear of offending the capricious queen, and still more from a positive distrust of Leicester. This was an awkward business on both sides. It was inevitable that endless jealousies and quarrels should grow out of it.

In truth, Leicester's administration had not been very successful, either in military or civil matters. Certainly it was not altogether his own fault that he had accomplished so little in the field, but he had to bear the blame. Then he had exasperated the Netherland merchants by financial measures which they considered damaging to the national prosperity as well as to their personal interests. His confidential partisans were regarded as unscrupulous adventurers by the opposition, and they called the others selfish and greedy seekers after gain.

Leicester was a Calvinist, like most of the people of the United Provinces; but, unlike the greatest and wisest of the Netherlanders, he was not willing to tolerate good citizens who were still Catholics, and was wont to denounce those who did. This was another cause of disagreement and alienation. Paul Buys, one of the prominent statesmen of the Provinces, was greatly obnoxious to the earl, who made no secret of his dislike. In writing to Lord Burleigh about having executed Baron Hemart, he added significantly: "And you shall hear that Mr. P. B. shall follow." Some time in the course of the summer this vexatious Hollander was arrested in his bed by a party of armed men, and people naturally felt sure that Leicester was at the bottom of it, in spite of his denials. "Mr. P. B." was kept in prison for six months without being tried or even accused; but was finally released at the request of Elizabeth herself.

Leicester had also a chronic and most vehement quarrel with Sir John Norris, and with the brother and uncle of Sir John. It grew to such a pitch that at last no one country could hold them all in peace. Indeed, his lordship was evidently addicted to falling out with people, and when he had an unpleasantness it was not likely soon to be gotten over.

The leave-taking between the earl and the States, however, was outwardly decorous and polite. He did not resign, neither did he promise a speedy return, if any return at all. The whole administration, both civil and military, was left in the hands of the State Council, whose decrees were to be issued in the name of his excellency and countersigned by Count Maurice. The States presented him with a magnificent silver gilt vase, "as tall as a man," as a parting gift; and about the last of November he sailed for England.

The queen received her favorite most graciously, for the tempest of royal wrath had blown over long before; and now she was almost as impatient of the limitations placed upon Leicester's authority as she had been indignant at his having dared to accept it at all. The whole affair, in its vehemence, its unreasonableness, and its speedy subsidence, was more like a lover's quarrel than anything else. "Never since I was born," wrote Leicester to Wilkes, "did I receive a more gracious welcome." The queen was really fond of "Rob," as she sometimes called him in her letters. In the previous July she had ended a business letter, written with her own hand, in the following affectionate style: —

> Now will I end, that do imagine I talk still with you, and loathly say farewell one hundred thousand times; though ever I pray God bless you from all harm, and save you from all foes. With my million and legion of thanks for all your pains and cares,
> As you know ever the same,
> E. R.

But while he was comfortably reposing himself "under the shadow of those blessed beams" of royal favor for which he had long pined, matters in the United Provinces were not going on as well as could be desired. While the State Council was supposed to govern in the absence of the governor-general, it was really only a board of consultation, having no power to enact decrees of its own. As to military matters, the English forces were nominally under the command of Sir John Norris, and the Dutch and German troops under that of Count Hohenlo. But as Leicester was on bad terms with both, as well as with the state councilors, he had on the eve of his departure signed a secret document forbidding the latter to revoke any military or naval commissions, or to remove any commanding officers of towns or forts, without special leave from himself.

This restriction unfortunately tied the hands of the administration in regard to a matter of great consequence which presently came up. Grave suspicions were afloat respecting the loyalty of two English officers in command of important posts. Sir William Stanley, commander at Deventer, was known to be a zealous papist, and the burghers had become distrustful of his intentions as well as discontented with his rather despotic management. Rowland York, who was in charge of the great fort opposite Zutphen, was said to be on such intimate terms with Colonel Tassis, the Spanish commander in the city itself, that it would not be surprising if he should present Tassis with the fort almost any day. York had fought under the Spanish flag before this, time and again, and had always possessed a decided facility for changing sides upon occasion. The effect of the secret paper was to render these commanders virtually independent of all control.

In the course of two months both Stanley and York actually did what had been apprehended. " Thus," wrote Parma to Philip, " Fort Zutphen, about which there have been so many fisticuffs, and Deventer, which was the real object of the last campaign, and which has cost the English so much blood and treasure, and is the safety of Groningen and of all those provinces, is now your majesty's. Moreover, the effect of this treason must be to sow great distrust between the English and the rebels, who will henceforth never know in whom they can confide."

Leicester had received timely warning of these apprehended treasons, and had been implored to empower the State Council to remove the suspected officers; but all in vain. As if still further to unsettle the confidence of the Netherlanders in any foreign allies, the important castle of Wauw, near Bergen-op-zoom, was sold to Parma about the same time by the French officer to whom it had been entrusted; and the city of Gelder was delivered up to the Spaniards by a Scotch officer temporarily in command. These lessons were well adapted to teach the young nation a wholesome and reasonable self-reliance, and though the experience was a severe one, it was doubtless worth all that it cost.

At this time Elizabeth was to a great degree absorbed in affairs at home. She was in an excited, anxious, irritable mood, and not at all likely to heed petitions or remonstrances from the Low Countries, however reasonable. She was spiteful to the king of

France and contemptuous toward Henry of Navarre. "Your lordship may see that our courage doth greatly increase," wrote Walsingham, with a grim humor, "for that we make no difficulty to fall out with all the world." She was cold and niggardly towards her Netherland allies, and strangely credulous in regard to the good intentions of Parma and his royal master. The war in the Netherlands was outrageously expensive. She must and would somehow get out of it; and to that end she was secretly trying to bring about a peace.

At the worst possible moment there arrived five deputies from the States, who politely intimated that should her majesty change her mind about accepting the sovereignty, upon reasonable conditions, the offer was still open to her. Having thus adroitly smoothed the way, as they imagined, the envoys proceeded to ask that the queen would double the number of troops formerly promised, and lend them sixty thousand pounds sterling for their operations the next year.

No sooner had the speaker concluded his address, which was given in French, than the exasperated queen rose and replied with great fluency and vehemence in the same language. She berated them soundly for their ingratitude and audacity in asking further aid, after having so illy used both the troops and the governor she had given them. Not content with denying the rumors that she was treating for peace without their knowledge, she went so far as to insinuate that certain of their chief men, "in the hope of bribes, had been favoring the Spaniards, and doing very wicked work."

"If ever I do anything for you again," she haughtily concluded, "I choose to be treated more honorably. I shall therefore appoint some personages of my council to communicate with you. And in the first place I choose to hear and see for myself what has taken place already, and have satisfaction about that, before I make any reply to what you have said as to greater assistance. And so I will leave you to-day, without troubling you any further." With this, she swept majestically from the apartment, leaving the astonished ambassadors to digest her speech as best they could.

The queen's statements about her troops having been left unpaid and unfed till many of them had been compelled either to pillage, to desert, or to starve, were perfectly true; but it was Elizabeth herself who was responsible for that, not the States. It had now been almost six months since she had sent them anything at all; and Wilkes declared that he had "pawned his very carcase" for the relief of her perishing soldiers. Out of previous remittances it was notorious that a handsome percentage always stuck to the fingers of the paymaster. And Leicester, who with all his faults was generous to the last degree, had spent a fortune in supplying, so far as he could, the funds which the queen had failed to furnish.

The envoys were astonished by the accusations which the queen made, and defended themselves manfully in a private interview with Lord-treasurer Burleigh two days later. Convinced that her majesty had listened to gross misrepresentations, they strove to enlighten her by voluminous statements in writing. In the midst of this affair came the news of the treason of Stanley and York. At the same time there arrived a very blunt letter from the States to Leicester. It was written by the eminent advocate of Holland, John Olden-Barneveld, and bore date, February 4, 1587.

Barneveld, who was always a clear-sighted and plain-spoken personage, was not disposed to mince matters now. He began by alluding to the boundless confidence and affection with which the United Provinces had received the earl, and had hastened to bestow upon him the office of governor-general. They had set aside all limitations to his authority, though they were sensible that designing persons might thence take occasion to promote their own interests, to the detriment of the country. This was what had actually happened. Upon the shoulders of these evil advisers the States-General professed to lay the blame of all that had gone wrong during Leicester's administration. They alluded to the distrust early implanted between their leading men and the earl, to the detested chamber of finance, or "back-stairs council," to the obnoxious embargo, to the embezzlement of funds furnished by themselves, to the sufferings of the English troops, to the violation of ancient rights, and efforts to sow discord and sedition. Then came the recent treasons at Deventer and Fort Zutphen, which Leicester's secret prohibition had rendered it impossible for the State Council to prevent.

"We doubt not that her majesty and your excellency will think this strange language," continued the letter. "But we can assure you that we think it strange and grievous that those places should have been confided to such men, against our repeated remonstrances. . . . At last, — feeling that the existence of the state can no longer be preserved without proper authority, and that the whole community is full of emotion and distrust, on account of these great treasons, — we, the States-General, have felt constrained to establish such a government as we deem meet for the emergency. And of this we think proper to apprise your excellency."

Prince Maurice had in fact been placed at the head

of the general government, and Count Hohenlo appointed his lieutenant. The States did not design, however, to withdraw from their alliance with England by this arrangement, which was only provisional; and in closing their letter desired Leicester to use his influence with her majesty to maintain her portion of the allied forces "in good order, and in better pay."

Another blunt letter, to the queen herself, accompanied this. In it they declared that although the loss of Deventer was a greater calamity to their cause than the fall of Antwerp, they were still resolved to maintain their liberties, and depended on the performance of her majesty's engagements.

But the queen was now more exasperated than ever, and declared that "these venomous letters" had settled it once for all that Leicester should never set foot in the United Provinces again. The earl, smiting his breast, fervently ejaculated in Latin: "From such an office, good Lord, deliver us!"

The States, however, stood the storm right manfully. They replied with firmness and dignity, under date of March 1, 1587: "We are accustomed, as our predecessors have been, to remonstrate freely with our princes and governors, in regard to disorders and encroachments upon our privileges, as we did with your excellency while here." And although the earl was very angry at first, it was not long before he said he would be willing to return, provided the queen would lend him a few thousand pounds to prevent the loss of the estates he had already mortgaged.

But her majesty's ill humor was not soon over. Her chief advisers were tormented by her perverseness and caprice, till they were weary of their lives. "Our sharp words continue," wrote Secretary Walsingham, "which doth greatly disquiet her majesty, and discomfort her poor servants that attend her. The Lord-treasurer remaineth still in disgrace; and behind my back her majesty giveth out very hard speeches of myself, which I the rather credit for that I find, in dealing with her, I am nothing gracious. . . . Her majesty doth wholly lend herself to devise some further means to disgrace her poor council, in respect whereof she neglecteth all other causes."

Walsingham in vain pressed her to advance the funds needed for Leicester's return to the Provinces, if only out of regard to her own safety and the interests of her realm. "She would rather hazard the increase of confusion there — which may put the whole country in peril — than supply your want. The like course she holdeth in the rest of her causes, which," he pathetically added, "maketh me to wish myself from the helm."

One good thing, however, Elizabeth did do: when

the envoys returned to the Provinces, about the last of March, she sent over Lord Buckhurst. This accomplished and upright nobleman was commissioned to inquire into the causes of complaint, and was apparently expected somehow to smooth over and hush up all the difficulties and troubles, so that the way would be clear for Leicester's return. The queen did not reflect that the delay thus occasioned would be a great boon to Parma. Perhaps she overlooked it purposely; for during all this year, while Philip was preparing his great invasion of England, the queen's head was full of schemes for some kind of reconciliation with Spain; and Buckhurst had even been instructed cautiously to sound the public mind on that point, and to do all in his power to " frame it to peace."

Buckhurst was an able diplomatist, and he honestly did his best to quiet party strifes, as well as personal animosities. The States-General were more moderate than might have been expected. They said they had written the letter of February in the bitterness of their souls, immediately after the treasons of Stanley and York. Yet they had used no more freedom of speech than was the custom of their race in dealing with princes. Buckhurst was prudent and conciliatory in his reply; he spoke in strong terms, however, of the goodness of the queen and of the merits of Leicester. Upon the whole, his influence did much good.

But the more Lord Buckhurst learned of the true state of affairs, the more cause he found to blame Leicester for sowing dissensions there, in order to promote ambitious designs of his own. Being too conscientious not to denounce wrong wherever he discovered it, he soon got himself into disfavor. Leicester was indignant because Buckhurst had attempted to mediate between Sir John Norris and himself, and had actually succeeded in reconciling the Norrises with Count Hohenlo. The queen scolded him soundly for not scolding the States-General enough. And when, in obedience to her majesty's express commands, Buckhurst had reluctantly and cautiously broached the subject of a possible peace with Spain, she bluntly told him he ought to have had the sense to keep still. Indeed, having discovered that she had made a mistake, she instructed Leicester boldly to deny that Buckhurst had orders to say anything at all upon the subject.

CHAPTER X.

THE LOSS OF SLUYS, AND DRAKE'S BUCCANEERING.

WHILE Elizabeth was quarreling with nearly all the world except her chief enemy, Alexander of Parma was silently and steadily carrying on Philip's grand scheme for the conquest of England.

In order that his army might be able to coöperate in this enterprise with the great fleet coming from Spain, it was necessary to secure a convenient seaport. Accordingly, early in the summer of 1587, Parma set about besieging Sluys. This city stood among a network of streamlets and canals, at the head of a broad inlet called the Swint, which afforded excellent anchorage for five hundred vessels. It was on the southern border of the Zealand archipelago, some twelve or fifteen English miles nearly southwest from Flushing, and about twenty-five east of Ostend. The island of Cadzand, opposite the city, protected the harbor.

Though the environs of Sluys consisted mainly of very dubious sandbanks, which were sometimes above water and sometimes below, the city itself stood upon good solid ground and was well fortified. It had a strong detached citadel, looking toward the sea. Parma had about five thousand foot, among whom were some of the most renowned regiments of Spain, and one thousand horse. The besieged could muster only about sixteen hundred regular troops, half of whom were English; and with this slender force they had to man two and a half miles of rampart, as well as all their forts and ravelins. However, there was a great deal of spirit and determination among both the citizens and the garrison. They made several brilliant sorties, in one of which a hundred Englishmen, headed by the gallant Sir Francis Vere, not only held at bay eight companies of a certain famous legion but even drove them from their position and took many prisoners.

The Netherland women in those days, if not "strong-minded," were doubtless remarkably able-bodied; and in the sieges of Harlem and Maestricht particularly had rendered much service. When the latter place was besieged by Parma in 1579 there were three regiments of female sappers and miners, who were officered by mine mistresses of their own number and did excellent work. In the present emergency the women of Sluys bravely resolved to do what they could. Having organized a band of pioneers under two female captains, the ladies took up their spades and actually constructed an important redoubt between the citadel and the rampart, which in compliment to its fair builders was named "Fort Venus."

But in spite of all that the brave little garrison, the sturdy burghers, and the women could do, Sluys was sorely pressed, and sent to the States-General urgent entreaties for help. Such was the condition of affairs, however, that there was little prospect that anything adequate could be done. On the fifth of June the State Council in session at The Hague appointed young Maurice captain-general until Lord Leicester or somebody else should be sent from England to take command. It also repealed all those limitations upon its own action which the earl had secretly made. Just then, however, there came letters from Leicester announcing his speedy return and summoning the Council and also the States-General to meet him on his arrival at Dort.

The sudden return proposed was even more surprising than the sudden departure had been; and the Council did not altogether believe in it. After dinner they resolved not to rescind their action of the morning, lest his excellency should change his mind and not come, after all. Just about this time Barneveld got hold of a private letter of the earl to his secretary, from which it appeared that he meant to be more absolute than ever. He also stated that the queen had bidden him flatly deny that she was privately trying to negotiate with Spain. This assurance would have been cheering to the Netherlanders, had it not been contradicted in the earl's private instructions from her majesty, a copy of which, also, Barneveld had managed to procure. In this document he was enjoined to do all in his power in favor of peace; and to inform all concerned that the queen would accept Philip's handsome propositions in behalf of her own realm, whether they did so or not.

It is not surprising that when, a month later, their ingenuous governor-general arrived he was not hailed with any great enthusiasm. The States-General did not come to Dort to meet him, as desired. In regard to measures for the relief of Sluys, there was plenty of disputing, but nothing was effected. The Leicestrians berated Maurice and Justinus of Nassau, and the States party threw the blame back upon them.

The Spaniards labored under no such perplexities as to whom they should obey; and Alexander declared that never in his life had he witnessed such heroism and endurance. Though almost up to their ears in the swamps and ditches, they delved away at their mines to such purpose that in the course of a month they were close under the walls of the town. Sluys had long carried on a great trade in foreign wines, for storing which immense cellars had been excavated beneath the city. On this account the peril of the inhabitants was the greater, as the miners might any day reach these subterranean vaults and blow up half the town at once. There was much hand-to-hand fighting underground, as well as upon the ramparts. Just about the time when Leicester returned from England the citadel was lost. "We were forced to quit the fort," wrote the gallant Welsh knight Roger Williams, "leaving nothing behind us but bare earth. But here do we remain, resolute to be buried, rather than to be dishonored in the least point."

Parma had closed the harbor by means of a bridge of boats, and Leicester ordered some fire ships prepared in hope of destroying it. But such were the misunderstandings and disputes that none of the measures for relieving the town amounted to anything. Only seven hundred of the garrison remained, and these were forced to live continually on the ramparts. There was a breach in the wall almost four hundred paces wide, besides two lesser ones; the powder was exhausted; the fleet designed to bring relief sailed away, leaving them to their fate. So at last the city was forced to surrender. Parma granted the most honorable terms; otherwise the citizens had agreed to burn the town and either fight their way in a body through the lines or perish in the attempt.

The loss of Sluys was a great blow to the United Provinces, and was likely to prove a very serious matter for England as well, though Elizabeth did not know it. Everybody was disposed to blame everybody else. There is no doubt that the city might have been saved but for the mutual distrust and jealousy of the two parties. The States would not coöperate with the earl, because they could not trust him; and the earl could not carry on affairs alone, had he been ever so well disposed. Maurice was only a boy of twenty, and though he was to become a great general, the time was not yet come. Count Hohenlo, though recklessly bold, was factious and headstrong; and both he and the Norrises were at swords' points with the earl. The only good thing about Leicester's second administration was that it was short. Before the year ended he returned to England, fully resolved never to set foot in the United Provinces again.

One good blow had been struck at the great enemy of England and the Netherlands during this year. On the second of April, 1587, Sir Francis Drake, the English admiral who had already done not a little damage to the Spanish possessions in America, sailed on another buccaneering expedition with a fleet of twenty-eight vessels. Four of these were equipped by the queen and the rest by private parties. When a few days out he learned from Zealand ships homeward bound that vast stores of munitions of war were accumulating in the harbors of Cadiz and Lisbon. Drake had no doubt as to what Philip II was intending to do with them, and instantly he resolved to pounce upon them. So he suddenly appeared in the port of Cadiz; and in the course of two nights and a day he burned a hundred and fifty vessels and sunk others containing great quantities of military stores prepared for the long-intended invasion of England. This was done in the face of a dozen huge galleys which were too clumsy to damage their nimble and audacious foes. At Lisbon he disposed of a hundred vessels more, taking as much of their cargo as he could conveniently carry and destroying the rest. Having put to sea with this booty, he had the further good fortune to meet and capture a great Spanish East Indiaman with a rich cargo. This was about enough for one voyage, and before midsummer the gallant privateersman was at home again; not so ready to boast of what he had done as to warn his government of the danger impending over England. One would naturally suppose that the queen must have been inexpressibly grateful to the brave admiral who had dealt her great enemy so hard a blow. But her head was still full of schemes for making peace, and she hastened to assure Parma that she never meant anything of the kind to be done. However, in doing it the English had become skillful in handling the big Spanish galleys, a lesson which stood them in good stead the following year.

The desire for peace on the part of Elizabeth was doubtless sincere, as the secret correspondence of the period shows. Nor did she deliberately intend to treat with Spain for herself without securing peace for the Provinces as well. For a long time she clung to the idea that she could effect both objects, and thus put an end to the war which made such incessant demands upon her limited resources.

On the other hand, Parma meant nothing at all except to gain time while pretending to negotiate. The longer he could keep up appearances, the more time there would be for getting ready to invade England. So he used to write affectionate letters to her majesty, assuring her a thousand times of his ardent desire to conclude a treaty; and the queen believed him. So did not a few of her statesmen, in spite of the news brought by Drake. In the autumn there began to be talk of sending over commissioners empowered to make a treaty. Lord Burleigh wrote to the queen's agent in Flanders that if Parma would only declare upon his princely honor that the military preparations in Spain were not intended for invading England, or if even he would advise Philip to desist from doing anything of the kind, the English commissioners should wait upon him without delay.

Now the prince of Parma had not the slightest doubt about his master's designs. The invasion of England had been a pet project for a long while. In May of this year Philip had written explicitly in regard to the proposed negotiations. He wished them to be carried on by all means, even to the appointment and meeting of peace commissioners. "This is the true way to take them in," he confidentially remarked. "But my intention is that this shall never lead to any result, whatever conditions may be offered by them. On the contrary all this is done — just as they do — to deceive them, and to cool them in their preparations for defense, by inducing them to believe that such preparations will be unnecessary. You are aware that the reverse of all this is the truth, and that on our part there is to be no slackness but the greatest diligence in our efforts for the invasion of England, for which we have already made the most abundant provision in men, ships, and money."

After instructing Parma in various details he added: "Thus, and in other ways, time will be spent. Your own envoys are not to know the secret any more than the English themselves. I tell it to you only."

Accordingly in February, 1588, the English deputies

actually came to Ostend to negotiate. Months were spent in tying and untying red tape, Parma now yielding one point and now insisting on another, so that matters were protracted as adroitly as could be desired, without any result.

CHAPTER XI.

THE STORY OF THE ARMADA.

IT was intended that the invasion of England should take place in the autumn of 1587. The month of October had been chosen, because the English barns would be full of grain and the fields of wheat would have been sown for the next year. But when the time came the Armada was not ready. Drake's exploits in the harbors of Cadiz and Lisbon had interfered seriously with Philip's navy; and not a little of the work had to be done anew. So the fleet was not ready till the next spring.

In the latter part of May, 1588, the great Armada set sail from Lisbon, where it had been waiting some weeks for a favorable wind. It numbered about one hundred and forty vessels, ranging in capacity from three hundred to twelve hundred tons. It was divided into ten squadrons, each commanded by an officer of distinction, with the Duke of Medina Sidonia as admiral. About sixty of the vessels were galleons; these were great, clumsy structures, with bulwarks three or four feet thick, and something like

THE DESTRUCTION OF THE ARMADA.

a castle built up at each end. Then there were four galleasses, very large, and each rowed by three hundred galley slaves, who sat on benches amidships. These also had enormous fortresses rising high at stem and stern and were equipped with heavy cannon. They contained splendid state apartments, cabins, chapels, and pulpits; and were elegantly furnished with awnings, cushions, streamers, and other paraphernalia for display. They must have been awkward and dangerous when there was sailing or fighting to be done. The galleys were much like them, only smaller.

The aggregate tonnage of the fleet was 59,120; the number of guns 3,165. There were nearly twenty thousand soldiers on board, together with more than eight thousand sailors and two thousand galley slaves. A band of volunteers from the Spanish nobility, with their attendants, numbered nearly two thousand more. And the vicar-general of the Holy Inquisition was also on board, with about three hundred friars and inquisitors, ready to go to work immediately on English heretics.

The Armada was to proceed to Calais roads, and there to meet the general of the expedition, Alexander of Parma, with his veteran army of seventeen thousand men. Crossing to Dover, Parma was to land with twenty-three thousand of the troops and to march at once to London. Meanwhile the duke of Medina Sidonia was to occupy the Isle of Wight, with the remainder of the army. So confident of an easy conquest was Alexander that he had provided gorgeous attire for the troops who were to figure in his triumphant entry into London. It is interesting to read how many thousand yards of cramoisy velvet, how much satin and embroidery, how many hundred-weight of gold and silver lace, and what quantities of pearls and diamonds were bought, to apparel himself and his train for that glorious occasion — which, after all, never arrived.

The one thing in all these careful arrangements which had not been provided for was the all-important junction of the two armies at Calais. A hundred and forty swift little cruisers of Holland and Zealand were watching every nook and cranny of the coast, so that Parma's light flotilla could not get out. His vessels were simply transport boats, small enough to navigate the inland waters of the Low Countries, and not at all able to resist an attack. Unless the blockading fleet should first be routed by the Spanish ships Parma's army could not quit the shore. But the Armada had no vessels that could venture among the dangerous shoals of that coast. They were too unwieldy for this perilous service. Parma had foreseen this difficulty long before; but he had not been able to make his royal master perceive it also. It could not be got into the king's head that there would be any blockading squadron there; or that Parma could not easily come out with his flatboats whenever he liked.

After the Armada had been about three weeks at sea, and had reached the dangerous neighborhood of Cape Finisterre, it encountered a severe storm. The largest of the four great galleys, the Diana, went to the bottom with all on board. Two of the others in the same squadron, the Princess and the Vasana, were also in imminent peril. On board the latter, among the wretched slaves toiling at the oars, sat one David Gwynn, a Welshman, who had been taken prisoner of war eleven years before. He was known to have been a sailor all his life; and in this desperate crisis the less experienced master of the galley condescended to ask his advice. David Gwynn was not slow to seize the opportunity for which he had waited all those wretched years. "There is no use in trying to overtake the rest of the fleet," replied he. "Unless we take in every rag of sail and trust to the oars alone, we are sure to go to the bottom. These soldiers cannot help us now; send them below, where they will be out of our way, and we will do our best to reach the nearest port." The anxious captain dared not refuse; and accordingly all the soldiers, except a few who sat on the benches among the chained rowers, were ordered beneath the hatches.

There was scarcely a man among all the gang who had not contrived to fashion for himself some rude weapon, which he secretly wore, ready for any chance of escape. At a signal from Gwynn each slave stabbed the soldier nearest him, while their leader killed the captain. Then rushing below they overpowered and put to death all the rest. By this time the commander of the fourth galley, the Royal, suspecting foul play on board the Vasana, sent a broadside which killed nine of the mutineers. But Gwynn and his men were now as well armed and as desperate as men could be. They boarded the Royal, and with the help of its own slaves mastered the vessel and put the soldiers to the sword. The gale had now abated. The brave Welshman made his way toward the French coast with his two great galleys and landed at Bayonne. Of that luckless squadron only one was left to join the fleet, which was finally reassembled at Coruña.

A full month was spent in repairing damages, and it was not until July 22 that the Armada again set sail. Seven days later the Spanish fleet first caught sight of English shores, as they entered the Channel.

England had been much in doubt about the threatened invasion, but by this time people generally were at least anxious. But they had heard of a terrible storm in the Bay of Biscay, and hoped the Armada, wherever it might be going, had been disabled for a long time. During that very week orders had come down from London to the admiral at Plymouth to disarm the four largest ships, as they were sure not to be needed before another year. Fortunately this had not been accomplished, when on Friday afternoon, July 29, a merchant ship came full sail into Plymouth Bay with news that the dreaded Armada was already in the Channel.

Then England awoke. There was no longer any doubt. Not a moment was lost. "The blaze of ten thousand beacon fires, from the Land's End to Margate, and from the Isle of Wight to Cumberland," says Motley, " gave warning to every Englishman that the foe was at last upon them." Macaulay's fine poem, The Armada, vividly pictures the instant rising of our brave ancestors against their mighty foe : —

Night sunk upon the dusky beach, and on the purple sea;
Such night in England ne'er had been, nor e'er again shall be.
From Eddystone to Berwick bounds, from Lynn to Milford Bay,
The time of slumber was as bright, as busy as the day;
For swift to east, and swift to west, the warning radiance spread,—
High on St. Michael's Mount it shone, it shone on Beachy Head.
Far o'er the deep the Spaniard saw, along each southern shire,
Cape beyond cape, in endless range, those twinkling points of fire.

· · · · · · · · · ·

The sentinel on Whitehall gate looked forth into the night,
And saw, o'erhanging Richmond Hill, that streak of blood-red
  light.
The bugle's note and cannon's roar the deathlike silence broke,
And with one start, and with one cry, the royal city woke.
At once, on all her stately gates, arose the answering fires;
At once the wild alarum clashed from all her reeling spires;
From all the batteries of the Tower pealed loud the voice of fear,
And all the thousand masts of Thames sent back a louder cheer;
And from the farthest wards was heard the rush of hurrying feet,
And the broad streams of flags and pikes dashed down each rous-
  ing street;
And broader still became the blaze, and louder still the din,
As fast from every village round, the horse came hurrying in.

While the Armada was slowly sailing onward toward the appointed rendezvous at Calais, there was great activity in Plymouth harbor. Before sunrise sixty of the best ships had left port. That Saturday afternoon the hostile fleets had their first sight of each other through the dimness of a drizzling rain. At nine the next morning they met. There were one hundred and thirty-six Spanish ships, ninety of which were large; the English had only sixty-seven sail.

The Armada offered battle, but the English declined, aware that with vessels so light and swift they could choose their own time for a regular fight. For the present they preferred hanging upon the rear, to tease, harass, and then elude their clumsy foes. The huge towering galleons were an easy mark for the English artillery, while the Spanish gunners were not expert enough to do much harm to their brisk little enemies. Admiral Oquendo, vexed at seeing most of his balls quite thrown away, blamed his master gunner for careless firing. The gunner, enraged by the reproof, quietly laid a train to the powder magazine, and after lighting it threw himself into the sea. Two decks blew up; the great castle at the stern rose into the clouds, and with it went the paymaster of the whole fleet, a vast amount of money, and two hundred men. In trying to assist the survivors several other ships became entangled and much damaged. The great galleon of Don Pedro de Valdez, commander of the Andalusian squadron, was at length forced to surrender. On the whole, this first " small fight," as Hawkins called it, was quite encouraging.

On Monday, the first of August, both fleets moved on along the coast, the English still hanging on the rear, but refusing to come to close quarters. They were well aware that in a hand-to-hand grapple the great Spanish ships would prove the stronger; so they contented themselves with what they could do in less hazardous ways. The Armada must needs go on to Calais; its audacious pursuers in their slender and swift-sailing craft could fight or leave off fighting whenever they liked. Doubtless they found it great fun to pelt the big galleons with a saucy broadside and then to slip through the very fingers of their unwieldy and exasperated enemies.

So it went on till Tuesday morning, when the first general engagement took place. They were sailing between Portland and St. Albans Head when the Armada, taking advantage of a change of wind, attacked the English fleet. The battle was protracted, but indecisive. "We had a sharp and long fight," wrote Hawkins in an official dispatch to Walsingham. "If her majesty's ships had been manned with a full supply of good gunners," remarked an old artillery-man long after, "it would have been the wofullest time ever the Spaniards took in hand, and the most noble victory ever heard of would have been her majesty's. But our sins were the cause that so much powder and shot were spent, so long time in fight, and in comparison so little harm done."

At night the English got the weather gauge again and continued the pursuit. Their fleet now numbered more than one hundred sail; yet few of these were ships of war, and the merchantmen that had been hastily equipped for service were chiefly useful to make a show. On Wednesday there was but little fighting; but on Thursday, off Dunnose, on the Isle of Wight, a few of the principal vessels on each side had a skirmish closer and sharper than any before. The English inflicted much harm, but suffered little.

At last on Saturday afternoon the Armada dropped anchor in Calais roads, where it was to be met by its commander-in-chief. It lay at a short distance from shore compactly drawn up in a half-moon. The English, who had been reinforced by Lord Henry Seymour with a squadron of sixteen vessels, lay only a mile and a half below.

Matters were evidently coming to a crisis. As soon as Parma and his veteran army should appear upon the scene the Armada was to cover the passage of his flotilla across the straits to Dover, which would require only a few hours, and then the chief difficulties would be over. It would be no great trouble to conquer England when once landed upon her shores.

So all eyes were strained with gazing eastward to catch the first glimpse of Parma's fleet, bringing the splendid army that was to subdue England. All through the calm moonlight night they watched, and all through the bright tranquil day that followed, with an impatience that grew sharper every hour. But nothing was seen or heard of Alexander. Messengers had been dispatched to him day after day ever since the week before; but not one had come back. It did not occur to them that they might attempt to clear the way for him; and so they simply waited. Meanwhile the English had a little scheme of their own.

That Sunday evening the sky became dark and

lowering. The Spaniards grew uneasy. They had reason enough; for Calais harbor was not a safe place for such a fleet in a storm, even had there been no enemy in the neighborhood. At one o'clock in the morning their sentinels caught the sound of distant oars. While they were anxiously listening a sudden glare lighted up the black waves and six blazing vessels burst into view, almost among them. The Spaniards knew only too well what fireships might mean. They remembered the floating volcanoes at Antwerp three years before; and it flashed upon their shuddering memories that Gianibelli, their inventor, now lived in England.

Panic-struck, they shrieked: "The fire ships of Antwerp! the fire ships of Antwerp!" The cry rang throughout the fleet; and on the instant, frantic with terror, they cut every cable, and every vessel made haste to flee. Two were set on fire by the flaming ships and consumed; several of the galleons became entangled and helpless; and the rest of the fleet, in wild disorder, drifted before the rising wind toward the fatal quicksands of the Flemish coast.

This was the beginning of the end. In the morning the English overtook their flying foes off Gravelines. They had by this time collected their vessels as well as they were able and gave battle. It was a long and severe engagement. The Spaniards were extremely anxious to get back to Calais; but the English, having now both wind and tide in their favor, stood decidedly in their way. The Armada lavished incredible quantities of powder and ball without destroying a single English ship or killing a hundred men. Their own best remaining vessels were severely damaged, and at least sixteen utterly destroyed. Not less than four or five thousand of their men perished.

The engagement lasted from ten in the morning till nearly five in the afternoon. The Armada, its small shot having been exhausted, now took to flight. The ammunition of the English also was almost spent; but, as the lord-admiral afterward told the story, they "put on a brag countenance and gave them chase, as though they had wanted nothing." Another officer remarked that "the Almighty had stricken them with a wonderful fear." Still driven apace before the westerly wind, the next morning the Spanish fleet was close upon the fatal shores of Zealand. The wind veered toward the south just in time to allow them to gain the open sea once more. But still they fled before the breeze, followed still by their triumphant foes. On and on, through the North Sea they were driven, closely pursued for four days longer by the gallant Howard, Drake, and Frobisher, who found it not difficult to maintain the "brag countenance" now.

On Friday, August 12, the remnant of the invincible Armada was still flying northward between the Scotch and the Danish coasts. The English fleet, having no longer either food or fire, concluded to let it make the rest of its homeward voyage alone. It was destined to find but cold consolation among the Orkneys and Hebrides. On the Sunday following a most violent storm arose, which was followed by successive tempests for more than a fortnight. Forty of the remaining vessels were wrecked upon the Irish coast, September 2, and nearly every soul on board perished. Only fifty-three of the one hundred and thirty-six vessels which left Coruña in July ever returned. Of the thirty thousand men on board probably not ten thousand ever saw their native land again. Spain was filled with mourning from one end to the other.

So ended the career of the great Armada. "Their invincible and dreadful navy," said Drake, "with all its great and terrible ostentation, did not so much as sink or take one ship, bark, pinnace, or cockboat of ours; or even burn so much as one sheepcote upon this land." One can hardly fail to be reminded of the message sent in answer to the prayer of Hezekiah: "Therefore thus saith the Lord concerning the king of Assyria. He shall not come into this city, nor shoot an arrow there, nor come before it with shield, nor cast a bank against it. By the way that he came, by the same shall he return, and shall not come into this city, saith the Lord. For I will defend this city, to save it, for mine own sake, and for my servant David's sake." [1]

Even thus did God defend England in this time of her peril. The greatest empire of the world had done its utmost to destroy a little seagirt kingdom, then ranking only at a third or fourth rate among European nations. And though the undertaking had utterly failed, at the outset there was every prospect that it would succeed. To contend with the Armada, whose numbers and strength have been mentioned, the navy of England could produce only thirty-four men-of-war, none of which exceeded eleven hundred tons, and some were even below one hundred. Its aggregate tonnage was scarcely one fifth that of the Spanish fleet; its total number of guns but one fourth. The greater part of the vessels otherwise furnished were not so equipped as to be of much service. Had the Spanish army effected a landing, there was little to oppose their progress. At the very time when the Armada lay in Calais roads, England's army, such as it was, had not even been mustered into camp. There was abundant patriotism, it is true; but nothing like an organized, disciplined, well-appointed army was to

[1] 2 Kings 19: 32–34.

be found. There were no fortresses, no commissary, no systematic preparation of any kind. It would seem that Parma's veteran troops might have marched to London without much trouble had they once landed.

What if the great schemes of Philip II had been carried out? Of course, we say, the history of England, Holland, and America would have been very different from what it is. But our answer should come nearer home than that. It would have made a great difference to us who are now living. Would it have been a small matter to us if the Bible had not been translated into our mother tongue, as it was in the time of Elizabeth's successor? Parma on the English throne would never have given us that. There would have been plenty of racks and gibbets and stakes; there would have been a great many more Englishmen in "the noble army of the martyrs." Instead of trial by jury would have been the Inquisition; in place of parliaments and congresses and ballot box would have been imperial "edicts" with foreign armies to enforce them. Well may we thank God that he defeated the "invincible Armada"!

NOTE. — An interesting and valuable collection of official documents entitled "La Armada Invincible" has lately been compiled by Captain Duro, of the Spanish navy. It has been reviewed by Mr. Froude in a series of articles entitled, "The Spanish Story of the Armada." The discrepancies between the Spanish and the English accounts are in general but slight. It is interesting, however, to learn that the duke of Medina Sidonia took command of the expedition greatly against his will, and protesting that he had not one qualification for the post, a statement which seems to have been entirely correct. He declared that his health was bad, he was always seasick, he knew nothing of naval warfare or of navigation or of anything else which he needed to know. Had the old admiral who preceded him lived long enough to conduct the enterprise in person, it might have succeeded. As it was, the fleet sailed with water and food which had been put on board four months before; and a great amount of illness resulted. Many other things naturally went wrong, though Philip fancied that, between his own explicit instructions and Parma's generalship, there would not be much for the admiral to do.

The Spanish account states that news did come from Parma on that Sunday when the fleet lay in Calais roads; he said he was at Bruges, his transports at Dunkirk, and nothing ready. Nothing is said of the Dutch cruisers, which would have stood very much in their way, had they been ready.

CHAPTER XII.

HOW BREDA WAS TAKEN.

WHILE the English and the Netherlanders were rejoicing over the defeat of their common enemy, they became very cordial toward each other for a time. The queen sent over Sir John Norris soon afterward to thank the States for their assistance, and invited them to join in a naval expedition against Spain the following spring. Nothing could have been more to their liking than an enterprise of this kind. They knew that however good the Spaniards might be as soldiers, they did not count for much at sea compared with the English or themselves.

Unfortunately for the mutual confidence just now restored, a fresh instance of treason occurred to unsettle it. The city of Gertruydenberg, whose English commandant had refused to acknowledge the authority of Prince Maurice and the States-General even after Leicester had resigned the government, was treacherously given up to the Spaniards. Naturally this awakened afresh the indignation and distrust of the Netherlanders toward their English allies, and the joint expedition was not as heartily undertaken, or as well managed, as it might otherwise have been.

The special design was to stir up a revolution in Portugal, now subject to Philip II. In order to accomplish this they were to take with them as a candidate for the Portuguese crown Don Antonio, the famous pretender. About one hundred and sixty vessels were mustered in Plymouth harbor in April, 1589, of which forty were from Holland. Only six were regular men-of-war, the rest being merely armed merchantmen. They carried some fourteen thousand men, including fifteen hundred of the Dutch. Norris and Drake were in command, assisted by other noted officers.

It was the eighteenth of April when they left Plymouth, and for some reason they stopped at Coruña, in England commonly called "The Groyne," instead of hastening toward Lisbon. They destroyed some shipping supposed to be intended for Philip's next invasion of England; took and pillaged the lower town; and routed a large Spanish force at Burgos. Meanwhile they lost some of their men by desertion, and a great number by fevers and dysentery. Thus they were delayed so long that the Spaniards had time to get ready for them at Lisbon. So the outcome of the expedition was not what had been expected. They had braved their old enemy, and had done him some mischief; but they had not effected a revolution in Portugal. "As a freebooting foray," says Motley, "it could hardly be thought successful; although it was a splendid triumph compared with the result of the invincible Armada."

Shortly after the return of the fleet startling news came from France. On the second of August King Henry III had been assassinated at the palace of Saint Cloud by a Dominican friar named Jacques Clement. This event greatly concerned not only France, but England and the Low Countries as well. In order to explain the connection, let us revert to the situation in France.

For a long period France had been almost continually distracted by civil war. There were three distinct factions, then known respectively as the Royalists, the Leaguers, and the Huguenots. The first consisted largely of the king's favorites, who held offices about him; the second, of the ultra-Catholics; the third, of the Protestants. The head of the Royalist party was of course Henry III of Valois; the head of the Leaguers was Henry, duke of Guise; and the head of the Huguenots was, at this time, Henry of Navarre. Sometimes each party would fight both of the others. Sometimes two of them would join forces for a while in order to beat the third, after which they could fight each other to their hearts' content until the third had rallied again.

The king had no children, and at his death the house of Valois would become extinct. The next male heir was Henry of Navarre, who was at this time a Protestant. It was this fact which led to the formation of the League, secretly, December 31, 1584. It was formed between the duke of Guise together with several of his family, on the one hand, and the deputies of Philip of Spain on the other. By this compact the Leaguers bound themselves to place on the throne of France at the death of the present king the old cardinal of Bourbon, instead of Henry of Navarre, the true heir. It was further agreed that all heretics, both in France and in the Netherlands, should be exterminated. Philip promised to furnish at least fifty thousand crowns a month toward the expenses of the League. The whole matter was kept profoundly secret; even Parma was not informed for some time.

Philip had various reasons besides his devotion to the Romish Church for his interest in this matter. In his opinion a civil war in France was always a good thing, whatever it might be about. So long as his neighbors there had their hands full of fighting to do at home, they would not be likely to meddle with any of his affairs. Accordingly he was careful to furnish the funds he had promised, to keep up the operations of the League, although this secret outlay cramped his military movements in the Low Countries not a little. Parma was forced to do as he could, and was sometimes reduced to extremities for want of money and supplies. And now that Henry III was dead, Philip hoped that by prompt and shrewd maneuvering he might get France for himself.

So Parma was privately directed, much to his vexation, to invade France at an early day as if to uphold the League. This diversion of Spanish troops and resources from the long-standing war in the Low Countries, for a year or two, gave the patriots a little respite, during which they contrived to strike some good blows for their cause.

Young Maurice of Nassau had been devoting himself with great ardor to the study of military science under the learned Simon Stevinus, of Bruges. He and his cousin Lewis William, the young stadtholder of Friesland, were to revolutionize military matters in the United Provinces at no distant day. Just now occurred an opportunity for a daring exploit.

Breda was a city of Brabant lying only a few miles inland from the network of waters embracing the islands of Zealand. It was upon a stream called the Merk. From the days of old it had belonged to the house of Nassau. Its splendid castle had been built by Henry of Nassau fifty years before. At present it was occupied by five companies of Italian

HOW BREDA WAS TAKEN. 145

infantry and one of cavalry, commanded by Lanzavecchia, who was also governor of the neighboring city of Gertruydenberg.

One day in February, 1590, a boatman named Adrian van der Berg came secretly to Prince Maurice to disclose something of importance. He lived some eight or ten miles from Breda and for a long time had supplied the castle with turf, the customary fuel of the country. It had occurred to him that as his vessel was hardly ever inspected it would be possible to conceal some soldiers in the hold, and thus get possession of the castle.

Prince Maurice consulted Barneveld, who agreed with him in liking the idea, and proposed Captain Charles de Heraugière to undertake the matter. Only a few persons were taken into confidence, and the arrangements were made as rapidly as possible. Captain Héraugière selected his men one by one, in part from his own company and in part from other troops. There were only sixty-eight in all. They were to have embarked on the night of February 25, but the boatman failed to keep the appointment. The next night, being perhaps a little faint-hearted when the moment arrived, he sent two daring nephews in his place.

The men stowed themselves away in the hold of the boat where they had not room even to sit upright.

A flooring of boards overhead supported a quantity of turf, which seemed to be the only cargo. After a little a head wind sprang up, bringing blocks of ice from the sea. This made navigation so dangerous that the boat had to lie still till Thursday, when the men were forced to get out and straighten their cramped limbs for a few hours at a lonely castle called Nordam. That night the wind became favorable and they embarked once more. But it was not till about three o'clock on Saturday afternoon that they found themselves in the outer harbor at Breda.

The officer came on board, as a matter of form, talked a little about the turf, stepped carelessly into the small cabin, which only a sliding trapdoor separated from the hold where the soldiers were, and went away, promising to send men to tow the vessel into the castle dock. But while moving slowly along the boat had the ill luck to strike some obstruction under water and sprang a leak. The men in the hold presently found the water up to their knees. The boatmen were forced to pump with might and main lest the vessel and all should go to the bottom. In the course of two hours the soldiers sent from the castle succeeded in towing it into the inner harbor as unsuspectingly as the luckless Trojans are said to have dragged the wooden horse full of Greeks into Troy. The laborers now set to work so eagerly at unloading the turf that, although it was almost night, they were likely soon to reach the bottom of the cargo and discover what was underneath. Besides, the soldiers in the hold were beginning to sneeze and cough in the most alarming manner. Lieutenant Held, finding it impossible to suppress his cough, entreated the man at his side to stab him to the heart. But the cool boatmen overhead contrived to keep up so much noise by pumping and shouting that the crowd standing by did not hear anything suspicious; and as soon as possible the laborers were dismissed with drink money, and orders to come in the morning to finish.

Night closed in around the little vessel and the strong citadel. The fateful moment when the bold adventurers must either triumph or die was close at hand. There was no chance of retreat. One of the boatmen had secretly stolen away to carry word to Prince Maurice that they were within the precincts of the castle, and that the governor had suddenly gone to Gertruydenberg, leaving his young nephew to command Breda. Captain Heraugière said a few words to his comrades — words befitting a gallant leader of brave men in such a moment, and about midnight the soldiers silently stepped on shore. They formed in two parties. Heraugière led one company to attack the guardhouse, while Captain Fervet went to seize the arsenal with the other.

Encountering a sentinel in the darkness Captain Heraugière quickly overpowered him and forced him to tell, in a whisper, how many soldiers composed the garrison.

"Three hundred and fifty," gasped the sentinel, with Heraugière's hands still clutching his throat.

"How many did he say?" eagerly whispered the men behind.

"Only fifty of them," replied their leader, striking down at a blow the captain of the watch, who had just emerged from the guardhouse. The alarm brought others with lights, but they quickly retreated into the guardhouse. The assailants fired upon them through windows and doors, and in a few moments every man of the watch had fallen. Meanwhile Fervet and his little band captured the magazine; and the young Lanzavecchia having been wounded, a panic seized the garrison and they fled across the bridge that joined the citadel to the town. Two hours before dawn came Count Hohenlo with the vanguard of Prince Maurice's troops. Soon the prince himself arrived with several officers of note and a larger force, marching briskly to the ringing music of "Wilhelmus van Nassouwen." Before sunrise Breda was won. Forty of the garrison had fallen, but not one of the patriots.

The terms of surrender were favorable, and the burghers promised two months' wages to every soldier of the prince's party. Maurice guaranteed protection of person and property, as well as freedom of conscience, to all who would show themselves loyal citizens. Public worship according to the Roman Catholic ritual was suspended for the present, however.

The morning found young Maurice in possession of his patrimonial city and castle, and there was great rejoicing throughout the United Provinces over the brilliant exploit. Parma, who was then preparing to lead an army into France, was deeply chagrined at the loss of Breda, and expressed his opinion of the behavior of its defenders by publicly beheading three captains in Brussels and by removing Lanzavecchia from the command of Gertruydenberg.

CHAPTER XIII.

PARMA IN FRANCE, AND MAURICE AT HOME.

THOUGH Henry of Navarre was evidently the rightful heir to the throne of France, he had yet to win it by the sword. As previously agreed, the party of the League set up the old and infirm cardinal of Bourbon as king, with the title of Charles X. But Philip claimed that nothwithstanding the Salic law, his eldest daughter, Isabella Clara Eugenia, ought to succeed to the French crown in the right of her mother, who was a daughter of Henry II. The cardinal of Bourbon was not likely to live long; and could the claims of Henry be set aside, Philip was ready to take possession of France in his daughter's name.

Henry of Navarre had almost nothing of material resources, but he was full of courage and hope. He was at present busy in besieging Paris. By gaining possession of the strategic points around it, especially along the Seine and Marne, he had cut off its supplies and reduced the inhabitants to extremities. It was estimated that out of about two hundred thousand inhabitants, as many as twelve thousand had starved to death before the end of July. The Leaguers, under the duke of Mayenne, had been severely defeated by Henry in the famous battle of Ivry, and were anxiously waiting for Parma to come to their assistance.

Alexander could not set out till the beginning of August, for want of funds. It was so long since his army had been paid that, in spite of their attachment to him, they had become demoralized and many of them were even mutinous. He was forced to pawn his own jewels and furniture to keep them from perishing. His urgent entreaties in their behalf were unheeded by his royal master, who only reiterated the command to relieve Paris and capture Calais and Boulogne. "Talk no more of difficulties, but conquer them," was Philip's cold reply to all his complaints.

At length Parma set out for France with twelve thousand foot and three thousand horse, having received funds enough to make shift for a time. He joined Mayenne not far from Paris, on the twenty-second of August. A few days later, on the right bank of the Marne, their allied forces encamped within a mile or two of the army of Henry. He was eager to give them battle, but, as their camp was well protected, he was forced to wait until they should give him the opportunity. After seven days of waiting, the troops of Parma and Mayenne appeared and deployed to the right and left in two great wings, as if about to form their line of battle. But by an unforeseen maneuver they proceeded to occupy a position at a village directly opposite Lagny and connected with it by a stone bridge. A heavy cannonade from this point, together with a flanking movement by another body of their troops, soon carried Lagny, and Paris was relieved.

The cavaliers of Henry, many of whom were volunteers serving at their own expense, were so much vexed and disheartened at having Lagny thus taken before their eyes without a chance to fight, that they rapidly fell away from his army. Meanwhile, Parma captured Corbeil after a month's siege, which opened the Seine also. Immense quantities of provisions poured into starving Paris, so that there was no longer any danger of its being taken at present. As Parma had now accomplished the objects for which he had been sent to France, and as there were many sick among his troops, not to mention his own failing health, he set out on his return to Brussels in November. But hardly was his back turned before the Huguenot forces recaptured both Lagny and Corbeil. The rivers Seine and Marne having thus been closed again, Paris was once more threatened with famine. So Parma's task was all undone in less time than he had spent in accomplishing it.

Meanwhile Prince Maurice had been effecting a good deal in a different line. Heretofore there had not been much system, and still less science, in the war department of the United Provinces. The army had been made up chiefly of domestic militia and foreign hirelings. They were poorly drilled and badly governed, as well as irregularly paid. During his years of study and thought the young Maurice had become convinced that things might be much better managed. It was evident that a good deal of fighting was yet to be done, and he resolved that his country should have the benefit of whatever was anywhere known of the art of war. He had been studying with this sole end in view. His cousin Lewis William, the young stadtholder of Friesland, was also hard at work in the same line.

Whatever the Romans knew in their day, or the Macedonians in theirs, about laying out camps or building bridges or executing difficult evolutions, Maurice and Lewis William dug out of books and revived. It had been the custom for troops to move in great solid squares, wheeling slowly and clumsily all one way, and scarcely able to wheel at all unless they had ample room. Lewis William sensibly reflected that in a country full of swamps, dikes, and other inconvenient features, it would be well to teach the men how to manage when they were in a tight place. So he drilled them in small bodies, teaching them a variety of useful maneuvers which could be executed when grand evolutions were out of the question. When the old colonels saw what could be done in this way they ceased to object to the new tactics.

Prince Maurice found occasion to reconstruct almost everything connected with the army, from the general organization down to the minor details of equipment and pay. In some points the Spanish army may have served him as a model, as it served the English. But in at least one it served as a warning. The Spanish soldiery had always been notorious for marauding and mutiny. The dreadful "Antwerp Fury," in which some eight thousand citizens perished, was the work of mutineers. During this very summer of 1590 a considerable portion of Parma's army was in open mutiny at Contray. The cause was simply that the king allowed his troops to go unpaid, sometimes for two years together. In such circumstances the soldiers could hardly be blamed for rebellion. Maurice resolved, as the first step toward insuring good order and obedience, that the Netherland armies should henceforth be promptly and fairly paid, come what might. He established efficient discipline, and severely punished any who were found guilty of plundering. His soldiers, being well and promptly paid, had no occasion to steal, and his camp had the orderly air of a well-governed city in time of peace. The farmers would bring their produce for sale in preference to seeking any other market, so sure were they of being well treated and honestly paid.

Some changes of importance were also made in respect to the arms used. At this period, though gunpowder had been invented a long time before, the weapons and armor of earlier ages — the lance, pike, halberd, buckler, and coat of mail — had not disappeared from the field. Men had not fully learned how much more could be effected by calling the forces of nature to fight for them than by human muscles and sinews. Most of the infantry still fought with pikes and halberds. Prince Maurice doubled the number of firearms, though he retained thirty pikemen in each company, as well as three buckler men to attend upon the captain for his personal protection. He did much more with artillery, also, than had been attempted before. His siege guns were 48-pounders and 24-pounders, his field pieces 12-pounders; and he took care to provide a course of instruction for military engineers at the university of Leyden.

The matter of transportation was no longer left to take care of itself, for Maurice perceived how much might be done by using the canals for conveying troops and supplies. These watery highways everywhere enabled his men to move hither and thither without fatigue or noise; their appearing and disappearing seemed almost magical. But perhaps the greatest of his innovations was in connection with the use of the spade. He considered earthworks and trenches of so much importance that he made the pay of the miners greater than that of the common soldiers. If a soldier served in that work, he had a handsome daily addition to his ordinary wages.

So between the strict discipline, the superior drill, the improved arms, the better engineering, and the prompt payment, the army of the United Provinces shortly became a model for the rest of Europe. In the campaign of 1591 the young commander gave some illustrations of the way in which he might be expected to proceed.

There were several different matters on hand, and Parma was to be kept in doubt as to which Prince Maurice would undertake first. In the region of the river Waal lay three important cities still held by the Spaniards: Gertruydenberg, Bois le Duc, and Nymwegen. Upon the river Yssel, which flows northward through the province of Gelderland to the Zuyder Zee, lay Zutphen and Deventer, whose Spanish garrisons controlled the river, and in great measure shut off communication between the provinces on either side of it. Then away to the north was Groningen, and some other fortified points still to be won.

At the opening of the campaign Prince Maurice threatened Gertruydenberg and Bois le Duc so seriously that Parma was obliged to send to those places reinforcements which he could not well spare. This was precisely what Maurice desired; and before any change of plan was suspected he was in the vicinity of Zutphen with something of an army.

Early one morning the guard at the gate of the great fort opposite Zutphen saw a few peasants outside with their wives, having for sale baskets of eggs, butter, and cheese. So the soldiers as usual came out to buy. While they were bargaining over their market stuff, all of a sudden one of the supposed women drew a pistol and shot a soldier dead. At the signal the rest of the pretended peasants threw off their disguises, and in a few minutes all the guard were overpowered. The troops lying in ambush darted in, and presently raised their flag over the great fort of Zutphen, without having lost a man. Within a week the town also surrendered to Maurice, who at once marched down to Deventer, seven miles below, and sent his artillery and munitions by boats.

Deventer was commanded by Count Herman van den Berg, who was own cousin to Prince Maurice, his mother being a sister of William the Silent. There were several of these young Van den Bergs in the Spanish army, and it repeatedly happened, as now, that they had to fight against their Nassau kinsmen. At this time a Spanish officer jocosely remarked: "We shall now have a droll siege — cousins on the outside, cousins in the inside. There will be one or two sham fights and then the cousins will make it up and arrange matters to suit themselves." The young Count van den Berg was deeply hurt at this gibe; and at mass next morning, in the presence of all the officers, solemnly vowed never to give up the city until he was obliged to be carried from the walls.

He was as good as his word, but Prince Maurice and Count Lewis William were too much for him. The prince had not studied military engineering in vain. Within a few days the town was completely invested, the batteries began to play, and a breach was soon made in the walls. An assault followed, and though it was not completely successful, the citizens saw that it would not be possible to hold out much longer, and clamored for a capitulation. Van den Berg had been wounded in the eye, so that he was wholly blind for the time; and he did not refuse to surrender. His cousins received him very cordially at headquarters, and he was afterwards sent in Maurice's own coach to a place of safety, and attended by the prince's own surgeon. While the cousins were together they chatted freely about military matters. "I've often told Verdugo," said Count Herman, "that the States had no power to make a regular siege, nor to come with proper artillery into the field; and he agreed with me. But we were both wrong, for I now see the contrary."

Verdugo and the Van den Bergs had occasion to see this a good many times. Count Louis, a younger member of the family, lost his life in an unsuccessful defense of Steenwyck the next summer; and Count Frederic was obliged to surrender the strong fortress of Coeworden to his Nassau cousins. It was the more mortifying because when Maurice had first summoned the place to surrender Count Frederic had boldly replied: "Tell him first to beat down my walls as flat as the ditch, and then bring five or six storms. Six months after that I will consider whether I will send a trumpet."

The veteran Verdugo soon conceived a high respect for the military prowess of the young commander. "I have been informed," he wrote in an intercepted letter, " that Count Maurice of Nassau wishes to fight me. Had I the opportunity, I assure you that I should not fail him; for even if ill luck were my portion, I should at least not escape the honor of being beaten by such a personage. I beg you to tell him so, with my affectionate compliments."

The skill, the boldness, the celerity of Maurice's operations amazed everybody. While he was busy in reducing several places far to the north, around Groningen, Parma thought it safe to make a diversion by laying siege to a fort which Maurice had built near Nymwegen. Hardly had he begun the siege, when, in spite of broad rivers and vast quagmires lying between, Maurice and his army were on the spot, and by a shrewd stratagem compelled him to retreat. And now, while everybody was waiting to see him besiege Nymwegen, he suddenly appeared before Hulst, twelve miles from Antwerp, and took it in five days. Steenwyck and Coeworden fell in the following campaign.

CHAPTER XIV.

THE CLOSE OF PARMA'S CAREER.

THERE was now at hand an event which had an important bearing upon the fortunes of the Netherland war. The great general who for fourteen years had been faithfully serving Philip of Spain was about to leave his unfinished task forever. There were circumstances of peculiar hardship and injustice to embitter his last days. For a long time his health had been impaired, yet his remarkable determination, as well as the urgency of his duties, forbade him to rest. But the treatment of Philip was harder than all. It had been evident to Parma for two or three years that underneath the smooth words of the king were concealed a deep-seated distrust and ill will. Although proudly conscious that he had never swerved in the least from his loyalty, he knew that the ever-suspicious monarch had set spies to watch his every movement, under pretense of giving their counsel and aid. The king had requested him to confer regularly with Mendoza, Tassis, and Moreo; he had enjoined it likewise upon them "to assist, correspond, and harmonize in every way" with Parma; but they understood very well what was really to be done, and were more than willing to do it. "I must make bold to remind your majesty," secretly wrote Moreo in June, 1590, "that there never was an Italian prince who failed to pursue his own ends, and that there are few in the world that are not wishing to become greater than they are." Yet the personage against whom this insinuation was aimed had once been on the point of putting to death with his own hand one who had ventured to propose his securing the sovereignty of the Netherlands for himself.

In the course of that year Commander Moreo suddenly died, but slanders regarding Parma did not cease. Other pens eagerly carried on the work of detraction. Alexander, aware of the misrepresentations made to the king, indignantly remonstrated with him for not putting a stop to them, or at least apprising him of the sources from which they came. It was not in Philip II to deal truly with anybody; and so he carelessly replied that he did not remember receiving any such communications, or at any rate he had paid so little regard to them that he had lost the letters. His well-beloved and faithful nephew need have no fear of such calumnies doing him the smallest damage.

So the spies continued their sly insinuations as to Alexander's motives and aims; and after a year or two Philip resolved to remove him from his command. But instead of doing it frankly and openly he set about the matter in the crooked, stealthy way which he always chose. In February, 1592, he wrote with seeming affection: "Nephew, you know the confidence which I have always placed in you, and all that I have placed in your hands; and I know how much you are to me, and how earnestly you work in my service; and so, if I could have you at the same time in several places, it would be a great relief to me."

After this artful beginning he went on to say that just then it was very necessary that Alexander should come to Spain, in order to advise with him about several important matters. Accordingly he was to put all the Netherland matters into the hands of the old Count Mansfeld, who was to be assisted by the marquis of Ceralbo; and as soon as possible he was to set out for Genoa, where he was to embark for Spain.

Now this marquis of Ceralbo was another of Philip's spies, lately come from the court on purpose to carry on his secret designs against his "dear nephew." At his setting out from the Netherlands the king had given him minute instructions in writing, how to manage the removal of Parma. If Alexander should consent to go to Spain as desired, Ceralbo would only need to assist his departure, and was to expatiate meanwhile on the honor of being summoned to take counsel with his majesty. But otherwise Ceralbo was to tell him plainly that he could choose only between going to Spain voluntarily and being taken thither in public disgrace.

However, this carefully prepared program was not carried out. In the latter part of January, 1592, Parma went for the second time into France, in order to relieve the city of Rouen, then closely besieged by Henry. It was done by the command of Philip, and quite against his own judgment, since during his absence Maurice could do what he liked, almost unopposed. Although hampered by lack of men and money, as well as the necessity of consulting Mayenne, who commanded the French Catholic forces, he at length relieved Rouen, made a masterly retreat from a difficult position, and returned to the Low Countries early in the summer.

Ill health compelled him to go at once to Spa, to try the medicinal waters; and the plan for removing him from the command was still delayed. Then Philip resolved to send him on a third campaign into France; and late in the autumn, after Parma had gained a little strength, he began to prepare for it. A complication of diseases rendered him wholly unfit for such a task; but with dauntless resolution the great general caused himself to be daily lifted into his saddle, and gave his personal supervision to the preparations for the approaching campaign. But his exhausted frame could endure no more. At the close of a busy day — December 3, 1592 — in the city of Arras, he went to his couch as usual, but presently fainted and expired. He was only in the forty-seventh year of his age, but his labors and hardships had been so excessive that his early death was not strange. He was interred at Parma; and, as he had desired, his body was robed in the garb of the Capuchin monks.

Had Philip possessed the ordinary sensibilities of human nature, he must have felt a keen remorse on remembering what he was about to do, if Parma's death had not deprived him of the opportunity. Whatever the great commander had been to others, there can be no doubt that he was absolutely loyal to his master. But Philip probably could not appreciate the fidelity which certainly he had never deserved. As little could he comprehend the vastness of the work which Alexander of Parma had accomplished. A place was now vacant which, whether Philip realized it or not, nobody else could fill. So much the worse for the despotic king; so much the better for the struggling republic whose people desired above everything else to be free.

For a little more than a year after Parma's death the management of affairs in the Obedient Provinces was in the hands of old Count Mansfeld, between whom and the other Spanish generals there was endless quarreling. Philip was meanwhile endeavoring to pave the way for another nephew of his to rule over France as well as the Low Countries. His plan was to have the Archduke Ernest, brother of the Emperor Rudolph, marry the Infanta and claim the French crown as a descendant of Henry II. But nobody in France could see any possible use in making Ernest king; and on the whole Philip decided to keep his daughter for some more promising party. However, early in January, 1594, he sent the archduke to govern the Low Countries and carry on the war, as the successor of the great Alexander of Parma. He presented a striking contrast to his predecessor, being a rather weak character, of a mild and melancholy turn, and physically unfitted for military life. Besides, being poor, he could furnish neither men nor money for carrying on the war, however strongly his devotion to Romanism inclined him to do so. He rather disliked the Spaniards, partly perhaps on account of his disappointment about marrying Philip's daughter, and thus becoming king of France. He made himself disagreeable rather than otherwise to his Spanish officers; and although he tried to be agreeable to the people of the obedient Netherlands, he did not succeed.

Upon the whole the brief administration of Archduke Ernest did not amount to much. There was nothing done in the military line, except that most of the Spanish troops joined in an open and well-organized mutiny on account of their having gone without pay till they were ready to starve. The council at Brussels was forced to negotiate with the mutineers, who would hear of no submission until their back pay, amounting to three hundred and sixty thousand crowns, should be handed over. While they waited they lived at their ease in fortified cities, compelling the government to support them handsomely in order to keep them from utterly devouring the country. This state of things continued till long after the appointment of the archduke's successor.

But in the days of Archduke Ernest a good deal was attempted in what Motley calls "the department of assassination." Philip had often pondered upon the probably happy results of removing Queen Elizabeth from the stage where she was so frequently interfering with his cherished designs, and had more than once attempted to open the door for the great queen's exit, as he had done for that of various other inconvenient personages. A fresh scheme was carefully arranged now, the assassin hired being Dr. Lopez, the royal physician. He was to be paid fifty thousand crowns, besides a handsome dowry for his daughter. While he was eagerly waiting for the money, which was to be paid in advance, the conspiracy was discovered, a number of persons being involved in it, and they were executed at London in the spring of 1594. Another of Philip's elaborate plots was arranged for the murder of Prince Maurice. In this case also the assassin was detected before he had committed the deed, and was executed in June, 1594. A second attempt in the autumn came out in the same way. Upon the whole, the department of assassination, though more active, succeeded no better than that of military affairs. Queen Elizabeth, Prince Maurice, Barneveld, young Frederick Henry, and other obnoxious personages continued to live, in spite of all that Philip could do.

Henry of Navarre, now Henry IV, had often been in peril of his life by dagger or poison in the hands of Philip's paid assassins; but since his professed conversion to the Roman Catholic faith in 1593 — a politic measure that had been a grievous blow to the Protestant cause — Philip had contrived a scheme of quite a different nature. It was nothing less than to marry his daughter Clara to Henry IV, thus insuring a lasting peace between France and Spain, and finally detaching Henry from his Netherland allies.

Philip secretly sent to propose this plan, and Henry actually listened to the proposition. Presently it was whispered about the Low Countries that the French king had very privately dispatched a confidential agent to Spain, and the Dutch statesmen were shrewd enough to guess what it meant. Soon they received positive information that Henry had been promised the hand of the Infanta and a good bargain for his kingdom of Navarre, provided he would abandon his alliance with the United Provinces and Queen Elizabeth. It was further stated that the Infanta, herself would not object to the marriage.

At this time, however, Henry IV was sending an envoy to the Dutch Republic and to England with the most profuse and conciliatory explanations regarding his recent conversion to Romanism and his purposes for the future. He assured them that he would never think of a peace with Spain in which they should not be included, and he should have as much care for their interests as for his own. In fact, he did not think it at all probable that he could ever be on good terms with Philip under any circumstances, and he earnestly solicited the States still to assist and coöperate with him, as they had generously done heretofore, in fighting their common enemy.

Of course it was a great object with the States to have war openly declared by Henry and vigorously pushed. So they received his assurances as if they fully believed them, and promised to send him a force of three thousand foot and five hundred horse with which to carry on the campaign of 1594 in the provinces of Artois and Hainault. But military operations went on languidly, and nothing was accomplished in that quarter during the year.

The secret negotiations for peace, with the hand of the Spanish princess, came to nothing, and at last Henry took a decided stand. The year 1595 opened with the formal declaration of war against Spain, which the Netherlanders had so long desired that Henry should make. Its language was strong, setting forth his grievances through Philip's intrigues to keep up civil wars in France, and actual attempts upon Henry's life. Certainly there was weight in reasons like these, and the States could now depend more upon Henry's alliance than they had been able to do before.

Archduke Ernest died February 20, 1595, at the age of forty-two, having been governor-general of the Obedient Provinces scarcely a year. Count Fuentes was left in charge of affairs till the pleasure of Philip should be made known. The count was a very stirring and vigorous personage, though more than twenty years older than Ernest. But the grandees of the Provinces were vexed at the appointment of a Spaniard, especially a near relative of the terrible duke of Alva, whom Fuentes resembled somewhat in person as well as in character. So his temporary administration was neither acceptable nor very successful. His military movements were chiefly within the French borders, where he captured Dourluy and Cambray. Nor was any marked advantage gained by Prince Maurice during the year.

CHAPTER XV.

THE FIRST YEAR OF ARCHDUKE ALBERT.

NEARLY a year after the death of Archduke Ernest, Philip II made up his mind to appoint another of his Austrian nephews to fill the vacant place ; and in January, 1596, the new governor-general arrived at Brussels. He was the Archduke Albert, brother of Emperor Rodolph, and cardinal of Toledo. In due time he was also to espouse the Infanta of Spain. In order to marry he would of course be obliged to lay off the robes of his ecclesiastical office, and with them to give up the princely revenues of the richest see in Christendom. But he made a prudent arrangement with his expected successor, by which he would still receive about one sixth of the annual income after resigning the office.

Archduke Albert was at this time about thirty-five years of age. He was a small, thin man, with light hair and beard, a pale complexion, and the heavy lower jaw of the house of Burgundy. Having lived much at his uncle's court, whom he greatly admired as the most illustrious of sovereigns, he was haughty and taciturn, as it was considered the correct thing for a high and mighty Spaniard to be. Whenever the mask of reserve was not sufficient to hide his real feelings he could add lies. These traits did not endear him to his people; he reminded them too much of Philip himself. To do him justice, however, he had his good points. He was industrious and liked to manage affairs; he was regular and temperate in his habits, he knew several languages, had given attention to mathematics, and claimed to be something of a general. But the great officers and statesmen who had figured in the Provinces in past years were now gone; and though there were plenty of nobles hanging around the court seeking offices and emoluments, the new governor-general did not find himself ably assisted when anything serious was to be done.

Before long Albert took the field in person, with an army of fifteen thousand foot and three thousand horse, which he had assembled at Valenciennes. For months the French king had been besieging the town of La Fère, an important position in the north of France, which was still in the hands of the League. In order to draw him away from the siege, Archduke Albert detached De Rosne, with four thousand men, to attack Calais, which had an inexperienced and rather weak commander. De Rosne soon got possession of the fortress commanding the harbor; and of the city itself, all but the citadel, into which the garrison retreated, agreeing to surrender at the end of six days unless sooner relieved. Henry IV, then at Boulogne, lost no time in demanding assistance from his friends the Netherlanders, as well as from Queen Elizabeth. Prince Maurice responded in person; his expedition arrived off Calais April 17, 1596—the very day its garrison retreated into the citadel. The great fortress commanding the port being already in the enemy's hands, not a vessel could enter. As to Queen Elizabeth, she had promptly mustered six thousand troops; but before sending them across from Dover she dispatched Sir Robert Sidney over to Boulogne to explain to the impatient Henry that she was quite willing to do her best to save Calais from falling into Spanish hands, but in that case she expected that city to be henceforth hers. If Henry could not keep it without her help, she would relieve him of it altogether, with great pleasure.

Henry was astonished and indignant at this cool proposal and did not scruple to say so to the queen's envoy, who reddened with shame and could not look the king in the face. How could the queen thus take advantage of her ally's distress? To accept such a proposal would be as disgraceful on his part as it had been on hers to make it. Better lose Calais a hundred times than to save it thus.

Sidney suggested with embarrassment that possibly her majesty would be satisfied if she might keep Calais for her lifetime, or even for a single year. But the king grew only the more indignant, and Sidney had to return without having extorted any pledge from him, notwithstanding which he assured Henry that the earl of Essex, with eight thousand troops, would soon arrive. Meanwhile, on the fifth night of the truce, two or three hundred soldiers were gotten into the citadel, not without extreme peril. The young commander was so rash as to begin fighting again the next day on the strength of this trifling reinforcement. As the six days had not expired, the Spanish commander was enraged at this breach of faith, and after a severe cannonade ordered the citadel to be stormed. The first assault was repulsed, mainly by the desperate valor of some Dutch companies of the garrison, most of whom perished on the spot. The second carried the citadel and there was a great massacre of both citizens and soldiers. Calais was once more in the hands of Spain, which was no less disastrous for the Netherlands and for Queen Elizabeth than for Henry himself.

Nevertheless, there was a project already on foot which promised partly to offset the loss of Calais, so far as the English and Dutch were concerned; it was nothing less than a naval foray upon the southern coast of Spain. Before the close of this same month of April, the Netherland fleet, consisting of twenty-four ships of war and four tenders, arrived at Plymouth to join their English allies. They brought two thousand two hundred picked veterans from the garrisons of the Netherlands, who, although English, belonged to the army of the States; and three thousand of the best sailors in the world, from Holland and Zealand. The admiral of the fleet was John Duvenwood, seignior of Warmond, and Sir Francis Vere was one of the vice-admirals. The whole fleet included fifty-seven men-of-war and fifty transports, carrying ammunition and other supplies. Lord High Admiral Howard and the earl of Essex were joint commanders, and were aided by many noble volunteers, including Sir Walter Raleigh and Count Lewis Gunther of Nassau. They sailed June 13, 1596, and on the last day of June arrived off Cadiz, in whose harbor was then lying a splendid Spanish fleet. There were thirty great war ships and fifty-seven well-armed Indiamen ready to sail, whose cargo was valued at 12,000,000 ducats.

Four of these Spanish men-of-war were famous great galleons; they bore the names respectively of Saint Philip, Saint Andrew, Saint Matthew, and Saint Thomas. The first of these was the wonder of its day for size and strength. It had a crew of twelve hundred men and carried eighty-two guns. But the English and Dutch, undismayed at so formidable a force, rushed upon the enemy. They soon captured two of the galleons, and ran aground and burned the other two, one of which was the Saint Philip. The allies were eager to seize Cadiz; and in spite of the other men-of-war they soon effected a landing. In a short time young Nassau had planted the banner of William the Silent on a bastion of the city. There was not much of a fight. The garrison and many of the inhabitants fled to the citadel in a panic; and the very next day they surrendered. The duke of Medina Sidonia refused to ransom his fleet by paying two million ducats, and deliberately burned thirty-two ships, with all their equipments. Twelve hundred cannon and arms for five or six thousand men went to the bottom.

The victors sacked Cadiz, but found less treasure than they expected. They burned churches, convents, and hospitals, but refrained from cold-blooded murders and barbarities, such as the Spaniards used to commit in the Netherlands. Essex wished to hold Cadiz, and the Dutch admiral approved the plan. But as most of the English were opposed to it, the fleet soon set sail for home, having taken millions of booty and caused the destruction of one third of Philip's fleet, with little loss on their own side. Had they retained Cadiz, they might perhaps have exchanged it for Calais, or made it a basis of operations in Spain.

Though the capture and sack of Cadiz produced no immediate results, its military importance was immense. It encouraged the Dutch to undertake still bolder and more extensive schemes in after years.

The Dutch admiral received a letter of thanks from the queen's own hand; the States-General were proud to preserve it in their archives. Their part in the foray had been an important one, although the English historians gave them hardly as much credit as they deserved.

The army of the archduke, after some other successes in Normandy, was meanwhile besieging Hulst, a little place in Flanders. At the end of six weeks its commander, Count Solms, surrendered, to the great indignation of his countrymen. Had its officers been as resolute as its defenses were strong, it might have held out a good deal longer. For want of the troops and officers who were gone to Cadiz, Prince Maurice did not find it practicable to raise the siege; nor was he able to put into the field any large force during the whole year.

There was much negotiating, if not much campaigning, from May to October. Certain treaties had been signed which were believed to be of great importance.

Henry IV was now openly at war with Spain; Queen Elizabeth too was practically so, and with good reason, though she had put forth no formal declaration as yet. Both Henry and the States-General longed to have her take a decided stand and form an alliance with themselves against the enemy of all three. Early in May, Henry had sent an envoy to England to urge this on his own behalf. Indeed, she had herself proposed something of the kind to him in February. And although their quarrel about Calais had happened in the interval, she now smoothed it over to the French envoy by saying that she only wished to keep Calais safe while the king's troops were too busy elsewhere to attend to it themselves. The envoy politely accepted this view of the matter as if he knew nothing to the contrary, and began to confer with the English diplomatists about the treaty. Once everything was broken off, and the French envoys had their farewell audience. But before they had set out on their return Elizabeth changed her mind and summoned them to her presence once more. Before the end of May articles were agreed upon and sent to Henry for his approval.

It seemed as if this treaty would amount to a good deal. The French king and the English queen proposed to defend each other's domains, to join against their common foe, and to invite other princes and states who might be inclined to make a stand against Spain to share in the league. An army was to be put into the field at once in order to invade the Spanish territories, and the queen was to furnish four thousand infantry to serve in Picardy and Normandy, paying them for half a year before sending them. At the end of the six months the king was to refund this amount.

In August, after the treaty had been ratified by Henry, Elizabeth solemnized it with a grand public display. There was first the fine spectacle of the French ambassador and his suite in seven splendid barges, moving in a stately procession along the Thames, from the Tower to Greenwich. Then followed a religious ceremony in the chapel of the royal palace of Nonesuch. A special pavilion had been prepared in the chapel, and the queen, standing there with her hand on her heart, solemnly swore to maintain the treaty which had been concluded with the king of France. Then she gave her hand to the representative of Henry IV, who reverently clasped it in both his own, and the royal chapel was filled with the thrilling music of psalms rising from organ and choir. A magnificent banquet was afterwards served, the French ambassador alone sitting at the queen's table, where the dishes and the wine were presented by the great nobles of the realm. At another table in the same hall sat many distinguished guests, among whom was Count Lewis Gunther of Nassau.

"In the midsummer twilight," says Motley, "the brilliantly decorated barges were again floating on the historic river, the gayly colored lanterns lighting the sweep of the oars, and the sound of lute and viol floating merrily across the water. As the ambassador came into the courtyard of his house he found a crowd of several thousand people assembled, who shouted welcome to the representative of Henry, and invoked blessings on the head of Queen Elizabeth and her royal brother of France. Meanwhile all the bells of London were ringing, artillery was thundering, and bonfires were blazing, until the night was half spent."

The young republic of the Netherlands was urged by the queen to join the league, and on October 31 the articles were signed at The Hague. The States agreed to furnish the same number of troops promised by the queen for the service of the king of France, but the king was to return them to the Netherlands, in case the chief part of the enemy's forces should be there.

It is humiliating to learn that none of the parties negotiating, except the Netherlanders, had entered into the treaty with entire sincerity and good faith. Henry and Elizabeth had made a secret treaty which reduced the published one to a mere sham. In fact Elizabeth had engaged simply to furnish two thousand troops who were to be quartered in two cities on the French coast — Boulogne and Montreuil — assisted by an equal number of French. If his majesty should at any time be personally present in Picardy with an army, they might serve in that province, but nowhere else.

The Dutch had thus been induced to unite in the League and to promise aid in proportion to that ostensibly pledged by Elizabeth with so much pomp at London. But the great queen was in her turn imposed upon by the king of France. Neither party was to treat with Spain unless with the other's knowledge and consent; yet Henry was soon listening to the secret messenger of the archduke so cordially and encouragingly that Albert presented him with a splendid suit of burnished blue armor of the newest style. Henry accepted the gift with affectionate assurances of his personal friendship and his ardent desire for a general peace, so that all Christendom might be at leisure to fight the Turks. The truth was that, being now a professed Catholic, the king found himself in an awkward position, and almost as soon as he had signed this treaty with England and the Netherlands against Spain he began to wish himself out of it. And yet it would never do to let Spain overpower either those countries or France.

Before the affair at Cadiz, Philip had been fitting out another armada to conquer England. The destruction of one third of his navy on that occasion of course had not lessened his desire, though it had somewhat diminished his resources. On the fifth of October of this same year his fleet set sail from Lisbon. There were one hundred and twenty-eight ships with fourteen thousand infantry and three thousand cavalry on board. They were to land in Ireland, where the Roman Catholic populace would easily be roused to share in the enterprise. Possibly also King James of Scotland would like to do something by way of revenging his mother's tragical death. After the Spanish troops had landed most of the fleet would return for the winter to Ferrol, on the northwest coast of Spain. In case the English fleet attacked them on their way, they were just to demolish it immediately.

But the second armada was destined to a fate hardly less dismal than that of the first. Almost at the beginning of the voyage it encountered a terrible storm. Forty of the ships, with five thousand men, went to the bottom; the rest, shattered and disabled, took refuge in the harbor of Ferrol.

Philip heard the tidings quite composedly and spoke of renewing the attempt the next spring. Indeed he fancied the archduke might manage to invade England himself with no great trouble; he could just send some forces across from Calais in almost any kind of vessels that might be at hand. This, however, the archduke did not find it convenient to undertake.

It was during the last decade of the sixteenth century that a great interest was awakened among the Dutch in exploring the northern seas, in the hope of finding thus a back way to India. The Spaniards and Portuguese knew how to reach India by the Cape of Good Hope, but they were careful not to tell the secret to anybody else. But it was evidently a very long voyage, and the Dutch were confident of saving several thousand miles if they could only discover the northeast passage. Linschoten, the author of a book on the East then just published, thought so too. He had lived thirteen years in Bombay, as a member of the suite of the archbishop of Goa, and had collected a vast amount of information about the country. His work was illustrated with maps and charts; it gave a great and lasting stimulus to maritime explorations. The first expedition to the polar seas was undertaken in the summer of 1594. There were only three vessels and a fishing yacht. The leaders were Linschoten and Barendz. Though they did not make a long voyage, only about a hundred and fifty miles beyond Nova Zembla, what they related excited so much interest and hope that the States-General took up the matter. The next summer they not only sent out seven ships, but even loaded them with linen, broadcloths, and tapestry, to be used in trading with China. They had been late in setting out on account of these preparations; and between the icebergs and the polar bears they were compelled to return without having found the northeast passage.

The States-General did not help them in the next voyage, except by promising a handsome reward to any navigator who should discover the passage; but Barendz and others set out with two ships in May, 1596. They got within ten degrees of the pole, but finding the ice closing around them they made their way back to Nova Zembla, where their ships were frozen in and they passed a long and dreadful winter. It was not until November, 1597, that the survivors reached home. It was the last effort to get to China that way; but some of the Dutch navigators had already made the voyage by way of the Cape of Good Hope, and a brisk trade had been begun. It was destined to produce results of the greatest importance at no distant day.

CHAPTER XVI.

A VICTORY AND A MARTYRDOM.

EARLY in 1597 Prince Maurice had a brilliant success by which his countrymen were not a little cheered.

It was discovered that the archduke had assembled some regiments of his best infantry and several squadrons of horse at a village called Turnhout, about twenty-five miles south of Gertruydenberg and nearly as far east of Antwerp. It was not clear what he was going to do with this choice little army, of which his general-in-chief of artillery, Count Varax, was in charge. By some it was surmised that he was intending to assault Breda, which was only twenty miles to the northward.

Whatever the archduke might be planning to set Count Varax about, Maurice and the council of state resolved to interfere with it, if they could. Before daybreak on the twenty-third of January the Dutch forces moved from Gertruydenberg towards Turnhout, plodding through rain and mire, for it was a time of thaw and the roads were all submerged. At nightfall they reached Ravels, less than a league from the enemy's camp. It seemed likely that the Spaniards, who had discovered their coming and were fresh for a fight, would fall upon them without delay. The prince was on the watch all night, weary as he was, while he planned the movements to be made in the morning, should they be unmolested so long. Very early he sent out a party to reconnoiter. Much to their surprise they discovered that Varax was already gone from the village, and was retreating with his entire force towards the south.

Beyond the village a small river had overflowed its banks, and could be crossed only in one narrow place, where a few planks had been hastily laid. The Spanish infantry had crossed, almost in single file, while the cavalry had plunged through the water and mire. Their rear guard was just disappearing among the thickets beyond when the prince's troops came in sight. It was known that an upland heath, three miles across, lay just ahead; and it was supposed that the Spanish army would wait there to attack them as they should emerge, one by one, from the narrow crossing. Varax had indeed left a guard there; but when Sir Francis Vere and Marcellus Bax dashed through, followed by a small detachment, they found that the main body of the enemy was not drawn up in battle array, as they expected, but in full retreat.

Maurice had no mind to lose his game thus; and

being aware that the only opening on the other side of the heath was as narrow as the entrance, and led into a swamp, he sent Count Hohenlo with most of the cavalry to make a rapid detour behind the thicket bordering the heath on the left, and thus cut off the enemy's retreat. In a few minutes Hohenlo and his squadrons dashed into view in front of the retreating foe, while their rear guard was assailed by the troops who had meanwhile emerged from the pass. None of Maurice's infantry were yet on the field, and the enemy outnumbered his men four to one. But the Spanish legions, veterans as they were, fell into a terrible panic; and though many escaped to the swamp, two thousand fell on the field, Varax among them. Five hundred were captured, with all their standards and most of their arms. Thirty-eight Spanish banners were the next week hung up in the castle at The Hague.

There was immense rejoicing at this victory, won in so unequal a conflict with the best regiments of Spain. Its moral effect was far more important than the material damage inflicted on the enemy. It was the first time that the Netherlanders had gained such a victory, over such a foe, in the open field. Never again could it be said that one Spanish soldier was worth five or ten Dutchmen. One needed only to point to those thirty-eight banners captured on the heath of Tiel.

Philip himself had just taken a step which in a certain way aided the Netherlanders, although that was the last thing in the world which he meant to do. It was nothing less than a public repudiation of all his debts and a resumption of all the revenues and mortgages that he had pledged as security for the interest. This was announced in a very solemn manner, and with an air of perfect uprightness, as if he were one who had come to bankruptcy solely on account of his superhuman efforts to save the true religion from destruction. He said the usurers had been growing rich at his expense, and he was now compelled to revoke all the securities which he had given them for money loaned, and let them get on as best they could.

In consequence of this royal fraud it became impossible for the archdukes to get money anywhere; two and a half millions of Albert's bills of exchange came back protested in a single day. In Frankfort, in Genoa, in Antwerp, and all over Europe there were more failures than ever had been heard of before. "There was a general howl of indignation and despair," says Motley, "upon every exchange, in every countingroom, in every palace, in every cottage of Christendom."

Philip had cut "the sinews of war" at a very inconvenient time; for there was urgent need that the archduke should raise an army to relieve Amiens, in the north of France, which Henry was now besieging in the most determined manner, the Spaniards having taken it by a shrewd trick not long before. Albert was living in great magnificence at Brussels; but now he was forced to pawn jewels, plate, and furniture to meet the daily expenses of his establishment. In this state of affairs Maurice had little to apprehend from the enemy, and could undertake almost anything he liked for the time. "The repudiation of Philip's debts," says Professor Thorold Rogers, "was a turning point in the history of the War of Independence."

Not far from this time the emperor of Germany sent a solemn embassy to the States-General, offering his services as mediator, to obtain for them a peace with their offended sovereign, Philip of Spain, who, as all the world knew, was wonderfully gentle and ready to forgive. The statesmen of the little republic replied as usual, with great politeness and at considerable length, that neither Philip nor anybody else had ever been their king; and that the gentle and forgiving monarch of Spain had manifested his disposition by putting to death, in the days of Alva, nearly twenty thousand Netherlanders; not to mention a hundred thousand who had since been massacred in battles and sieges.

The friendly king of Denmark also tried to persuade the sturdy Protestant republic to think of submission and peace, and with no better success. The king of Poland, whose daughter was soon to marry the prince of Spain, pressed the matter more than either of the other sovereigns had done. His ambassador, Paul Dialyn by name, had a grand reception at The Hague in July. Magnificently attired, he appeared in the council chamber, where he delivered a long and grandiloquent Latin oration before Prince Maurice and the States, keeping his eyes fixed upon the ceiling. This pedantic and gorgeous personage afforded much inward amusement to his audience by the airs he assumed while he tried to persuade them to cease their contest with the benignant Philip of Spain, and go to fighting the Turks as all good Christians should.

Not discouraged by the obduracy of the Netherlanders, the envoy proceeded to England and held forth in the same conceited manner before Queen Elizabeth. His Latin oration had no sooner been concluded than her majesty, indignant at his presumption, yet forcing herself to speak with dignified moderation, made a spirited reply in the same language:—

"Oh, how I have been deceived!" she began. "I expected an ambassador, and behold, a herald! In all my life I never heard of such an oration. Your boldness and unadvised temerity I cannot sufficiently admire. But if the king your master has given you any such thing in charge, — which I much doubt, — I believe it is because, being but a young man and lately advanced to the throne, not by ordinary succession of blood but by election, he understandeth not yet the way of such affairs." The rest of her speech was not less severely satirical, and the confounded envoy doubtless left the royal presence with a different air from that with which he had entered. The queen's reply, though given on the instant, was no less correct and fluent than spirited and fearless. And no doubt her ministers were delighted at the lecture which the pompous ambassador had received.

During this same summer of 1597, when there was so much effort to reconcile the Netherlanders to Philip and the Catholic religion, an event took place in the "obedient provinces" which revived the memory of the old days of the edicts and the Inquisition. Many a year had passed since any one had been put to death for being a Protestant; and to the children and young people the terrible stories of those times seemed as unreal as a hideous dream after it is over. But the edicts had not been repealed, though they had been a dead letter ever since the Pacification of Ghent in 1576. At this time the Jesuits were so strong in the obedient provinces that they undertook to make an example of somebody as a warning against heresy.

In the family of two maiden ladies living in Antwerp, who had once been imprisoned as Protestants and were now professed Catholics, there was a maid-servant of middle age, named Anna van den Hove. She had been brought up in the Reformed faith and was evidently less pliable than her mistresses had proved. The Jesuits thought her a promising case to take in hand; they denounced her to the civil authorities and got her condemned.

They took her to Brussels and informed her that she was to be buried alive unless she would recant her heresies and enter the Roman Catholic church. She replied meekly that she daily read her Bible and prayed for help to understand its teachings and obey them. But she did not find there any commands to pray to the Virgin Mary and the saints; there was nothing about indulgences or purgatory or various other matters insisted upon by the Roman Catholics; and although she did not wish to interfere with the beliefs of other people, she could not renounce her own faith. The poor soul, in her lowly stedfastness, perhaps had never heard how easily King Henry IV had been converted to Romanism when the crown of France was to be won. But the prize to which she aspired was that crown of righteousness which the Lord would give to those who had kept the faith. It seemed real and near.

So one bright summer morning they led her out of the city to die. Remembering how her Master "suffered without the gate," she willingly went forth, "bearing his reproach." Walking between two Jesuits and followed by other priests, who reviled her as they went, she at length arrived at the spot where, in the grassy fields, there was a great heap of freshly turned earth beside a strange deep pit. The executioner stood by. She was made to descend into that living grave, and he shoveled in the earth till she was buried to the waist. Then, for the last time, the Jesuits invited her to save herself by abjuring her faith; but she was stedfast. Gazing upward, like Stephen of old, she seemed to have a vision of heaven. The pit was fast filling up; the executioner heaped the earth upon her, as if in haste to cover from view that radiant face. It was soon done; then he stamped down the soft earth again and again till it was all made smooth and firm.

Whether or not the impression made upon the public mind by the death of Anna van den Hove was what the Jesuits intended, they did not repeat the experiment. It is said to have been the last of the Netherland martyrdoms.

CHAPTER XVII.

NEGOTIATING WITH ELIZABETH.

IT began to be evident that the alliance formed with so much solemnity the previous year had not amounted to much. The States-General had done their part in furnishing troops, but Elizabeth had done only what the secret treaty bound her to do, and Henry had busied himself with taking Amiens, which was mainly his own affair. The English and Dutch had together sent out another expedition, under Essex, to attack the Spanish coast; but ten days of tempestuous weather had prevented its success.

In August Prince Maurice began his autumnal campaign on the eastern frontier; and as the archduke was not able to interfere with it, in the course of three months he took nine strongly fortified cities and five castles, opened the navigation of the Rhine, and put matters in better condition all along that boundary.

This was cheering, so far as it went. But there was now much distrust of their French ally. And

Elizabeth was out of humor with the States, and still more so with Henry. His envoys at London and also at The Hague had admitted that their royal master was talking about making peace, at least for himself; it was doubtful whether or not it would include the Netherlands. Being now a Catholic, he could have the pope's good offices in negotiating with Philip, if he chose, but his holiness could not be expected to exert himself on their behalf too.

Now the Netherlanders had as little desire for the mediation of the pope as the pope had to intercede for them; but it was no small grievance to be abandoned by their ally. Matters were not made more comfortable by their learning, about this time, how they had been deluded in the league. They felt that they had good reason for displeasure and distrust toward England as well as France. The queen and her people complained because the Dutch still carried on their lucrative commerce with Spain, which was strictly forbidden to Englishmen. Thus they were making fortunes for themselves, and at the same time feeding the enemy. It was urged on the other side that the Netherlands had nearly all their revenue from their foreign traffic, and would be fatally impoverished should commerce with Spain be stopped; while that country would have supplies from other nations, if not from them. Thirty thousand sailors were employed in this trade alone; must all these be forced to choose between starvation and the service of the enemy? It had been only with the utmost effort and sacrifice that the republic had carried on the war till now; if their foreign commerce were to be cut off, it would be all over with them.

Vexed as the queen was, she said to Caron, the Dutch envoy, that she would do her best to dissuade Henry from concluding the peace which he was arranging with Spain; and that she would faithfully tell Caron whatever Henry's special ambassador should communicate to her. She would not help to deceive them respecting Henry's intentions, unless she were herself deceived.

"I feel indeed," she added, "that matters are not always managed as they should be by your government, and that you have not always treated princes, especially myself, as we deserve to be treated. Nevertheless, your state is not a monarchy, and so we must take all things into consideration, and weigh its faults against its many perfections."

The States-General decided to send a special embassy to France to prevent, if possible, the conclusion of this fatal treaty with Spain. They would promise Henry even more assistance than they had already pledged, if he would abide by the league and continue the war. If necessary, they would bring their whole military power to sustain him, whether in sieges or campaigns.

The two envoys sent on this momentous errand were Barneveld, their greatest statesman, and Admiral Justinus of Nassau, a soldier at once brave, wise, and patriotic. They were to sail for Dieppe the last of January, 1598, but persistent head winds detained them more than six weeks. Henry was at Angiers, two hundred miles southwest from Dieppe; and it was not until April that they had an interview with him. They were soon convinced of the hopelessness of their mission. To make peace with Spain was decidedly for Henry's interest, and that was enough. Moreover, Elizabeth had told his ambassador that she had no means with which to help him carry on the war, and that she was quite inclined to make peace herself, if she could.

So the disheartened envoys turned their faces toward London, where they arrived in the latter part of May. Her majesty was already in a bad humor, and on hearing the news they had brought from France she became really angry and abusive. Why should not the States themselves try to make peace? Probably it could be so arranged that Prince Maurice and their other great men could still keep their offices; while the Spaniards could be sent out of the country. Why should not that suffice?

Barneveld replied that it would involve submission to the pope, as well as to the despotism of Philip — the identical two points about which they had been fighting for the last forty years.

"The queen here broke forth into mighty oaths," says Motley, "protesting over and over again, by the living God, that she would not and could not give the States any further assistance; that she would leave them to their fate; that her aid rendered in their war had lasted much longer than the siege of Troy did; and swearing that she had been a fool to help them and the king of France as she had done, for it was nothing but evil passions that kept the States so obstinate."

Barneveld answered adroitly, complimenting her majesty's eminent sagacity, but begging her to think of the difference between a monarchy and a republic. For them to accept a sovereign would be putting themselves under his absolute control, and giving up all the religious and political freedom for which they had struggled so long.

But the queen grew only the more furious, especially when entreated to suffer the republic to raise soldiers within her kingdom, at its own expense. "How am I to defend myself?" she cried; "how are the affairs of Ireland to be provided for? how am I ever to get back my money? Who is to pay the garrisons of Brill and Flushing?" And here she left the room, telling the ambassadors that they might confer with her counselors.

It was true that the queen's aid had amounted to a large sum in the course of these fourteen years. She herself reckoned it at nearly fourteen hundred thousand pounds sterling; and it was not surprising that she wanted the debt paid. Yet had the Netherlands been subdued by Spain, she would have been forced to spend much more money and lose many more soldiers in fighting Spain on her own account. It was her cause as well as theirs.

The next interview was not so stormy; but the queen still urged that the States might somehow reconcile themselves to their ancient ruler without letting him tyrannize over them as before. Suppose Philip should transfer his title to his daughter and her affianced husband, the archduke: would not that remove the objection? To this Barneveld replied that they had no more confidence in the princess and the archduke than in Philip himself.

After long and laborious negotiating it was at last agreed that the States should pay the queen thirty thousand pounds annually till they should have paid four hundred thousand. After this was done they should arrange for the payment of four hundred thousand more. In case England should be invaded by the king of Spain, the States promised to furnish the queen with thirty ships of war, five thousand infantry, and five squadrons of horse. But the queen refused to promise that if England should make peace with Spain, she would restore to the republic the towns which she held as security for her claims.

Henry's treaty with Spain was finally signed at Vervins, May 2, 1598; it included restitution of all places taken by either party within the realms of the other, since the treaty of Câteau-Cambresis in 1559. So Henry recovered Calais and many other places, and gave up the country of Charolois. The famous edict of Nantes, to protect the Protestants of France, was signed about the same time, though it was not proclaimed till the following year.

CHAPTER XVIII.

LAST DAYS OF PHILIP II.

FOUR days after concluding the treaty of Vervins the king of Spain executed a deed giving to his daughter Isabella Clara Eugenia all his Netherland domains, including the seven provinces that had long ago renounced his sway, as well as the ten called "obedient." The princess was about to marry the Archduke Albert, and to rule over the Low Countries jointly with her husband. Her brother gave his written consent to the transfer; and everything was transacted in due form, so far as legal documents and royal signatures and seals could go. The consent of the millions of people supposed thus to be handed over to a new sovereign was not asked; of course it was no concern of theirs.

This was the last public act of Philip's life. Though the bloody drama was not soon to close, in which, though rarely seen, he had for forty-three years been the chief actor, his exit from the stage was at hand. He was nearly seventy-one years of age, and his health — always delicate — had long been failing. He now grew worse rapidly, and resolved to leave Madrid for the retirement of his favorite palace, the Escorial. This was twenty-one miles northwest of the capital.

It was a tedious and distressing journey. He was borne in a litter with the utmost care, traveling only three or four miles a day. The gout had been one of his lifelong maladies, and now he could scarcely bear so much as the pressure of a linen sheet. Thus, suffering and helpless, he was borne for the last time through the stately portals of this royal cloister of his own building, which was intended to be at once a palace and a tomb.

The Escorial, often called the Escurial, was twenty-one years in building, and cost six million ducats. It was finished only fourteen years before Philip's death, and for magnificence was regarded as the eighth wonder of the world. Philip built it in fulfillment of a vow to Saint Lawrence, at the battle of Saint Quentin; and to commemorate the instrument of the saint's martyrdom he ordered it made in the form of a gridiron. It forms a huge rectangular parallelogram, measuring seven hundred and forty-four by five hundred and eighty feet. The long open courts, stretching from end to end, represent the spaces between the bars of the gridiron, while towers at the corners indicate the legs, and the handle is a range of buildings projecting from the middle of one end. This last is the royal dwelling; there is also a splendid royal chapel, as well as a pantheon, in which only kings and kings' mothers are entombed. The Escorial is still one of the great sights of Spain.

Philip's symptoms grew more alarming day by day, and soon a low fever fastened upon him. His constitution was evidently giving way. At the joints and upon the breast abscesses gathered; these did not heal, after being opened, and notwithstanding all that could be done by the imperfect surgery of those times they swarmed with maggots, which fed and multiplied in the flesh of their living prey. "No torture ever invented by Torquemada or Peter Titelmann could exceed in acuteness the agonies which the most Catholic king was now called to endure. . . . That the grave worms should do their office before soul and body were parted was a torment such as the imagination of Dante might have invented for the lowest depths of his Inferno."

Amid these sufferings the month of July wore away. The king asked his physician's opinion. Evidently he foresaw the fatal result; but it was not until the first of August that his confessor told him plainly what the doctor dared not utter. With surprising composure and gentleness Philip thanked him for ending the suspense, and thus enabling him to devote himself to preparing for the solemn event.

After sending a courier to Rome to ask the pope's

PHILIP II, KING OF SPAIN.
From Bor's History of the Netherlands, 1621.

blessing the king spent three days in confession. The father confessor had prepared a very long and searching list of questions to guide him in his self-examination, that no sin might remain undiscovered and unforgiven. Strange to say Philip declared both to his confessor and to his son that, so far as he knew, he had never in all his life done a wrong to anybody. Perhaps the Netherlanders could have helped his memory with a few facts, had they been desired. And certainly many of his subjects in Spain could have done the same. But in those days it was supposed that a monarch had a right to do almost anything he liked. At least that was evidently Philip's view. "'This internal conviction of his general righteousness," says Motley, "was of great advantage in the midst of his terrible sufferings; and accounted in a great degree for the gentleness, thoughtfulness for others, and perfect benignity which, according to the unanimous testimony of many witnesses, characterized his conduct during this whole sickness."

As a Roman Catholic, devout beyond most men of his time, Philip depended much on holy relics, which he had long been assiduous in collecting. There was a bone of Saint Alban, given him by Clement VIII, to be the special comfort of his dying bed; there was also an arm of Saint Vincent of Ferrara and a knee bone of Saint Sebastian. All these were thought to possess great virtue, and Philip often gazed upon them as he lay on his sick bed, or had them applied to his torturing sores. He had always been fond of planning all the arrangements for any great procession or other spectacle; and during the period of his failing health he had not forgotten to write out full directions for his own funeral. One day while enduring the ceaseless agonies of his relentless disease, he had this paper read aloud in his presence; so that his children, his ministers of state, and other great personages in attendance might understand precisely how all the ceremonies were to be conducted.

"Having governed my kingdom for forty-three years," began the document, "I now give it back in the seventy-first year of my age to God Almighty to whom it belongs, recommending my soul into his blessed hands, that his divine majesty may do what he pleases therewith."

Then followed directions for the funeral procession, which was to be led by the bishop holding a crucifix aloft and followed by the clergy. The Adelantado next should bear the royal standard, trailing it along the ground; then the duke of Novara should carry the crown on a silver salver covered with a black cloth, and another nobleman should carry the sword of state. Eight Spanish grandees, robed in mourning and holding lighted torches, should bear the royal coffin; and the heir apparent, attended by the new archbishop of Toledo, should follow. Thus the procession was to enter the chapel and approach the stately tomb prepared for the royal dust. "Mass being performed," continued the king's instructions, "the prelate shall place me in the grave which shall be my last house until I go to my eternal dwelling. Then the prince, third king of my name, shall go into the cloister of Saint Jerome at Madrid, where he shall keep nine days' mourning. My daughter and my sister, the ex-empress, shall for the same purpose go to the convent of the Gray Sisters." Then followed directions that thirty thousand masses should be said for the repose of the king's soul; that five hundred galley slaves should be freed, and that five hundred maidens should receive marriage portions.

Several times during the latter part of his illness the king received the sacrament of the Lord's Supper, and twice the rite of extreme unction, by which he was inexpressibly consoled, and felt himself ready for his departure. But he still lingered, suffering undiminished tortures. Toward the middle of September it became evident that death was near. The king bade an attendant bring from a certain shrine the crucifix which his father had held when dying, that it might be at hand to soothe his own last moments, and also a candle of Our Lady of Montserrat which also he desired to hold when the hour should come. Then he added directions about the enshrouding of his body, being aware that decomposition had already begun. He desired that it should be enclosed in a well-soldered metallic coffin, and that, in the coffin of state, which he ordered brought to his chamber that he might examine it. It was to be lined with white satin and trimmed with gold lace and gold nails; a certain brocade of black and gold, in the jewel room, was to be used for his pall.

On the twelfth of September, less than twenty-four hours before his death, he again received the Lord's Supper and gave his dying blessings and farewells to his children. He charged the Infanta never to relax her exertions to maintain the Roman Catholic religion in her Netherland domains, and bade her impress this, his dying command, upon the archduke, soon to become her husband.

When the last hour approached, the crucifix of Charles V was placed in his hand and he said: "I die like a good Catholic, in faith and obedience to the holy Roman Church." Presently came what seemed the last struggle and he lay motionless, as if life were gone. They had covered his face when he suddenly opened his eyes, grasped once more the crucifix, and pressed it with fervor to his lips. The death agony returned and he spoke no more, lying insensible till five o'clock on the morning of Sunday, September 13, 1598, when he ceased to breathe.

What shall we think of such a life, closed by such a death?

Certainly Philip had shed the innocent blood of thousands in the Netherlands alone, by the excecutioner's hand; he had many a time procured, or attempted, assassinations; he had, with much expense, kept civil war raging in France for private ends; he had plundered multitudes by confiscation, whose opulence was their only offense; and he had been a notorious adulterer.

Yet we must not forget the difference between those times and our own. Then a great deal used to be said about the prerogatives of kings; it had hardly occurred to anybody to inquire into the prerogatives of human beings. The king of Spain was virtually an absolute monarch. If he chose to take the life or possessions of a subject, no one dared complain. And though he sometimes assumed the attitude of a penitent toward God, he doubtless felt it his privilege to do what he pleased toward men. He was quite superior to the moral code which mankind in general is bound to observe. Kings, of course, could not be expected to live by the Ten Commandments.

In that age the manual by which royal personages were wont to guide their steps was Machiavelli's famous work, The Prince. This celebrated Florentine philosopher had died the very year that Philip was born. One might fancy that The Prince was incarnated in Philip of Spain. Machiavelli taught that since all men are liars, scoundrels, and idiots, ever ready to deceive and yet easily duped, he is alone fit to be king who excels in deceiving. According to this rule Philip deserved the world-empire which he had so ardently desired. Falsehood was the all-pervading element of his character. Not even to his most valued servants was he true. His secret correspondence, laboriously deciphered within the nineteenth century, shows that he was not sincere even with Alva, with Don John, or with Alexander of Parma. From Machiavelli he had learned that " in order to maintain power it is often necessary to act contrary to faith, contrary to charity, contrary to humanity, contrary to religion." Again, " Every one sees what you seem, few perceive what you are. . . ͵ A prince ought therefore to have great care . . . that to see and hear him he should appear all piety, all faith, all integrity, all humanity, all religion. And nothing is more necessary than to seem to have this last-mentioned quality." You must not really have it; it would sometimes be very much in your way. You would be obliged to do justly, to love mercy, and all that. You would love your neighbor as yourself, and so you could not hire assassins to stab, shoot, or poison him, nor could you seize his estates or kidnap his child. But you must *seem* very religious all the same.

Here perhaps we may find a key to the mystery of Philip's saintly departure from this life. Since hypocrisy had pervaded his whole career he could hardly be expected to drop the mask before he left the stage. Aware that every word and deed would be recounted to the world, he would naturally desire to act the devoted Catholic to the last. Moreover the habitual deceiver often ends by deluding even himself. He has acted his part so long and so well that he at last thinks he really is what he has pretended to be. He can no longer discern between the true and the false. Once a conscious hypocrite, he is now self-deceived. We may be sure that the father of lies is careful that his victim shall not be roused too soon. And thus it may have been perhaps that Philip died in the serene expectation of heavenly bliss as the reward of such a life.

CHAPTER XIX.

CAMPAIGNING IN FLANDERS.

IT was in September, 1599, a year after Philip's death, that Archduke Albert arrived at Brussels with his bride the Infanta of Spain. He had been absent for a twelvemonth, and the admiral of Aragon, Francis de Mendoza, had meanwhile managed military affairs. This stirring and vigorous personage, during the autumn of 1598, had made a fine campaign in the German duchies of Cleves, Juliers, and Berg, which bordered upon the United Provinces. The States-General, hampered by various difficulties, could put only a small force into the field, amounting to six or seven thousand men; but the admiral was laying waste the adjacent duchies with nearly four times as many.

Prince Maurice was adroit enough, however, to keep the Spanish army out of the republic by watching every movement and harassing the enemy whenever there was a chance to do so. He effected so much with his little army as to make it appear like a large one. Queen Elizabeth declared that Maurice deserved to be called the first general in all Christendom. "Never before was it written or heard of," said she, "that so great an extent of country could be defended with so few troops, and an invasion of so superior a hostile force could be prevented; especially as all the streams and rivers were frozen."

At length the enemy went into winter quarters. Campaigns merely defensive are not apt to be regarded with perfect satisfaction; fault-finding is easy and natural, especially when taxation is heavy. In the struggling little republic it was more difficult than ever to raise the money for carrying on the war. Of late, it had been found necessary to lay a tax of one-half per cent upon all property, and two-and-a-half per cent on all sales; yet this self-imposed addition to burdens which had long been enormous did not suffice. It has been remarked by a great authority in such matters that "No nation ever bore so much in the way of taxation without flinching. . . . Every Hollander was taxed from the cradle to the grave, for every act of his daily life, and even for the voluntary and involuntary incidents of it."[1] What made a great difference in the finances at this time was that there was no longer any commerce permitted between the United Provinces and Spain or Spanish dependencies. It had been forbidden first by the Spanish

[1] Thorold Rogers, in The Story of Holland.

government, and in retaliation by the Dutch also. So a large part of the foreign traffic that had brought money into the Provinces was cut off; and the annual revenue was now far too little to support the war efficiently.

The Obedient Provinces were poorer still. Though they had made a fine show of rejoicing on the arrival of their new sovereigns, they were already murmuring loudly about their extravagant style of living. The "archdukes"—for so, with amusing impartiality this wedded pair used to be called—kept house in almost imperial state. It was said to cost two thousand florins a day just to feed the multitude of cooks, lackeys, pages, and fine gentlemen in their retinue, not to speak of wages and salaries.

Isabella was at this time thirty-three years of age, and Albert was thirty-nine. She was considered handsome, gifted, and wise, at least by her courtiers. In her haughty bearing, her tastes, and her habits, she was altogether Spanish, and on that account less winning to her subjects than if she had adopted some of the Flemish ways. It was much the same with her husband. They were fond of each other, and remarkably harmonious in their views and aims; these of course included, above all, the subjugation of the remaining seven sturdy little Provinces to their sway and to the yoke of Rome.

Early in the year 1600 Prince Maurice recovered two forts, whose garrisons, being mostly Walloons, and in mutiny against the archduke, were persuaded to come over to the service of the States. They formed a legion about twelve hundred strong, which was placed under the command of young Frederic Henry of Nassau, who was then beginning his illustrious career. This legion somehow got the name of "the new beggars," in allusion to the derisive epithet borne by the nobles who in 1566 ventured to ask for a little of the liberty since then so bravely won by the Dutch republic.

As to any foreign aid, the prospect was gloomy enough. It was known that secret messages were going to and fro between Brussels and London. Furthermore, an English envoy named Edmunds was visiting various cities of the Obedient Provinces on some mysterious errand; and they were making a great parade wherever he went. So Caron, the representative of the States in England, respectfully asked the queen what it meant. Elizabeth happened to be in a bad humor with Edmunds, who had not duly informed her what he was accomplishing while parading about the Netherlands so triumphantly. She replied to Caron that she did not herself know what it meant, unless the people regarded Edmunds as a phenomenon, and were carrying him about for a show.

Perhaps they wanted to have it appear that she was trying to make peace with the archdukes, which, she added, was very wide of the mark. But she admitted that, as she had so often been approached on the subject, she thought she would find out, once for all, what they had to propose.

What they did propose was that the queen should be base enough to put into Spanish hands the towns of Brill, Flushing, and Ostend; which, together with the castle of Rammekens, she had long been holding as security for the money she had lent the republic. She was further to forbid all trade and intercourse between her subjects and the Netherlanders, and never again to let any Englishman fight in their cause. On these conditions peace might be made between England and Spain.

Now Elizabeth had formerly assured the Dutch envoy that if such things were proposed to her, she would reply in a way that would be talked of for a good while. "Before I consent to a single one of those points," said she with vehemence, "I wish myself taken from this world! Until now I have been a princess of my word, who would rather die than deceive such good people as the States."

She did reply to the Spanish commissioner that she would not attempt to treat for peace so long as Spain insisted on those three points; but she did not declare that she would not negotiate at all, and so the talk about a treaty still went on. Yet she used to be furious if any rumors were heard of the States-General listening to proposals from the archdukes. One day when Caron was to have an audience, the queen called out almost before he entered the door: "Have you not always told me that the States never could, would, or should treat for peace with the enemy? Yet now it is plain enough that they have proceeded only too far in negotiations." It was not true, but Caron had hard work to remove her suspicions; and she swore a great oath that if the States should deceive her, she would have such revenge that men should talk of it forever and ever.

Nor was Henry IV at present a comfort to his Dutch friends. He was now so ardent a Catholic and so grateful to the pope for absolving him from his former heresies and confirming him upon the throne of France that he declared he would be willing to proclaim in his kingdom the very decrees of the Council of Trent. "I desire it more ardently," said he, "than I pressed the edict for the Protestants."

More than ever it seemed to the leading statesmen of the republic that all must now depend upon their own efforts. As the season for campaigning drew near they began secretly to plan a great military movement which, if it succeeded, might almost finish the war. Barneveld, the leading spirit in the States-General, had contrived a scheme which he was extremely anxious to have accomplished; it was to carry the war into the enemy's country by a sudden invasion of Flanders, the province from whose ports came swarms of privateers to prey upon their commerce. Could they but capture Nieuport and Dunkirk, — for Ostend had always been theirs, — it would not be difficult to subdue that whole province, from which a great part of the enemy's supplies came. And the archdukes were at this time in an uncommonly bad plight, not only as to money but as to forces, many of their troops having mutinied. In short, Barneveld, wise and cautious as he generally was, persuaded the States that this was the thing to be done.

In vain did Prince Maurice, Lewis William of Nassau, and Sir Francis Vere present the objections. They urged that the whole army would be required, except the small garrisons of the principal posts; so that a defeat would be not merely disastrous, but fatal. The sagacious Lewis William declared that it would be to suspend the very existence of the republic upon a hair. Certainly, generals could better judge than statesmen; nevertheless, the statesmen decreed and the generals obeyed. But they undertook the campaign with heavy hearts, aware that all was to be staked on a single throw of the dice. This was the feeling of the populace too. While the troops summoned from various posts were marching through Holland and Zealand, on their way to the rendezvous near Flushing, they were met by the people with dismal forebodings instead of enthusiastic confidence.

A great fleet was assembled at Flushing to convey the army readily to Nieuport, the point to be attacked. In all there were about thirteen hundred vessels, including a multitude of transports and flat-bottomed barges, beside the war ships. The army numbered fourteen thousand troops, well trained, well equipped, and well paid. Prince Maurice had with him two of his cousins, Count Ernest and Count Lewis Gunther of Nassau, the younger brothers of Count Lewis William, stadtholder of Friesland. The latter remained in charge of the eastern frontier, and Count Hohenlo of the southern. The prince's half-brother, young Frederic Henry, was in the army with his legion. And Sir Francis Vere, who was a soldier of great experience as well as valor, had charge of the rear guard during the march.

All was ready on the twentieth of June, and the army on the point of embarking for the voyage of thirty-five miles; but the wind was directly ahead. For two days they waited, hoping it would change. Then they resolved to effect a landing upon the nearest point of the Flemish coast within their reach, and proceed the rest of the way by land. They could sail southeast, if not southwest; and so on the twenty-second of June they passed up the western Scheldt and disembarked at the Sas of Ghent, near a fort which Count Ernest had taken the day before.

The fleet was sent away as soon as possible and ordered to make its way toward Nieuport as fast as the wind would permit. In fact, it anchored in that roadstead July 1, the same morning on which the army arrived; and thus nothing had been gained by the change as to time. The army had marched more miles than the original voyage was to be, and had been obliged to do some work in building bridges on the way, as well as to take a few of the enemy's forts. Ten days had thus been consumed, and of course their approach was no surprise.

Nieuport was a well-fortified little city, a mile or two from the sea, and surrounded by low and marshy land. At high tide the creek upon which the city stood was broad and deep enough for vessels to ascend. Maurice sent the greater part of his forces across to the western side of the water, leaving the rest under the command of his cousin Ernest. He ordered a good bridge to be built, so that the two divisions might not be separated at high tide, and marked out the lines of entrenchments for the intended siege. This was on the day they arrived, and much besides planning had been done before night came on.

The archdukes were not supposed to be in a condition to take the field, and it was hoped that they did not yet know how their territory had been invaded. They had been looking for an attack upon their eastern border indeed. But Albert now bestirred himself so actively and Isabella seconded him so well that before the invading army dreamed of such a thing he was almost in sight, with forces nearly as numerous as their own.

Albert had succeeded in reclaiming a great part of the regiments in mutiny by appealing to them in the name of their holy Catholic faith, and their loyalty to the Infanta Isabella, as well as to himself. They had stipulated and he had promised that the long arrears of pay should be met as soon as possible, that they should be led by their own officers, and should have the place of greatest exposure on the field. On the twenty-ninth of June, near Ghent, the archduke reviewed an army nearly twelve thousand strong. Albert spoke a few stirring words reminding them of their duty to their church and their sovereign; and Isabella, splendidly attired, and mounted on a white palfrey, galloped along the lines. She declared that rather than let them remain unpaid she would sacrifice her personal effects, even to her earrings and the plate daily used at her table. Loud cheers rose in response to her words and the army began its march with enthusiasm.

On the first of July the archduke and his army approached Oudenburg, a fort which Prince Maurice had taken and garrisoned two or three days before. As nobody had any idea that there was a Spanish army within twenty miles, the commanding officer had allowed most of the garrison to go out foraging or plundering; so he was compelled to surrender at once. The same thing occurred at several other points the same day. Favorable terms were offered, but when once the forts were theirs the Spaniards butchered nearly everybody as usual.

On the evening of the first of July, after the tired generals and troops had gone to rest, the hurrying footsteps of a terrified fugitive were suddenly heard approaching Count Ernest's quarters on the eastern side of the harbor. It was a soldier escaped from Oudenburg, who brought the astounding news that the enemy had recaptured that fort and all the other forts and redoubts in that vicinity. Count Ernest, with the fugitive, at once sprang into a boat and was rowed across to Maurice's headquarters, where the officers immediately gathered to hold a council of war.

Oudenburg lay between Nieuport and Ostend. If the enemy had really taken possession of it, retreat was impossible, and there must be a great battle instead of a leisurely siege.

CHAPTER XX.

THE BRIDGE AT LEFFINGEN.

STARTLED by the hasty summons to headquarters, the other generals gathered with anxious faces around their commander-in-chief while he repeated the tidings.

Most of them doubted whether there could be any Spanish force at Oudenburg, except the troops stationed in that region. Probably these had been trying what they could do under pretense of belonging to an approaching army. Sir Francis Vere was fast asleep in his tent, but was specially sent for to give his opinion. He said he had no doubt the archduke was coming in force; he had expected nothing else from the first. Then he went back to take a second nap, leaving the other officers still consulting. At midnight they summoned him again; there was no longer any doubt. A messenger had arrived from Ostend, where thirteen members of the States-General, with Barneveld himself, were staying to watch the progress of the campaign which they had planned. He had brought the written terms of the capitulation of Oudenburg, which the Archduke Albert himself had signed, and had violated almost before the ink was dry.

Evidently Albert was following the very track which Maurice's army had traveled the morning before; and his progress would be assisted by what they had done in making roads and bridges. Maurice recollected a certain spot, a few miles back, where they had crossed a deep and dangerous river; and resolved if possible to secure that bridge before the enemy could reach it. He ordered Count Ernest, whose division was on the east side of the harbor, to march thither with all speed. A small force in such a spot might possibly hold at bay a considerable army for a time. He also sent to Ostend an order for four hundred cavalry stationed in that city to hasten to Leffingen and destroy the bridge before the enemy should arrive. Had this order been received, the plan might have succeeded; but it did not reach Ostend for ten days. Indeed, the States-General, who were intensely anxious, themselves ordered out the horsemen; but, as the latter were not accustomed to receive orders from that body, they could hardly be gotten into their saddles at all; and nothing would induce them to ride farther than Fort Saint Albert.

Count Ernest well knew that he was going on a desperate enterprise, but he needed no urging. He set off at once, with two regiments of infantry, one being Scotch and the other Zealanders, four squadrons of Dutch cavalry, and two pieces of artillery. It was over difficult ground that he had to pass; and when, about eight in the morning, he came in sight of the bridge, the enemy was there. Nothing was to be seen of the cavalry expected from Ostend.

It was plain that the enemy's force outnumbered his, six or eight to one. He might perhaps still retreat into Fort Saint Albert, or even to Ostend. In that case, though he might save his men for future service to the republic, there would be nothing to hinder the foe from pressing on and falling upon the main body of Maurice's army, at this moment struggling across the harbor in the ebbing tide. And if they did, there might not be a republic to fight for another day. So the gallant Ernest of Nassau, with a self-devotion worthy of the house to which he belonged, resolved to perish then and there, if he must, in order to hinder the advance of the enemy, and gain a little time for the main army before Nieuport.

He drew up his men in order of battle, behind a dike, upon which he placed his two fieldpieces, directly in face of the advancing foe. The Scotch regiment was on the right, the Zealanders on the left, with four companies of horse. They were within a carbine-shot of the stream, and the passage from the stream along which the enemy must march was not more than a hundred yards wide, with a swamp on each side. So resolute was the air of the little army awaiting attack that the archduke paused for a few moments, to make sure that he was not about to engage the whole force of the States. Then his battalions moved on, and were met with four volleys in succession from the fieldpieces mounted on the dike.

For a moment they were staggered; but confident in their overwhelming numbers, they rushed upon the dike and captured the guns. The attack began upon Count Ernest's left; and the cavalry, fearing they were going to be cut off from all chance of retreating to the fort, suddenly turned their backs in a disgraceful panic. In another moment a senseless terror fell upon the whole Zealand regiment; and bravely as they had often before fought, they now took to their heels, threw away their weapons, and rushed across the sands toward the sea, hotly pursued by their exulting foes. Even the Scots, beside themselves with terror and despair, joined in the flight, though all their captains and company officers strove to rally them, and themselves were slain on the spot.

"No viler panic," says Motley, "no more complete defeat, was ever recorded. The glory of Thermopylæ might have hung forever over that bridge of Leffingen. It was now a pass of infamy, perhaps of fatal disaster. The sands were covered with weapons thrown away by almost every soldier as he fled, to save the life which after all was sacrificed." Not less than a thousand of Maurice's best men perished, and the Spaniards claimed that they destroyed nearly twice that number; the artillery, ammunition, and thirty flags were captured. The archduke triumphantly sent word to Isabella at Ghent that he had utterly defeated the advance guard of the States' army, scarcely losing a man himself. He expected in his next bulletin to announce the final overthrow of Maurice; and she might count upon seeing the rebel stadtholder soon brought before her a prisoner. Isabella said to her ladies that she wondered how Maurice of Nassau would carry himself in her presence as a captive. The archduke had decided to put to the sword all prisoners except Maurice and his brother Frederic Henry, and gave instructions to that effect to his army.

The report of the victory was dispatched in haste to Ghent, to Bruges, and other cities; in response, the bells rang joyfully and cannons thundered, as if the thousand men killed that morning had not been fellow countrymen of those who rejoiced. The archduke held a council of war, to consider whether to press on without delay and engage the main army of the States, or whether a few hours of rest should be allowed after the hurried march and the exciting affair of the morning. Since Maurice was not likely either to take Nieuport or to escape into Ostend, as matters now stood, it seemed safe to wait a little. They would need simply to entrench themselves for the night where they were, since he could take no other route if he marched at all. Should he venture to attack them, it would be with troops already wearied and disheartened by the defeat of Count Ernest's division; or if he should stay where he was, he would soon be starved into submission, especially should the archduke recapture Fort Saint Albert, as he might easily do. Meanwhile their own rear guard of three thousand men would come in to reinforce the present army.

These arguments were urged by Zapena, a veteran marshal of the camp. But most of the officers, as well as the men, were eager to push on. They feared the enemy would skulk away on board of his fleet, and so slip through their fingers. While the debate was going on, from their position on the edge of the downs they actually descried a few ships moving slowly along as if bound for Ostend. Most likely the rebel commander was on board, said the eager chieftains; but possibly they might yet intercept the main body of his army. So the order to march was given, and the army was speedily on the way.

Had those few companies of horsemen at Ostend

but been brave enough to sally out and hang upon the enemy's rear, they might have hindered him a good deal and perhaps compelled him to detach part of his own cavalry in self-defense. But not a step would they stir, however pressing the commands and entreaties of the States-General. That honorable body was now in great anxiety as to the result of the Flemish campaign which they had started. A contemporary writer [1] says: "Since in such extremities, when human resources fail, there is no better course than to take refuge in the God of armies, therefore my lords the States, with their suites and many others who were present, withdrew into their chamber where they were wont to assemble; and after the chaplain Uytenbogart had offered prayer for the preservation of his excellency and the other lords and captains who were with him and likewise for the whole army, they committed all to God, expecting a favorable issue."

[1] Les Lauriers de Nassau, fol. 197.

THE FINAL CHARGE IN THE DUNES.

CHAPTER XXI.

THE BATTLE OF NIEUPORT.

WHILE Count Ernest had been absent much had been going on in the army before Nieuport. The first problem was, how to get across the haven in the speediest way. The brief midsummer night would soon be gone, the tide was nearly full, and there were neither bridges nor boats by which to cross. There was no way except to wait until the tide had nearly gone out, before attempting the passage. At the earliest possible moment, which was not till after eight o'clock, Count Lewis Gunther rode across with eight squadrons of cavalry, the horses swimming where the water was still beyond their depth. Then the advance guard of infantry under Sir Francis Vere, five or six thousand strong, slowly waded across, the water being up to their armpits and in places nearly over their heads. Owing to the delay of the enemy at Leffingen, the army of Maurice all reached the eastern shore of the haven before the archduke's vanguard came in sight.

Count Lewis Gunther and his cavalry, sitting motionless upon their horses, their line of battle stretching across the beach from the downs to the sea, first perceived that far along the shore troops were coming from the direction of Ostend. He hoped it might be that his brother Ernest was returning victorious from his morning's work at the bridge. But shortly, two breathless horsemen galloped along the strand with news that the whole army of the archduke was coming. Without letting them tell more of their evil tidings they were sent to the prince to deliver their message to him alone. And now at last Maurice knew that the worst had befallen Ernest's expedition, and that nothing but utter ruin could be expected.

In that supreme moment, when a weaker spirit would have given way, the prince stood unmoved. He quietly told the two horsemen as they valued their lives not to open their lips to a single soul, and sent them under guard to a man-of-war lying outside the harbor. Saying not a word of the great disaster, nor asking counsel of any man, he sent orders to the fleet that every vessel, of whatever kind, should instantly put to sea. Having thus deliberately cut off the last chance of escape for himself as well as for his men, he went on with the arrangements for the impending battle.

The field was a peculiar one. The hard, smooth beach stretched along toward the northeast in an almost unbroken line for many miles. A little above the line of high tide began the downs, seven hundred yards in width, and parallel to the beach. Here the sands, deep and soft, were ever drifting hither and thither in fantastic heaps and hollows at the caprice of the winds. It was no place for the evolutions of cavalry, nor could infantry perform regular and well-timed movements while wading in the hot sand and tangled in the prickly broom which grew profusely all over it. Beyond the downs lay a belt of level green meadows, with a stream flowing sluggishly through them towards the harbor.

Before noon the army of the United Provinces had been drawn up in battle array, confronting that of the archduke, now in full view. The day was bright and warm, a gentle southwest breeze was blowing, and the sails of more than a thousand vessels gleamed upon the blue sea. The prince rode through the lines arrayed in complete armor, sword in hand, the orange plumes waving from his helmet and the orange scarf across his breast. There was no need of many words. Behind his army lay the harbor of Nieuport, now again flooded by the rising tide; at their left was the sea, whitened by the sails of the departing fleet; before them the enemy. Either victory or death awaited them. They would be put to the sword if captured; better perish bravely fighting for their fatherland.

"I am here to share your fate," said the prince. "I shall conquer or perish with you this day. I trust in the God of battles and in your brave hearts and strong arms to win the greatest victory we have ever achieved."

"Lead us on!" shouted the troops eagerly, "we are ready!" And the legion of the New Beggars, so lately on the Spanish side, at a word from Marquette their commander all lifted up their hands and solemnly swore to live or die that day at the feet of Prince Maurice.

Several nobles had joined the prince's staff as volunteers, including the duke of Holstein, the prince of Anhalt, and others; these were urged to withdraw while it was yet possible to send them on board the fleet. Among them was young Frederic Henry, a boy of sixteen, on whom the hopes of the house of Orange would depend, should Prince Maurice fall. He implored his brother to let him remain, however great the peril. At last Maurice gave his consent; a son of William the Silent could hardly be excluded from the field where the fate of his country was about to be decided. Nor did any of the other nobles withdraw.

Count Lewis Gunther, with his eight squadrons of cavalry, had at first held a position somewhat in advance; but afterwards he yielded to the judgment of Sir Francis Vere and drew up his troops at the left flank of the vanguard, as close as possible to the sea. Vere himself commanded the vanguard; it consisted of more than five thousand men, their ranks extending quite across the beach and into the downs. Just at the edge of the downs and in the narrow border of hard beach above high-water mark was a battery of six demicannon. Vere had stationed groups of musketeers and pikemen on all the hillocks of the downs, and ambushed in every hollow were arquebus-men and carabineers. Two pieces of artillery stood on the highest point, for it was foreseen that the battle might be fought mainly in the downs.

Behind the vanguard was the center, commanded by George Everard Solms, and then came the rear guard under Tempel. In all divisions of the army many of the men were foreigners, some Germans, some Swiss and French, and many English. To the English, certainly, it must have seemed that the cause was in a sense their own, however it may have been with the rest.

In the other army, meanwhile, Archduke Albert, in splendid armor and mounted on a white horse of wonderful beauty, was riding to and fro to cheer and stimulate his troops. He rode with his helmet off, that he might at once be recognized by the men. His vanguard was commanded by Mendoza, the admiral of Aragon, and noted warriors had charge of the other divisions of the army.

The two armies had been standing face to face and at no great distance for some time, when, about two o'clock, the archduke ordered his columns to advance. Maurice had directed that a small body of Lewis Gunther's cavalry should at the outset make a charge upon the enemy and then retreat as if in a panic, in order to draw the Spaniards towards the battery at the edge of the downs. Then the battery was to open upon them suddenly while they were close to it. This was expected to throw them into some confusion, during which the soldiers hidden in the hollows were to rush upon their flank, and all the cavalry to charge upon them in front and drive their advance guard back upon the center. But the battery men, getting too eager, fired a volley before the detachment of cavalry had time to make their pretended charge and retreat. And so nothing came about as was intended. The effect was to make the downs shortly the chief scene of the conflict, and thus to oblige Maurice to change his front. But the well-drilled troops accomplished it in tolerable order, leaving only a few companies of foot on the beach, now almost covered by the rising tide.

The Spaniards were now obliged to face the southwesterly wind, which blew sand and smoke into their eyes, and to meet the full glare of the July sun. While their infantry was charging that of the States under Vere, Count Lewis Gunther was sent across the downs to the meadows beyond, with six squadrons of horse. He found a large body of the enemy's cavalry there, and made a brilliant charge upon them by which they were put to flight. In the ardor of pursuit he found himself surrounded by the enemy, and only ten of his own men near. He was fortunately rescued by another company of horse, just arrived; but his troops were so long returning from the pursuit that he could not push the advantage.

In the downs, meanwhile, the infantry of both armies were fighting terribly in a hand-to-hand conflict among the hillocks and hollows, where they were knee-deep in the hot sands. It was impossible to fight according to regular and scientific methods. Three times the Spanish infantry retreated in confusion, but each time they rallied and drove back the republican forces. The latter recovered themselves in their turn and renewed the struggle. The downs were strewn with the dead and dying. Sir Francis Vere was fighting in the very front all the while, though twice shot through the leg; at last, and seemingly at the most critical moment, his horse was killed, and fell so that his rider was held fast to the ground. Fortunately he was found by one of his friends and carried off the field.

While the battle was thus raging on the downs, Lewis Gunther, having at length rallied his scattered forces, was impatient to charge again. Maurice, who was watching the infantry as they fought, desired him to wait till he should see a favorable moment. At last yielding to his young cousin's importunity, he gave the coveted permission; and with three picked squadrons the count made a furious charge upon the enemy's cavalry, now drawn up close to their musketeers. But he did not this time succeed in putting them to flight; and the musketeers poured a heavy fire upon his troops, who faltered and began to wheel upon the companies behind them, thus throwing all into confusion. Seeing this, the archduke now sent in his last reserves of foot, and charged afresh upon the infantry of Vere, now exhausted by long fighting in the extreme heat. Some of the English and Netherlanders fled in a panic, never stopping till they reached the sea; but most retreated slowly and in some degree of order, as they were driven from one ridge to another, till at last they made a stand behind the battery at the edge of the downs.

It seemed as though all was lost. Vere had been carried off the field, Count Lewis Gunther routed, and the whole army broken and dismayed. But the prince never faltered. He had simply three squadrons of cavalry left; he now put himself at their head. In that moment of unspeakable peril it was given him to utter such words of cheer, of entreaty, of love for fatherland and freedom, of upbraiding to those who were deserting the sacred cause in its greatest need, that part of the fugitives rallied once more. So dauntless was the bearing of the prince that the enemy, struck by the sight, unconsciously paused an instant to gaze.

Maurice saw that the battle was now to center around his battery on the beach, and ordered the reserved squadrons to charge in that direction. Just as the battery was about to be deserted, the first squadron thundered along the beach and fell upon the Spanish infantry near the guns. Then followed the second and the third. Many of the enemy were killed or captured; and the Zealand sailors who had been serving the battery now promptly opened fire once more. The Spaniards were staggered; the Zealanders shouted " Fall on ! " and others began to shout " Victory ! " while Maurice's cavalry charged again. Then the whole line of the Catholic forces suddenly broke and fled in every direction; the republicans who just now were retreating in panic rushed after the enemy with exultant shouts, and the hard-fought field was won.

The admiral of Aragon, whose horse had fallen upon him, was captured by two of his former servants, to one of whom he had been extremely cruel. He recognized them as he surrendered, and gave his scarf to one and the hanger of his sword belt to the other, in token that he belonged to them. According to the custom of the time, so great a personage as the admiral would have to pay a heavy ransom, some small part of which would go to these old servants who had captured him. He was sent to the rear, not so much dismayed as to spoil his appetite for a hearty dinner, which he called for at once, though the firing had not ceased. Later in the evening he supped with Prince Maurice in his tent, where, in the circumstances, he was not an unwelcome guest.

Archduke Albert himself was almost captured in the final rout. He had fought like a hero throughout the battle and had been slightly wounded early in the action. He was now hard pressed, and a Walloon pikeman, not recognizing him in the plain armor and shabby scarf which he had put on during the battle, seized his bridle and cried: "Surrender, scoundrel!" Just then came up a Flemish officer, Captain Kabbeljaw, who knew the archduke, and rushing to his relief killed the pikeman and four others on the spot. Then he was himself slain; but the archduke escaped along with a few officers and horsemen. They might have been easily captured at that bridge of Leflingen where he had been so triumphant a few hours before, had not the handful of republican soldiers guarding it (who had not yet heard anything of the victory at Nieuport) fled when they saw cavaliers riding hotly toward them. The archduke hurried on to Bruges and thence to Ghent, where, not precisely as a conqueror, he met his wife. Instead of bringing Maurice of Nassau as his captive he had left him master of the field. But Isabella met the disappointment coolly, as if she did not mind. This was a sample of the royal deportment which she had been taught to consider the correct thing on such occasions. True, her fine army had been utterly routed and at least three or four thousand of them killed, besides many captured; but why should her lofty spirit be discomposed by trifles like these?

At length the victors were exhausted by the battle and the chase; the sultry night was black with clouds; it was enough to have turned such a defeat into such a victory. The prince encamped on the field for the night. Through all the perils of that terrible day he had been firm and self-controlled; but when at length the legions of Italy and Spain had fled before the army of the republic he had been overcome. "Dismounting from his horse," says Motley, "he threw himself on his knees in the sand, and with streaming eyes and uplifted hands exclaimed: 'O God, what are we human creatures to whom thou hast brought such honor, and to whom thou hast vouchsafed such a victory!'"

The next morning the prince rode to Ostend, now wild with unspeakable joy, to join in the public thanksgiving for this deliverance. His chaplain, Uytenbogart, preached on the One Hundred Sixteenth Psalm, beginning, "I love the Lord because he hath heard my voice and my supplication." After the service a dinner was given in honor of the prince at the house of the States-General. The great prisoner, the admiral of Aragon, was a guest and had to put up with some keen though not ill-natured jokes. Considering that his own mode of dealing with prisoners had been to cut their throats, he might well submit to a little teasing. Prince Maurice remarked: " Monsieur the admiral of Aragon is more fortunate than many of his army; he has been constantly wishing these four years to see Holland, and now he will enter there without striking a blow." Others inquired what he now thought of their awkward Dutchmen and Zealanders who had long been admitted to fight well behind ramparts, but not considered equal to a pitched battle with Spanish troops in the open field. The admiral was not disconcerted and commented freely on the management upon both sides. He praised Maurice's prudence in holding some of his cavalry in reserve till the crisis, which the archduke ought also to have done. He observed that the archduke's artillery had been of little service for want of such platforms as had prevented Maurice's cannons from sinking deep into the sand. More than all he admired the prince's heroism in ordering his fleet to put to sea, leaving no alternative but victory or death.

Lewis Gunther wrote to his elder brother, Lewis William, stadtholder of Friesland: "I hope that this day's work will not be useless to me, both for what I have learned in it and for another thing. His excellency Prince Maurice has done me the honor to give me the admiral for my prisoner." To this Lewis William replied: "I thank God for his singular grace in that he has been pleased to make use of your person as the instrument of so signal a victory. . . . I am glad too that his excellency has given you the admiral for your prisoner, both because of the benefit to you and because it is a mark of your merit on that day. . . . You will now be able to free your patrimony from incumbrances when otherwise you would have been in danger of remaining embarrassed and in the power of others. It will be a perpetual honor to you that you, the youngest of us all, have been able by your merits to do more to raise our house out of its difficulties than have your predecessors or myself."

The admiral's ransom was afterward fixed at a hundred thousand crowns and he was released on parole.

But two years later it came about that the States-General, with the consent of the Nassaus, agreed to release Mendoza altogether without his paying the ransom, on condition that the Spanish government would discharge all prisoners of war belonging to the Dutch republic who were held in any of the Spanish domains. So Lewis Gunther freely relinquished the hundred thousand crowns that were to have relieved the house of Nassau so much, and took instead the exceeding joy of setting free a great many prisoners from the dungeons of Spain or from the galleys where they had toiled in chains so many miserable years.

The prince announced his victory to Lewis William in the most simple and modest way. "At length," he remarked after having written of the long battle, "it became a hand-to-hand struggle and was fought very hotly on both sides for the space of two hours. Finally God graciously willed that the victory should remain on my side."

It was five days after the battle when the news first reached England. The governor of Calais wrote to the French ambassador in London, and he told it to Caron, the ambassador of the States. Caron could hardly wait for daybreak; and in spite of bad weather he rode post haste from London to the palace at Greenwich, and waited on Sir Robert Cecil, who was still in bed. A rumor had reached Sir Robert, also, through the English ambassador in Paris; but it was that the archduke had won the day. In the midst of this agitating suspense there arrived a bearer of dispatches from the States-General, and a letter to Cecil from Sir Francis Vere. The queen heard that tidings had come, and sent down to know the particulars. Caron made hasty notes of the principal facts, and sent them up to her majesty, but nothing would satisfy her till she could see Caron. So he was obliged to appear in the royal presence booted and spurred, and bespattered from head to foot with mud. But the queen cared for nothing at present except to hear every word of Barneveld's letter to the Dutch ambassador. Caron read it aloud, translating from Dutch into French, and the queen listened with unbounded delight. It was natural that she should rejoice; the English and the Dutch had fought at Nieuport side by side, and it was Sir Francis Vere who had been next to Prince Maurice in command. Had the archduke won the day, it would have proved the overthrow of the Dutch republic, and England might soon have had reason to tremble for herself.

The queen declared that she thanked God on her knees for granting this splendid victory to the United Provinces. She lavished her praises on the wisdom and skill, as well as the courage, of the prince and the

Dutch government. "The sagacious administration of the States," said she, "is so full of good order and policy as far to surpass in its wisdom the intelligence of all kings and potentates. We kings understand nothing of such affairs in comparison, but require, all of us, to go to school to the States-General."

Henry IV also manifested great satisfaction at the news of the victory, in spite of his being now a professed Catholic. As he heard of it earlier than even the Dutch envoy at his court, the king amused himself by sending for that personage and reading aloud the account of Ernest's defeat at Leflingen; then he told him the whole, being unable to conceal any longer his delight at a victory which would prove such a check to the designs of Spain.

Three days after the battle Maurice returned to the vicinity of Nieuport; but as the garrison had been reinforced, and other circumstances were unpropitious, the States-General decided to abandon the enterprise on which they had been so determined. So far as recovering Flanders was concerned, it had completely failed. The moral effect of having conquered in a pitched battle certainly was great, in giving confidence to the soldiers of the republic for the future. Yet all who appreciated the extreme narrowness of their escape must have mingled many serious reflections with their rejoicings at the happy event.

For a time the great statesmen were willing to leave the planning of campaigns to the great generals.

It was probably just here that the alienation between Barneveld and Maurice began. The wise statesman doubtless felt the personal mortification of having made such a mistake in insisting upon the invasion of Flanders. He was well aware that the prince, when reduced to that desperate condition, might have said: " I told you so; " and though it had ended in a victory, the glory of it was upon Maurice's brow, not his own. Barneveld, patriot as he was, had still a little of human weakness; and Maurice had more. Each now began to fear that the other was aspiring to control things entirely according to his own judgment; and each feared, with good reason, that harm would thus come to the republic which both sincerely loved.

CHAPTER XXII.

BEGINNING OF THE SIEGE OF OSTEND.

THE next act of the great Netherland drama opened in July, 1601. It was destined to be a long and memorable one; and its scenes were nearly all to take place around the small seaport of Ostend, the only town of Flanders now held by the republic.

Ostend was situated ten or twelve miles northeast of Nieuport and about fifteen west of Bruges. For four or five hundred years it was merely a fishing village, with an ancient church built by Robert the Frisian in honor of Saint Peter. In 1445 it had been enclosed by a wall; and not far from 1580 it had been so well fortified by the States that the great Alexander of Parma, who made a sudden attack upon it in 1583, did not succeed. Its population numbered only about three thousand, aside from the garrison.

The archdukes wanted Ostend, not only because it was the only place in Flanders which still defied their authority, but still more because it controlled the coast and furnished a good base for forays into the surrounding region by its garrison.

The States of this province, according to the metaphorical style of those days, spoke of Ostend as a thorn in the paw of the Belgic lion, which they earnestly implored the archduke to extract. They offered to furnish funds to the amount of three hundred thousand florins a month as long as the siege should continue. They would also pay one hundred thousand as soon as the place should be invested, another one hundred thousand when a breach should be made, and the same on the surrender of the town. Albert himself, when informed that Parma had to spend eighteen months in reducing Antwerp, declared that he would cheerfully devote eighteen years, if necessary, to capture Ostend. *

During the preceding year a vast amount of damage had been inflicted upon the Dutch shipping by a notorious privateersman called Admiral Van der Waecken. He had twelve or fourteen armed vessels making their headquarters at Dunkirk and preying continually upon defenseless merchantmen and fishing smacks. His cruelties to the crews of these vessels were almost beyond belief. Sometimes he would nail the men to the floor of the cabin by their hands and feet, and then scuttling the ship, would let them all go to the bottom. Vengeance happily overtook some of these buccaneers; and the admiral himself, while escaping to Spain with most of his vessels, lost many of his men by desertion and shortly died. The memory of barbarities like these made the States only the more determined that Ostend should not be converted into such a den of pirates as Dunkirk.

Ostend lay at the mouth of a little river called the Iperleda. The original harbor, on the western side of the town, was now so choked with sand that it could hardly be entered save at full tide. There were high downs stretching along the shore like miniature ranges of mountains on either side of the town; but south of it the ground was so low and marshy that it was often submerged. Along the shore to the westward there was a dike forming a partial barrier to the sea. To the eastward the sand hills were so high that it had been found necessary to level them lest they should be of service to the besiegers. In consequence, the sea had broken over the lowered barriers on that side, flooding the suburbs. Even at low tide there now remained a deep and broad channel at the eastern side of the town, through which war ships might well pass. The new harbor thus formed completely supplied the place of the old one, and by opening a passage through the fortifications there was now a snug haven within the walls for vessels bringing supplies.

The little town, around whose walls one might walk in about half an hour, had a regular counterscarp, bastions, and casemates. It was further defended by a number of strong ravelins on the western side, where the old harbor no longer furnished any protection, being so nearly filled up. The principal ones were named the Sand-Hill, the Porcupine, and Hell's Mouth. Toward the southwestern part of the walls there were some detached works called the Polder,

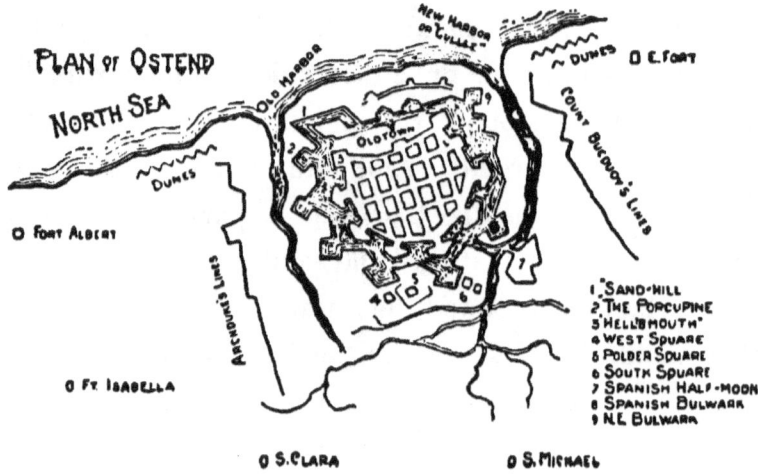

the Square, and the South Square. On the east side, bordering upon the new harbor, was a fortification called the Spanish Half-moon.

The archduke had built eighteen fortresses to the west and southwest of the town, the largest of which were named the Saint Albert, the Saint Isabella, the Saint Clara, and the Great Thirst.

On the fifth of July, 1601, just a year and three

days after the battle of Nieuport, Archduke Albert appeared before Ostend to begin the siege. He established his headquarters at Fort Saint Albert; and his wife was almost always at the fort, having the keenest interest in the enterprise. On the eastern side of the new harbor, Frederic van den Berg was in command, assisted by Count Bucquoy-Longueval, the archduke's chief of artillery.

The garrison of Ostend, commanded by Sir Francis Vere, included seven or eight thousand men, about one fourth of whom were English. The archduke's forces numbered usually two or three times as many. But however successfully Ostend might be invested on the landward sides, it was not easy to cut off its supplies. The new harbor, now called the Gullet, was too broad, too deep, its rushing tides too powerful, to permit it to be shut up.

There was a new contrivance, at that time considered quite wonderful, by means of which the besiegers hoped to advance their works closer and closer on each side, in spite of the sea. Huge baskets of wickerwork, twenty feet long, were packed full of bricks and sand and sunk in the water. These got the name of "sausages." Little by little they succeeded in thus building a foundation for some batteries in the bed of the old harbor. But before long the besieged managed to cut the sea dike in that quarter, and during storms and floodtides the waves would rush in, sweeping clean away batteries, gunners, brick-baskets, and all. Then the besiegers would do this work all over again; and some part of it would perhaps withstand the next flood, so that a little progress was really made.

On the east it was much harder. Bucquoy kept laying his sausages along the edge of the rushing water in hopes at length to have a dike and a platform there on which he could plant a battery. Then he would be able to keep away all vessels bringing reinforcements or supplies. But the guns on the Half-moon opposite were perpetually playing on his pioneers as they labored, killing not a few; and the high waves often demolished their works and drowned the men. Meanwhile the adroit Dutch skippers would coolly sail past and discharge their cargoes within the walls, just as if nobody had any objection. All sorts of provisions were abundant and cheap in Ostend, so regular and ample were the supplies sent by the States. The archduke's prospects of starving the city into submission did not look very bright.

There was much cannonading from fifty great guns, whose balls weighed from ten to forty pounds apiece. On an average, there used to be fired a thousand shots a day by the besiegers; and it is related that the Infanta would sometimes touch off a forty-pounder with her own dainty hand to stimulate the gunners. In that day it was thought a prodigious affair to use artillery to such an extent, and all Europe thought it worth while to gaze. But the cannons at Ostend would seem mere popguns beside those now in use, and their artillerymen would have thought the skill displayed at the present day simply miraculous. Yet no soldiers can be more daring, no patriots more devoted than were those who lived three hundred years ago.

Before the siege of Ostend was begun, the States-General urged Prince Maurice to make a foray into Flanders, in the hope of driving away the archduke before he had accomplished anything. But Maurice decided to devote himself to guarding the eastern frontier of the United Provinces, so as to hinder the sending of supplies from that quarter to the archduke. Early in June he appeared before Rheinberg and laid siege to it. In the midst of this he was obliged to send two thousand of his English troops, by order of the States, to reinforce the garrison of Ostend. He had now only eight thousand men, nevertheless he went on with the siege; and about the middle of July he exploded a mine which blew many of the garrison into the air. One of these victims alighted in the prince's camp, not much injured, strange to say; and was able to report the condition of the town at the moment when he left it so unexpectedly.

On the thirtieth of July the garrison of Rheinberg surrendered and the prince gave honorable terms, as he usually did in such cases. No citizen was required to leave the town, and the garrison departed with the honors of war. The public worship of the Roman Catholic church was not permitted, but there was not to be any inquiry into private services or individual beliefs. The next week the city of Meurs also capitulated. In November Maurice invested Bois le Duc; but a sudden frost sheeted the rivers and canals with ice, and fearing Holland might be invaded, he raised the siege.

All through the autumn the cannonading went on at Ostend with deadly effect. Many dwellings were burned and many people killed within the walls, and pestilence swept off more than fell by the enemy's shots. The governor, Sir Francis Vere, was at one time compelled to go away for six weeks to be cured of a wound. By December only three thousand of the garrison survived, and not more than eight thousand of the besiegers. The ravelin called the Porcupine, a very important work though small, was much damaged by the waves; and while the besieged labored incessantly to repair it, they were baffled by the rushing wintry tides, as well as by the efforts of the enemy, who set fire to a quantity of the materials for the work. For weeks no reinforcements arrived, and the garrison was dwindling day by day.

On the morning of December 23, Sir Francis Vere perceived that the garrison was no longer sufficient to hold the external works at the southwest part of the walls; and he gave orders that on the next day the men should withdraw from the Square and the Polder in order to concentrate within the walls. His own quarters had hitherto been in one of these detached forts; and to be forced to retire within the town seemed like defeat. But during the day he learned from a deserter that the archduke was intending to storm the place on all sides that very evening. If these forts must be abandoned to the enemy for want of men to hold them, they might as well surrender outright.

CHAPTER XXIII.

THE CHRISTMAS PARLEY.

THAT day — Sunday, December 23 — was an anxious one for Sir Francis Vere and for everybody else in Ostend. The situation was gloomy indeed. The course which Vere took has been variously represented and commented upon by different writers of that period and of recent times. The story is told in a work published at Leyden only eleven years afterwards, — Les Lauriers de Nassau, — in a way that seems in a great degree to harmonize the apparently conflicting accounts [1] of others.

It would seem that about two o'clock that afternoon, Vere sent four captains to examine and report upon the condition of the Porcupine, whether it could be held in case of assault. While they were there, about three o'clock, Captain Louis de Conture came to the same work, sent by Vere to ask a parley. It is expressly stated that "this was done without the advice of any of the captains." The archduke agreed to the conference, and two English officers, Ogle and

---

[1] United Netherlands, vol. iv, pp. 77-86, and The Fighting Veres, pp. 320-323.

Fairfax, were immediately sent as hostages to the archduke's camp. He received them with ceremonious politeness, and inquired if they were empowered to treat for the surrender of the town. They were not, they replied, but were only hostages for the safety of the commissioners whom it was expected that he would send to confer with Governor Vere. Accordingly, about five o'clock the same evening, he sent two highly respected officers, Don Antonio, quartermaster general of his army, and Matteo Serrano, the governor of Sluys, who was at this time serving in the besieging army.

As the days were at the shortest, it was dark when they arrived at Ostend, which they entered on the western side. On the way to headquarters they heard a great uproar and beating to arms on the eastern side of the town. They knew nothing about the cause of it, and were confounded and indignant when Vere, apparently in a great rage, declared that the Spaniards were deceiving him, and were about to storm the town in spite of the truce. Without giving them a chance to protest their innocence, the governor went on to declare that he would have nothing to do with them; and he directed the officers who had escorted them into his presence to take them back again immediately.

So much time was consumed in going to and fro through the dark and miry streets that when they arrived at the point where they had crossed the old harbor before, the tide was so high that they were unable to return that way. Vere had all the time been perfectly aware that they would find it so. Then they were conducted to headquarters once more; and being very tired they begged to be allowed to remain in Ostend till morning — in a guardhouse, if necessary. But the governor would not permit even this, and ordered the escorting officers to conduct them across to the new harbor, whence they might be sent in a boat to their own entrenchments. Moreover, he gave private instructions that they should be led thither by the most roundabout course; and so it was not until they had plodded long through the most filthy and dismal streets of the town, in the darkness and sleet, that they reached the Half-moon, quite worn out.

"Ah, the villainous town of Ostend!" ejaculated Serrano, surveying his bespattered condition with disgust. He begged the small consolation of a pipe of tobacco, but none was to be had at the Half-moon. However, four flagons of foaming ale were set before the two Spaniards, and after they had drunk they were rowed across the new harbor and committed to the sentries of Bucquoy's division. As it was now midnight, they remained there till morning, and then proceeded to the quarters of the archduke.

One would suppose that this would have ended the parley. But as Ogle and Fairfax declared that there must have been some unaccountable misunderstanding, the commissioners were sent back to the town, with orders to arrange for the capitulation as soon as possible.

It appears that Vere had called together all the captains, at one o'clock that Monday morning, and had presented the case, dwelling much on the weakness of the garrison and the difficulty of holding all the works, should there be an assault. He asked whether the officers would not think it wise to destroy certain of the outworks, which they could not well hold, and place those who had manned them in the fortifications where they were more needed. It was decided to raze the South Square; but this was not actually done, on account of an unforeseen circumstance.

At nine the same morning Vere summoned all the officers again to his quarters. He now told them why he had entered into communication with the archduke, which he had done on his own responsibility. He stated, as he afterwards wrote to the States-General, that he had thought it well to deceive and amuse the enemy, in order to gain time and be able to finish certain redoubts in the old town. Besides, he had some hope of being reinforced.

What the officers thought of this dishonorable stratagem is not known. If they regarded it as it would be regarded in our day, they must have been glad that they had not been partakers in the plot.

The commissioners did not arrive in the town the second time till rather late in the afternoon. When the sergeant major who had escorted them the night before announced that the two dignitaries had returned, and asked by what road he should conduct them to the governor's quarters, Vere replied that he must be careful to choose the softest and muddiest streets, lest their feet, accustomed to the sandy beach, should suffer from the rough paving stones. So this was explained to the commissioners, and in spite of their remonstrances they had to follow through miry and crooked ways, until at last they were brought into the presence of the commander.

Sir Francis Vere is described by Motley as "a man of handsome, weatherbeaten, battle-bronzed visage, with massive forehead, broad intelligent eyes, a high, straight nose, close-clipped hair, and a great brown beard like a spade." He wore usually a gold-inlaid corselet of Milan and a ruff of point lace. This time he received the Spaniards in the most gracious and affable manner, showing them every possible attention. They gravely acknowledged his civilities; and then Vere made excuses for the misunderstanding which had caused them so much inconvenience the evening before. Then they talked about the false alarm, each wondering what caused it; and thus time slipped away, just as Vere wished. After a while the commissioners came bluntly out with the question: "What terms of negotiation do you propose?"

"His highness has only to withdraw, and leave us, his poor neighbors, in peace," replied Vere. "This would be the easiest and best arrangement, to our minds."

"But the archduke sent us to treat for your surrender," urged the commissioners, "not for his withdrawal." And now the matter was discussed in good earnest, with hot and sharp words tossed back and forth for a long time. At length Sir Francis spoke of supper and urged the commissioners to stay.

As the next day would be Christmas, according to the new style of reckoning (which had not yet been adopted by the English), this evening was for all good Catholics a strict fast. So the Spaniards were offered fish, eggs, and other dishes permitted on fast days. Wine was abundant, however, and the servants in attendance were struck by the rapidity with which it disappeared. Governor Serrano was said to have drunk fifty-two goblets of claret, besides some beer; and instead of getting hilarious, he grew only the more dignified each time he drained his glass. While they drank they were still talking about the capitulation, but coming no nearer to an agreement than at first.

Vere remarked, in substance, "It is unreasonable in the archduke to demand that we give up the town, which is all we have."

"But Ostend, with all the rest of Flanders," rejoined the commissioners, "belongs to his highness by the legal gift of his late majesty, Philip II."

"Nevertheless," replied Vere, "it is at present ours; and in England they always say that possession is nine points of the law. Do you think we shall give it away?"

Then he went on to compliment the valor and perseverance of the besiegers in holding out so long in spite of dangers and hardships; but he added that since it was now winter, and they had so far gained nothing, they would do well to be content with the glory already earned, and betake themselves to winter quarters.

Serrano remarked that the archduke knew perfectly well how reduced the garrison had become, so that they could not hold their outer works any longer. Of course there could now be no hope for them; and they must needs burrow in the middle of their ruined nest, from which the besiegers were sure shortly to bring them, without any trouble.

By-and-by, between the hard drinking and the

fatigue, the Spaniards consented to remain for the night. Meanwhile it had been reported through all the country round that negotiations were in progress, and it was taken for granted that there would be no more fighting. The thorn in the lion's paw was as good as extracted, and great were the rejoicings that had begun. Next morning Archduke Albert, in splendid armor and with stately plumes waving on his helmet, was riding to and fro in the presence of a great concourse of people who had gathered before the town. Isabella was also there, well mounted and magnificently attired. A gay cavalcade of ladies of her court attended her, all gorgeously arrayed. They were every moment expecting a deputation from the town, submissively bringing its keys. Everybody, whether soldier, burgher, or peasant, was making merry, singing, skating, feasting, drinking; they were sure that Ostend was won and the war as good as ended.

But in the early morning the longing eyes of the besieged joyfully beheld three Dutch men-of-war coming to their rescue. The wind had changed during the night, and the long-delayed vessels, apparently crowded with troops, were sailing directly into the new harbor. The good news quickly reached headquarters. It was just what the governor had hoped might happen, but it had come even sooner than he expected. So he coolly told the commissioners that, having been reinforced, it would not yet be necessary for him to retire into his ruined nest. He would not detain them any longer; should he ever again be so sorely pressed, he felt sure that his highness would magnanimously grant all due clemency, as it seemed his nature to do.

That day Sir Francis Vere wrote to the States-General a letter which the historian Meteren quotes in full. The following is the chief part of it: —

> But forasmuch as this step [the abandoning of the detached forts] would inevitably cause the loss of the town, in order to prevent that calamity, we made use of this stratagem, to enter into communication with the enemy in order thus to amuse him and gain time, and to be able to wait for succor from your highnesses; and . . . to be able to repair and put in better defense all the places, . . . especially the old town, the Porcupine, etc.

Then after mentioning the arrival of the troops that morning, he adds: —

> For by this means we have had occasion to give a brief, peremptory, and full reply to those who had come here on the part of the enemy — to wit, that since we had received this morning what was in part lacking to us, we could not with honor and agreeably to our duty go farther in this negotiation.

This treacherous dealing was not commended even in those times. An officer who should do the like at the present day would hardly be able to hold up his head before either friends or foes.

The Spanish commissioners, agreeably to the custom of that reserved and haughty people, did not condescend to tell Sir Francis what they thought of him, but solemnly departed under escort, to report their ill success. The Dutch ships got safely past the batteries of Bucquoy, which did their best but only wounded two men; and sailed into the haven within the city walls. The festivities outside were broken off, the disappointed crowds scattered, the English hostages returned to Ostend; and meanwhile the archduke, highly incensed, shut himself up alone to growl over the perfidy of Vere and to meditate revenge.

His soldiers also were unhappy and full of complainings. They were ill-fed, unpaid, and altogether wretched, while the archdukes were living magnificently, even beyond sovereigns of former years. And every now and then the archduke would put some favorite of his own in the place of some veteran officer whom he was not at all fit to supersede.

Vere was continually on the alert, knowing that there might be a general assault almost any time. The six hundred men lately arrived enabled him still to hold the external fortifications; and he hoped soon to be further reinforced. Within a few days he found out that a grand assault was to be made the next week, and he did his utmost to prepare Ostend for the reception of its expected invaders. As the three chief ravelins fronting the old harbor would doubtless have to bear the brunt of the attack, he placed in them the best part of his troops. His brother, Sir Horace, was in command of twelve picked companies at the Sand-hill, which was the farthest north and the most important of the three.

There was living in Ostend a remarkable man named Philip Fleming, the auditor and secretary of the city, who was of great service to Governor Vere and to his successors throughout the siege. Though not a military man, he possessed enough courage, coolness, and sagacity for a general. He was so quick to discern dangers, to discover opportunities, to invent expedients, that he really filled a most important place in military matters without holding any office, save in municipal affairs. This " grim, grizzled, leathern-faced man of fifty" was in fact the commander's chief aid-de-camp, ever at his side in danger, unless he was more needed somewhere else, ready to do or dare anything, and often making suggestions of great value. Among his other duties Auditor Fleming took time to keep a regular diary of the siege, recording minutely the events of each day. This was afterwards published and is considered the best history of the matter that exists. Being in Dutch, however, it is of service to fewer readers than the accounts in French.

While Vere was hastening the repairs needed, Auditor Fleming remarked that it might be well to have in readiness materials to stop the breaches that the assailants would make in trying to storm the walls. Accordingly a few houses were demolished for this purpose, since there was no other way.

From morning to night of the seventh of January there was a great cannonading of the town. Two thousand shot were actually counted during the day. Vere knew what might be expected to follow. As the tide would be out at seven o'clock in the evening, the bed of the old harbor could easily be crossed on foot. Having gone the rounds to see that all were at their respective posts, he sat upon his horse at the Sandhill awaiting the onset of the foe. He had not to wait long. On they came through the darkness like a great surge dashing furiously against the walls. Now was the time! At a word from the commander a great blaze flared up from a heap of tar barrels and other inflammable materials which had been arranged for the occasion in the Porcupine. The vivid glare fell upon the long lines of pikemen rushing up to the works with their scaling ladders, and the gunners directed their fire full upon them with deadly effect. Behind them, reserved masses of spearmen could be discerned, ready to support the storming party; and still farther off strong squadrons of horse were visible.

As they came near, the assailants fell in heaps at each volley of musketry; and those who tried to storm any breach were met by men who fought even more desperately than themselves.

Thus the struggle went on for nearly two hours. Then the ever-ready Auditor Fleming, aware that the tide was now rising, desired leave to open the western sluice and thus cut off the retreat which he saw was about to begin. The sudden rush of the waters through the floodgate created a panic in the broken ranks of the storming party. They tried to run back across the harbor to their camp on the other side; but it was too late, and a great number were drowned. Those who had succeeded in getting into the detached forts on the south side were now overpowered and slain. On the east side the attack was not promptly begun, and the water in the new harbor being never shallow enough for wading, nothing of consequence was accomplished. Two thousand of the archduke's army were either killed in the fight or drowned; while the loss of the garrison was only sixty.

Then there was a long period of wintry tempests which prevented any important movement on either side. Pestilence raged in the camp as well as in the town. In March, 1602, Sir Francis Vere was called to service in the field, and Colonel Frederic van Dorp succeeded him in command at Ostend.

CHAPTER XXIV.

THE INDIA TRADE, AND THE PROGRESS OF THE WAR.

JUST about this time an event occurred which had a great deal to do with the future of the Netherlands and with the outcome of their great struggle for independence, though it was not at all of a military character. Within a few years the Dutch had learned how to reach the East Indies by way of the Cape of Good Hope, and already a profitable commerce was going on. A number of private companies had been formed for this purpose; and it was evident that a vast deal of money could be made in trading with the East Indies, if it could be carried on upon a much more extensive scale.

In England, whose people were also interested in commerce with India, the queen had, on the last day of the year 1600, chartered a company having the monopoly of that trade. There were reasons for granting the monopoly at that period; and those already engaged in the trade were invited to associate themselves with the great company and share in its undertakings.

The Dutch East India Company, following the same

general plan, but on a larger scale, was chartered by the States-General, March 20, 1602. Its original capital was five hundred and fifty thousand pounds sterling, while that of the English company was only seventy-two thousand. Half of this capital was subscribed in the city of Amsterdam alone; a fourth came from other Dutch cities, and the rest from the province of Zealand. A great amount of money had to be expended in permanent works, forts, factories, and the like, in the East Indies; and also a great deal in providing fleets, for it was necessary to have men-of-war to protect their commerce. And, like the English, the Dutch company founded in the East an empire larger than their dominions at home.

The Dutch company was far more under the control of the States-General than the English company was under that of their parliament; in the course of time harm came of this too close relation. There was a board of directors, who managed the business of the company; and the States gave them large powers to enter into treaties with the native sovereigns and even to make war and peace. There was a great demand in Europe for the various spices of the East Indies; and the company wished to get a monopoly of that trade, so as to put up the price enormously. Out of this effort grew many difficulties between the Dutch and English, which lasted for generations; and of course there was always trouble with Spain, as that power claimed the East Indies as her own private property, as well as much of Europe, and all of America.

In the course of this very year, before the company sent out its first fleet, a Dutch skipper named Wolfert Hermann, with five trading vessels, routed an imposing Portuguese expedition, numbering twenty-five ships, on its way to punish the king of Bantam, in Java, for having dared to trade with other European people; and this led to the founding of Batavia, the first trading settlement of the Dutch in the East Indies. Other Netherland captains, of whom Jacob Heemskirk was one, established friendly relations with native rulers in that part of the world, and one of them took back with him to the Netherlands several ambassadors from Sumatra, who were profoundly impressed by what they observed. Thus the way was still further opened for the new East India Company.

The States-General were again anxious that Prince Maurice should march into Flanders, hoping that he might thus be able to save Ostend. Vere also thought it might be done; but, as before, the prince and the sagacious Lewis William disapproved of running so great a risk. However, Maurice yielded to the States, and did enter the Obedient Provinces, advancing to the vicinity of Thienen, in Brabant. He had a splendid army, numbering eighteen thousand foot and five thousand horse; Lewis William commanded the center, Vere the right, and Ernest the left. He was now within a day's march of Brussels, the archduke's capital; and Albert felt obliged to quit Ostend for a time, leaving some one else to carry on the siege, in order to watch Maurice's movements. The admiral of Aragon was not far off, with fifteen thousand men in an entrenched camp; and he thought best to stay there. As his position was so strong, Prince Maurice did not make an attack; and before long he moved northward and laid siege to Grave. This important town had been lost by the treachery of its commander some time before; and after a very scientific and masterly siege, lasting sixty days, it surrendered on the eighteenth of September, 1602.

In the mean time there was a mutiny among the Catholic forces which became a most serious affair. As usual, the men had been long unpaid, and had become desperate enough to march away in large bodies. There were about three thousand five hundred who took possession of the city of Hoogstraaten. They established a strict government, and though they lived by daily plundering the country around, they divided it among themselves " with the simplicity of the early Christians." Anybody who took booty on his own private account was severely dealt with.

Albert denounced them as accursed outlaws, and offered rewards for their heads. The mutineers responded by publishing a bold and defiant manifesto, setting forth their grievances before the world. Their numbers increased to five thousand; and they found some sympathy. They opened negotiations with Prince Maurice, and for a considerable time were in the service of the States.

Through 1602, the siege of Ostend still went on, but the end seemed no nearer. On both sides, labors and hardships were immense. During the ten months following the appointment of Governor Van Dorp, not less than four thousand men died in Ostend and probably twice as many in the Spanish camp. But the besieged still held their outworks. When the Spaniards attempted to make subterranean galleries they would meet in the darkness alert and desperate foes, who had divined their stealthy approach and could mine as well as themselves. The enemy toiled incessantly to construct a firm foundation for batteries, so as to make the Gullet impassable; and the besieged over against them were working with might and main to prepare still another entrance from the sea, which might serve them if the present one should be closed. Both were perpetually under fire.

Queen Elizabeth died in March, 1603, and her kingdom passed into the hands of James Stuart, the king of Scotland. The great queen was nearly seventy years of age; her reign had begun even before the outbreak of the Netherland war. Though in her dealings with the Provinces she had often been capricious and ill-tempered, her assistance had been invaluable. There was not a little anxiety as to what her successor might do. No time was lost in presenting the case of the young Netherland republic at the court of James. Barneveld was accompanied by Count Frederic Henry of Nassau, Brederode, and other eminent personages. The other European powers, both small and great, were equally prompt in sending deputations to salute the new monarch, among which of course appeared those of the archdukes and Spain.

The interview of the Dutch envoys with the king was brief and not very encouraging. Barneveld's address, though beginning with compliment after the custom of the time, was an able and earnest plea for the continuance of aid to the Netherlands, whose interests were so intimately connected with England's own. The king replied cautiously and vaguely that he felt good will to the republic, certainly; and likewise to Spain. He did not feel prepared to say at once what he would do. In truth he was a student rather than a warrior.

This was discouraging; but after a time, through the influence of the French ambassador in London —

afterward known as the duke of Sully — Barneveld succeeded in bringing about an agreement between the English and French sovereigns jointly to help the United Provinces to some extent with troops. But as the French king was bound by a treaty with Spain, his aid was to be rather privately given. What Henry IV had in view was really to prevent James from making any treaty with Spain and to keep the Netherlanders from being overpowered; lest either of these events should increase Spanish power in Europe, which seemed to him quite too great already.

CHAPTER XXV.

THE SIEGE OF OSTEND, CONTINUED.

ONE day in April, 1603, a terrific gale put a stop to the fighting at Ostend for some hours. The sea deluged the ramparts, the wind tore off the roofs and chimneys, and the tower of the church came crashing down into the public square. Besiegers and besieged, alike helpless, were driven into such shelters as they could find. Toward evening, when the wind abated and the garrison ventured again to their storm-shattered ramparts, there seemed a suspicious stir in the hostile camp, and the sentinels sounded an alarm. It was not a moment too soon. All at once there rose a great blaze in the Porcupine fort near the northwest corner of the city. With their missiles the Spaniards had set on fire a great pile of wickerwork and building material, and now they were rushing on with loud shouts. There was a general rally of the garrison to the scene of danger; the governor himself was on the spot. The assault was repulsed with heavy loss on the part of the Spaniards, the flames were extinguished, and the danger was supposed to be over. But all this was only a trick of the enemy to divert attention from the real point of attack — the external works to the southward. While the besieged were straining every nerve to save the Porcupine, a swarm of invaders were nimbly climbing on rope ladders up the walls of the South Square, the West Square, and the Polder. There was a fierce struggle to retake them which lasted all that night. At least fifteen hundred men perished, but all in vain. The forts were lost. In the morning the Spaniards coolly butchered all the wounded and prisoners, and turned the captured batteries upon the town.

It was a great loss; but the besiegers had by no means taken the city yet, and the fighting went on much as before. When the second anniversary of the beginning of the siege arrived — July 5, 1603 — Ostend kept it as a day of solemn thanksgiving for having been enabled to hold out during two full years.

It was during this summer that the Spanish cabinet discovered the man who could take Ostend. At least they thought so, and almost without saying " By your leave " to the archdukes, they made him field marshal and commander-in-chief. All Europe was amazed at the news, for this new leader, the Marquis Ambrose Spinola, had never distinguished himself in any way. He was young, wealthy, and highborn; his younger brother, Frederic Spinola, had within a few months been doing much damage to the merchant vessels of the Netherlanders by means of a number of galleys which he commanded, coming forth from time to time out of the port of Sluys. On the twenty-fifth of May, during a desperate engagement with the Dutch admiral in command of the blockading squadron, the daring Frederic lost his life. Ambrose Spinola had looked on during a campaign or two in the Low Countries, like many other nobles from various parts of Europe; but he had never been an officer in any army. Yet strangely enough there was an indefinable something about the man which made people think he was the hero who would subdue Ostend.

So this elegant and fascinating young Italian was set over all the old warriors and generals in the Spanish army, though many of them had won laurels before he was born. They were naturally indignant. Their enemies were amused as well as surprised; and the more, when it came out that Spinola was not only going to conduct the siege to a happy termination, but also to furnish the money largely from his own coffers and from those of the great bankers of Genoa. This was indeed a consideration of weight, for the treasury of the archdukes was running low.

In fact, there was in the face and bearing of the new commander that which profoundly impressed those who met him. The archdukes accepted his services with cordial satisfaction. Early in October,

1603, the young general made his first inspection of the works surrounding the city. After examining the situation thoroughly, he decided that there was no use in trying to do anything on the eastern side, where Bucquoy had so long been laboring to shut up the new harbor. The water there was always so deep, the tides and storms so irresistible, that their floating batteries and bridges were swept away as fast as Bucquoy and Targone could build them. So it was determined to concentrate their efforts upon the western side.

Notwithstanding the dissatisfaction of the officers at the outset, they soon saw that Spinola knew what he was about, and could endure hardships and brave dangers as heroically as any of them. He was not long in winning their confidence and admiration. Winter with its storms and floods was too near to allow of any great undertaking just then; but there was incessant mining and countermining while the dreary months wore away. In February and March there were terrible westerly storms, the like of which had not been known for years; these damaged the defenses so much that had the besiegers found it out they might have taken the town. But Peter van Gieselles, the vigilant commander who had been in charge since New Year's, was prompt in repairing them, keeping the enemy busy meanwhile with frequent feigned movements. But on March 12, 1604, Spinola succeeded in storming the lesser Polder Bulwark. Most of its brave defenders lay dead within the little fort, though a few escaped to the next. On the twenty-first of March the brave governor was himself picked off by a sharpshooter as he was reconnoitering from the ramparts. His provisional successor, Colonel John van Loon, was mortally wounded within four days, and died on the fifth.

Then followed Sergeant-major de Bievry. Meanwhile, on the second of April, the Spaniards carried the Polder Ravelin, after a terrible fight with great loss on both sides. Spinola was evidently making progress. Then the acting commandant was severely wounded in a sortie, and had to be carried to Zealand to be taken care of.

A Flemish nobleman, the baron of Berendrecht, now took the command; he was an experienced officer, at once bold and watchful. But on the eighteenth of April the enemy captured the great Western Ravelin, so that now they were nearly up with the work called the Porcupine, having worked along almost the whole length of the counterscarp on that side of the town. The resolute Berendrecht considered it time to build a new counterscarp, since the present could not much longer be held. Prince

Maurice had foreseen this, and sent a noted English engineer named Ralph Dexter, with able assistants, to lay it out and build it. Drawing the lines with neatness and precision, they proceeded to cut off about half the space inclosed within the walls, and to build the new bastions and redoubts, calling each by the name of the one to which it corresponded. Whole streets had to be demolished, and the crowded houses that remained were crowded still fuller, in order to shelter the inhabitants. The men who were digging or building must be ready at any moment to rush to the defense of the walls. As the work required several weeks, common laborers were sent, in order somewhat to relieve the soldiers.

Before the middle of May the besiegers had possession of one corner of the Porcupine, and a mine was in progress beneath it, so that it was finally carried May 29. On the same day, however, the Spaniards were disastrously repulsed in trying to storm the great Polder; the losses would have been about the same on both sides, had not the batteries of the Porcupine been now turned upon the town. Three or four days after, the besiegers sprung the mine they had long been preparing under the great Polder Bulwark, making an enormous breach. They rushed in, expecting to carry the town at once; but to their astonishment and dismay they beheld new fortifications bristling behind the old, and found a flanking battery playing directly upon them. Ostend was not yet theirs.

Four days later the brave Berendrecht fell, mortally wounded, as he was returning from a reconnoissance. This was the fourth governor of the city who had fallen at his perilous post within less than four months. Colonel Uytenhoove, a rough, hard-fighting Dutchman, took his place; and it was now resolved to be ready with still another retreat, should the new works be carried. So a corner of what remained, close to the new harbor, was set off to be fortified. They named it Little Troy. Exact drawings of its miniature fortifications that were to be were sent to Prince Maurice. But there was nothing solid left with which to build — no stone or brick, no timbers or even earth. They were actually forced to use whatever the cemeteries contained, piling into the bulwarks of Little Troy disinterred bodies of the soldiers, so many of whom had fallen in these three years. Later, shiploads of materials began to arrive daily from Zealand.

On the seventeenth of June Governor Uytenhoove fell while leading his troops to repel an assault, and was thought to be dead. He was rescued, however, though too severely wounded to remain in charge of the town, which was now committed to the brave Marquette, distinguished at the battle of Nieuport.

It hardly looked like a town at all now. But the States were resolved to hold on, and the garrison and citizens were still cheerful and brave. It was something to keep Spinola and the army busy at Ostend, if only that they might not relieve Sluys which Prince Maurice was at this time besieging, and which as a seaport was worth a good deal more than Ostend had ever been.

CHAPTER XXVI.

SLUYS TAKEN AND OSTEND LOST.

SLUYS had now been held by the Spaniards for seventeen years. Alexander of Parma had taken it in 1587, as one of the preliminaries to the part which had been assigned him in connection with the invincible Armada. And though he had his labor for his pains, so far as that enterprise was concerned, — the Zealand fleet having kept him from stirring out of the harbor with his transports, — Sluys had been a valuable acquisition to Spain. The Netherlanders had never ceased to regret its loss.

In the spring of 1604 the States-General were again urging Prince Maurice to invade Flanders in order to relieve Ostend. Just to threaten Sluys might divert part of the besieging army. Maurice preferred, if any demonstration was to be made, to besiege Sluys in earnest. Accordingly, about the middle of April he mustered at Willemstadt an army of fifteen thousand foot and three thousand horse; and, as when he invaded Flanders four years before, he insisted that several members of the States-General should attend the expedition. His young brother Frederic Henry, and his cousins Lewis William, Lewis Gunther, and Ernest Casimir accompanied him, as well as other nobles.

Crossing the western branch of the Scheldt in multitudinous vessels of all sorts, he landed his army on the island of Cadzand, April 25, and got possession of it all in the course of two days. He was busy

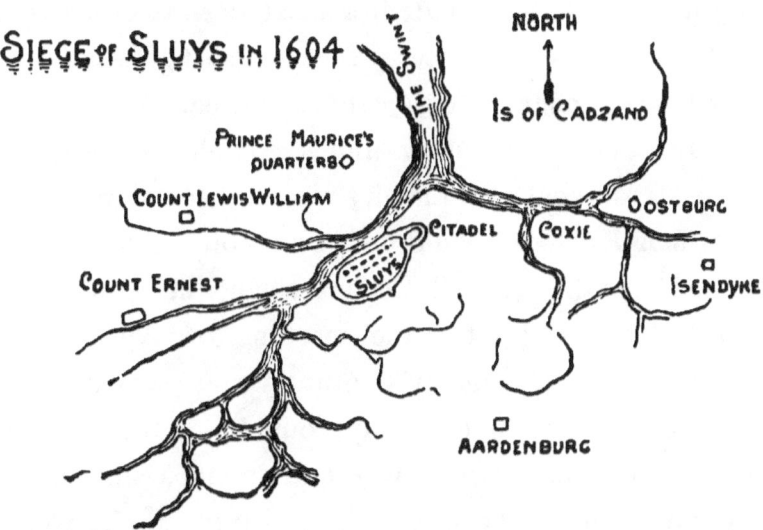

with the needful arrangements for making Cadzand his basis of operations, when he learned that Spinola had sent forces to hold the passage across the Swint, the great channel by which Sluys had communication with the sea. Had he approached the city immediately on his arrival, he might possibly have taken it by surprise; but it was his habit to make everything

SLUYS TAKEN AND OSTEND LOST. 287

secure before beginning a siege. It will be remembered that Sluys lay in the midst of a watery maze formed by many little fresh-water streams and several salt-water channels, interlacing endlessly among the quagmires and the rare bits of solid ground. Its excellent fortifications, its spacious streets and squares, and its great harbor made it a most desirable seaport.

While Prince Maurice was considering what was now his best course, there came to his camp a Flemish peasant, offering to show him a roundabout way on the east and south of the city where there were fords by which his troops could cross. So on the next day, guided by the friendly countryman, he proceeded toward Oostburg. On the morning of April 29 a small force of the enemy's infantry and cavalry were discovered; they were easily routed and pursued to the fort of Coxie, which was built upon a dike some distance east of the city. After capturing it, which was soon done, Maurice went forward as fast as the dangerous nature of the ground would permit, till his troops were confronted by the strong redoubt of Saint Catharine. After obtaining fieldpieces from Cadzand which the high water delayed for several hours, he ordered a cannonade, having given notice that the guerrillas who chiefly composed the garrison would receive no quarter. In response to this announcement a daring volunteer ensign sprang upon the ramparts and audaciously waved his banner in the face of the besiegers as he danced about. As there was no firm footing for either artillery or cavalry, Maurice was forced to order the guns taken back to Cadzand, leaving the fort until he could besiege it in a formal and deliberate manner.

But an odd accident almost immediately placed the fort in his hands. The garrison, hearing in the distance the shouts and uproar which the retreating cannoneers made while they were trying to rescue one of their guns from a quagmire, fancied that the great Prince Maurice was coming back with plenty of artillery to execute his threat. They were seized with a panic, and under cover of the night they abandoned the fort, which was at once occupied by the besiegers. Then Maurice went on and invested Ysendyke (or Isendyke), a strong position three leagues east of Sluys.

While Maurice's back was thus turned, two thousand troops were sent down the channel from Sluys to Cadzand in boats, in hopes of surprising the forces left there. Six hundred of them forced a landing; but a few companies of sturdy Scots stood their ground manfully and at length drove the attacking party off and sank some of their sloops with all on board.

When Ysendyke was summoned to surrender, one

of the garrison shot the prince's trumpeter, in gross violation of the laws of war. The musketeer who was guilty of this outrage was given up by the garrison the next day, when they surrendered. Aardenburg, four miles south of Sluys, submitted two days later, without making any resistance; and within two weeks the prince had taken the remaining posts on the southwest of Sluys, though some of them were held by strong bodies of troops. He now had control of the great sea channel and proceeded to lay out his lines, arrange his camps, and shut up the city completely.

During these two or three weeks there had been an attempt to reinforce the garrison, and fifteen hundred troops had reached the town. But no supplies had been received and now it was too late to get them in. The larger the garrison the worse off was the city, as provisions were scarce.

On the thirtieth of May Count Berlaymont set out from Dam at the head of four thousand men, convoying a large amount of food and military stores, while the garrison of Sluys sent out a thousand galley slaves with five hundred infantry into the overflowed fields to meet them. As usual, Prince Maurice was on the alert and at Stamper's Hook he met and routed a portion of Berlaymont's force, capturing two hundred. In the pursuit unluckily he took another path, so that

Berlaymont escaped to Dam, leaving some of his grain wagons behind. Those who had waded out from the city to assist the expected convoy made the best of their way back, but many of the galley slaves contrived to hide themselves and afterward went over to Maurice's side.

It had been the prince's intention to press the siege by means of various floating contrivances, but he was now so sure of the result that he could patiently wait till famine compelled a surrender. The distress within the town became extreme. As at Harlem and Leyden twenty years before, the besieged ate dogs, cats, rats, old boots and shoes, weeds from the graveyards, and finally even human flesh. All the while they were imploring help from the army at Ostend by beacons and signals of distress. June passed slowly away and then July, but no help came. Ostend was only fifteen miles distant, but it might as well have been a thousand.

At last the archdukes became sensible that unless they were willing to lose Sluys they must do something to save it, but of course without raising the siege of Ostend. There was no other way than to make a treaty with the mutineers at Grave; they were forced to grant all which they had before refused, and to give the city of Roermond as security besides three distinguished hostages. Early in August the Marquis

Spinola reluctantly left his siege in the charge of Bucquoy and Rivas for a little and marched with a large force toward Sluys. On the ninth of August he made a violent attack on Count Lewis William's camp, west of the city; but the count was equal to the occasion and Spinola had to withdraw with loss. A week later he suddenly moved around to the south of Sluys, seized the forts of Saint Catharine and Saint Philip, which were feebly garrisoned, and tried desperately to break the lines at Oostburg and thus make his way into Cadzand. At length he succeeded in crossing the waters and Maurice mustered his forces at Cadzand to meet him, for it was a vital position. The next day Count Lewis William while leading the advance guard of the States' army met Spinola with a larger force between two redoubts on Cadzand dike.

The fight was desperate and Lewis William was in the thickest of it when Colonel van Dorp came to his rescue, dealing terrible blows right and left with the great broadsword which he wielded with both hands. And then Maurice himself arrived with a Frisian regiment, so that Spinola had to fall back, leaving several hundred dead. He had fought bravely, but Lewis William and Maurice were too much for him. That was the end of his attempt to relieve the city. He withdrew to Dam and from thence returned to Ostend.

It was all over with Sluys. The next day, August 18, the town surrendered after a siege of three months. It might have held out for a long time but for the lack of supplies, and it might have been well provisioned beforehand had not the archdukes been altogether absorbed in besieging Ostend.

The prince gave favorable terms and on the twentieth of August the garrison, numbering nearly four thousand, marched out with the honors of war. It was a ghastly procession. The pale and emaciated forms seemed hardly to belong to living men. It is related by one writer of the period that not a few fell dead while they were going forth from the famine-conquered town. Its pestilential air proved fatal to one of the brave Nassaus. Count Lewis Gunther, who had led his cavalry so daringly in the battle of Nieuport, was attacked with a fever of which he soon died. Others were ill from the same cause, including the prince himself.[1]

On the twenty-second of August a violent north-east wind and a high sea did great damage to the remaining defenses of Ostend. This made the situation still more discouraging for its gallant defenders. The Sand-Hill, which was become a dense heap of cannonballs, had at length been carried by the enemy, and the walls of their final retreat, Little Troy, were

---

[1] Les Lauriers de Nassau, fol. 267.

not firm enough to endure long cannonading. Since they had now a much better seaport in Sluys, the States-General and the prince resolved not to prolong the struggle, and Marquette was instructed to capitulate. Meanwhile he sent off by sea not only guns, ammunition, and surplus provisions, but likewise such persons as could now be spared, including the engineers, artillerymen, and others. By September 20 the terms were settled; they were honorable and not in any respect severe. On the 22d Marquis Spinola entertained Governor Marquette with his officers at a grand banquet. The garrison departed by land, according to the terms arranged, having remained in Little Troy two days after the signing of the accord. They passed the Gullet by means of pontoons and boats. The French troops led the van, the Netherlanders formed the center, and the English and Scotch brought up the rear. In all they numbered more than three thousand, well-equipped and in good health. They retained with them four guns, but most of their artillery had been sent away by ship. The next day they arrived at the camp of Prince Maurice, and his highness in person welcomed them, standing with uncovered head while he took them by the hand and warmly thanked them for their faithful service to their country. Promotions and other rewards were liberally bestowed.

The citizens of Ostend hastened to quit the ruined town and most of them settled in Sluys.

"Thus ended this celebrated siege of Ostend, after having lasted three years and eighty days; a siege which will be talked of as long as the world shall stand, and which will seem incredible to those who shall read the account of it."[1] So says the author of a narrative published only eight years after Ostend fell. He says it "was called the Academy and University of Military Chieftains — so many governors, officers, engineers, surgeons, and the like, who had been only a few months in that school became masters." The lives sacrificed and the money sunk there can never be counted. A memorandum, said to have been found on the dead body of one of Spinola's officers before Sluys, made the number of officers and men in the archduke's army who had perished at Ostend 76,961. This was only to July, 1604, and did not include those sent away to hospitals. The losses of the besieged have been reckoned at 50,000 men; but it is impossible to be exact. The cost to the States is given at four million guilders, and the besiegers must have expended far more.

Though it seems a prodigious waste of money and of human lives, it had some important results. The long siege had so absorbed the attention and the

---

[1] Les Lauriers de Nassau, fol. 241.

resources of the archdukes that they could do little else. Prince Maurice was able to go on almost unchecked in his campaigns till he captured Sluys. Before the long-festering thorn of Ostend was removed from the paw of the Belgic lion it was pierced by another and a sharper one. As Markham has observed, though the States-General seem to have been mainly influenced by their desire to keep the Flemish port, " the result of their policy was to bring to a close the most memorable struggle in modern history. The siege of Ostend led directly to the twelve years' truce."

The archdukes as soon as possible came to survey the captured town. They found hardly more than a heap of stones and sand, thickly strewn with cannon-balls and bones of the slain. It is said that Isabella, ardent as she had been in the siege, wept at the sight. Steps were at once taken for the rebuilding and fortifying of the city, but it was not easy to find people who were willing to live there.

CHAPTER XXVII.

SPINOLA'S INVASION OF THE PROVINCES.

ABOUT the time of the capture of Sluys a treaty was arranged between King James and the archdukes — much to the disappointment and disgust of the Netherlanders. The archdukes had introduced the matter the preceding year, and now sent ambassadors to London to conduct the negotiations. The States' deputies did their utmost to prevent the conclusion of this treaty, and they were strongly supported by the French ambassador at the English court. Many of James' own subjects also opposed making peace with the archdukes, considering it far more essential to preserve friendly relations with the Dutch and to keep them from being overpowered. But James had no taste for fighting, especially none for fighting in behalf of the Dutch, whom he disliked. Besides, he had doubtless observed that the Englishmen who had served in the Low Countries brought home high notions about popular rights and civil liberty; and though not a very shrewd or far-seeing monarch, he instinctively felt that these ideas would be apt to make trouble some day or other.

The terms of the treaty with the archdukes were settled thus : — Neither party was to help the enemies or rebels of the other in any way ; the king promised that no English vessel should convey the merchandise of Holland into Spain, nor that of Spain into Holland ; as to Brill and Flushing, James would continue to hold them for the present, but their garrisons should take no part in the war ; however, if the States, after being duly warned, should fail to make peace with the archdukes within a reasonable time, he should consider himself absolved from Elizabeth's promise to restore those towns to the States, and none other.

In the course of the next year the results of this treaty were illustrated. It happened that a fleet of ten Spanish vessels bringing troops was attacked in the English Channel by Admiral Haultain. The fleet took refuge in the harbor of Dover. The admiral followed, and there was a fight, during which, strange to tell, the guns of Dover Castle were turned upon the Dutch, and more than a hundred of them were killed by their old allies. James declared that the neutrality of English shores was violated by the Dutch coming into the harbor. Yet this was no more than the Dunkirk pirates were allowed to do when they pursued merchant vessels of Holland and Zealand. Admiral Haultain was not inclined to show any mercy to the Spanish prisoners taken ; nor were those who had escaped to English shores permitted to pass through the United Provinces on their way to Flanders.

The Marquis Spinola now became the commander-in-chief of the archduke's army; and his vigorous administration of affairs wonderfully reformed many of its ancient abuses. While he was very strict in discipline, he was punctual in payment and liberal in rewards. Since his appointment was received from the king of Spain himself, it looked as if the ceding of the Low Countries to Isabella and her husband had been only a pretense.

When Spinola returned the next year from Spain to Brussels, he brought a large amount of money and fresh troops, so that he had now a larger army than had ever before been in service there. Maurice's forces were inferior in numbers, but by the celerity and adroitness of his movements he was generally able to keep Spinola in check. For some time the two armies were watching each other in the vicinity of Sluys, but as the prince had laid much of the region under water, Spinola suddenly moved northward, about the first of August, 1605, intending to invade Friesland and Groningen. No sooner was this ascertained than Maurice broke up his camp and followed. Spinola succeeded in capturing Oldenzaal and Lingen, the latter having no garrison worth mentioning, before

Maurice could overtake him. But strangely enough, the brilliant young general paused at Lingen for nearly a month, instead of pressing on to Coewarden, and thence into Friesland, as he could easily have done. Then leaving twenty-five hundred troops in Lingen, on the fourteenth of September he turned back toward the Rhine. Maurice, who had now been reinforced by his cousin, gladly hastened to Coewarden, and after making all secure in that quarter resumed his watch of the movements of Spinola, who was now at the point where the Ruhr empties into the Rhine.

Here the two armies remained for a fortnight, each waiting to see what the other was going to do. Maurice discovered that at Mülheim, a village on the Ruhr, there was a body of Italian cavalry, somewhat apart from the main army; he resolved to surprise them and thus bring on a general engagement. The movement was well planned, but it was not successful, owing to the failure of one division of the cavalry to arrive in time. The enemy's cavalry had news of its approach and was drawn up in battle array beforehand. So those who planned to surprise were themselves thrown into an unaccountable panic, and disgracefully fled. Maurice, coming up with the infantry, was almost beside himself with wrath at such a sight; he did his utmost to rally his forces, and some did make a stand for a few moments. But the drums and trumpets of Spinola's approaching troops revived the strange panic, and the day was lost. Young Frederic Henry, made conspicuous by his orange plumes and scarf, fought with splendid daring, and was in the greatest peril. Maurice was able to turn the rout into an orderly retreat; but five hundred of his best cavalry perished, and his banner was disgraced. The enemy lost at least three hundred, with the gallant leader, Count Trivulzio; but they claimed the victory.

Within three or four weeks Spinola took two other posts by siege. The troops of Maurice were so reduced by illness and losses that he was compelled to remain inactive. This was an unprecedented experience under his leadership; and there was much complaint on the part of the States-General. But Spinola did not turn his successes to much account, and hardly deserved all the praise he received at the Spanish court.

In the meantime matters in the East Indies were going on favorably for the Dutch. The third fleet of their East India Company was now busy there. Amboyna and the much-coveted Moluccas, where alone grew the cloves which were so precious in that day, had come into their hands. Wealth was flowing in upon them; but at the same time the ill feeling between their former friends, the English, and themselves was growing more and more apparent. Each of the great companies wanted all the India trade for itself, while the Spaniards and Portuguese maintained that all that part of the world was given to themselves by the pope a long time ago.

Spinola did not find funds for the war so abundant in Spain as he could have wished. Philip III was a mere nonentity; and his favorite, the duke of Lerma, found it easy to spend on his pleasures whatever money was within reach. Spinola spared neither his own purse nor his credit, to raise means for the next year's campaign. While returning, he had a dangerous illness in Genoa, and did not reach his army till June, 1606. Meanwhile, on the part of the Netherlanders, military movements had not been active. Their funds were not plentiful; the sovereigns of England and France were cool towards them; Maurice's recent ill fortune had weakened their confidence; and there was ill feeling between him and Barneveld. Moreover, it was more difficult than usual to enlist soldiers, on account of difficulties in the neighboring countries from which many of them ordinarily came.

One thing, however, did remarkably favor the cause of the republic. It rained in torrents week after week, so that Spinola's two armies, now well on the way northward, were forced to stay in their camps. The country was flooded; the roads were mere quagmires. After some time Spinola gave up invading Friesland, and made another plan for his campaign. If he could get across the Meuse and Waal, he thought he could readily march into Utrecht, and thence into Holland and Zealand — the very heart of the republic.

Maurice instantly saw through the scheme, and he was more than a match for Spinola. As the rivers were high, it was the easier to keep the enemy from crossing. Wherever he tried it the troops of the republic were on the spot. He tried to turn Maurice's flank, but was foiled. Early in August, after capturing a little town called Lochem, east of Zutphen, Spinola laid siege to Groll, or Groenlo, in the same region; and in eleven days, not without the loss of many men, he reduced the place. Thence retreating to the Rhine, he besieged Rheinberg. It was well garrisoned and tolerably fortified. Frederic Henry was there, and likewise some French noblemen who were serving as volunteers. Spinola was almost equal to Maurice himself at conducting a siege, and in six weeks he carried the town. Maurice could not go to its relief without the risk of letting the enemy slip into the province of Utrecht while his back was turned; and this would be much worse than to lose

Rheinberg. But there was a great deal of complaint about it.

In October it appeared that Spinola had exhausted his credit; he could get no funds, and so his troops mutinied. Six hundred men in a body went over to the republican army. And now Maurice found it practicable to make a few moves. He readily recovered Lochem and was laying siege to Groll when Spinola again advanced to relieve it. It was now November; the prince, who had been much delayed by the rains and had not begun his entrenchments, would not risk a general engagement, although his troops were eager to fight. Much to the vexation and disappointment of the States, as well as the army, he raised the siege and closed the campaign.

Though the prince was severely censured, abroad as well as at home, he had reasons of weight. There was much sickness among his men, the rains continued to pour, and he had lost confidence in his cavalry on account of their bad behavior at Mülheim. To lose the battle would have been fatal; and so he chose rather to endure the blame.

A memorable deed had been done upon the sea during the autumn of this year. Admiral Haultain was cruising off Cape Saint Vincent with thirteen war ships, to intercept the rich squadrons of merchantmen returning from the West Indies; but he had the ill luck to meet instead a great fleet of Spanish men-of-war, vastly superior to his own in numbers as well as power. The encounter was sudden, and it was blowing a gale. Eighteen huge galleons were bearing directly down full before the wind upon the Dutch fleet, and the enemy had many smaller vessels not far off. Most of the Dutch ships were scattered, but the vice-admiral, Klaaszoon, bravely faced the first galleons that came near, and there was a fierce fight at close quarters. Admiral Haultain came to his help with five vessels, and Klaaszoon had a short respite. But it was an unequal contest at best. It was nearly dark and Klaaszoon's ship was already disabled by the loss of its mainmast, when the galleons attacked him again. The rest of the Dutch vessels bore away as fast as they could from the hopeless conflict, but the gallant vice-admiral would not think for a moment of surrender. For two days and nights he kept his colors flying on the stump of his mast, and continued to send broadsides at the enemy. At length the ship began to sink; he was promised quarter if he would surrender. There were only sixty of his men alive. The enemy did not attempt to board, fearing he would blow up the ship, which indeed he had resolved to do. He called his men together, and all agreed to die rather than haul down their colors. Together they knelt upon the deck and the commander offered a prayer. Then Klaaszoon lighted the powder magazine, and the awful explosion scattered far and wide the fragments of the ship and its gallant crew. Two sailors, terribly mutilated, were picked up by the Spaniards, but lived only long enough to tell the tale.

The wise and venerable Count John of Nassau, the last of the brothers of William the Silent, died during this year. He was the only one of the five who did not fall in battle or by assassination. Count Hohenlo who was the brother-in-law of Prince Maurice, also died, and had done many daring deeds in the service of his country.

CHAPTER XXVIII.

HOW THE TWELVE YEARS' TRUCE WAS MADE.

IT was at the opening of the year 1607 that the first step toward a peace was actually taken, though there had been more or less talk about it in certain quarters before that. The war had been going on for forty years; only the elderly people could remember its beginning. All parties felt nearly worn out. The Spaniards did not see where money to carry it on was going to be found, and even the thrifty Dutch, with their wonderful willingness to tax themselves to the uttermost, were perplexed. Besides, their rapidly expanding commerce opened to them great opportunities, which of course seemed inviting.

But the "peace party" of the young republic had no idea of accepting any arrangement which would not secure their independence, and not all the people belonged to the peace party. Many had no faith in the Spaniards and felt that any supposed treaty would prove only a delusion and a snare. Besides, should they stop fighting for a time it would give the enemy opportunity to recruit his exhausted resources, and perhaps enabled the Obedient Provinces to become their rivals in certain directions.

Prince Maurice did not favor the idea, for these reasons as well as certain others of a personal nature. He was still in his cradle when the war began, and he had been educated for a general; his fame had been won in military life. If peace should be made, his vocation would be gone; he would lose his rank and power as commander-in-chief, as well as much of his income. He did not believe it would be the best thing for the republic; he was certain it would not be for himself.

Barneveld, being not a warrior but a statesman, saw things in a different light. He was in favor of a peace, provided independence could be ensured and all that independence implied. He appreciated, no doubt, the wonderful openings for their commerce which lay before them. If, notwithstanding the heavy burdens of taxation to support such a war, their material prosperity had been so great, what might it not become during years of peace?

The first move was made by the archdukes. In January, 1607, they secretly sent to The Hague two envoys, Van Wittenhorst and Gevaerts, who were to introduce the subject. They said that the archdukes, as the States were well aware, claimed only what really belonged to them, and that they were ready to entertain proposals for either a peace or a truce, whichever might be preferred. To this the States, perceiving that the archdukes were still assuming that they owned the Netherlands, did not make a very gracious response; they sent back word that in order to treat with them, the archdukes must begin by recognizing their independence.

This was a hard thing for the archdukes to do. It would be equivalent to admitting that they were in the wrong, and the world would of course infer that they must be in great straits if they did. But this was the simple truth. Toward the close of February, having chosen a more adroit diplomatist, they sent him to The Hague with letters to the prince and Barneveld. It was John Neyen, a Franciscan monk, born at Antwerp. He looked frank, though really artful. The interview was profoundly secret. The monk was attired as a burgher. The letters stated that the archdukes consented to treat with the States of the United Provinces " in the quality and as considering them free provinces and states, over which they had no pretensions." They would consider the question of either a peace or a truce for twelve, fifteen, or twenty years. They would appoint ambassadors on their own part, and the States were desired to choose for themselves an equal number. And in order to have time for the negotiations they proposed an immediate armistice of eight months.

After Neyen's credentials had been shown to the States-General, and various little difficulties regarding them had been settled, the States agreed to the armistice so far as promising not to begin any siege or build new fortifications during that period, provided the king of Spain would likewise ratify the agreement within three months, and make the same concessions as to their independence.

This took a long while, for in those days it was a journey of several weeks from The Hague to Madrid. Besides, Philip III, like his father, required a good deal of time to make up his mind. When at last the document arrived it was far from satisfactory. The king proposed to treat the United Provinces as independent only so long as the truce should last. Besides, he had signed it as if it were an edict to his subjects, "*Yo el Rey*,"[1] and he had affixed only the small seal.

This naturally tended to confirm the distrust of those who believed the talk about peace was only a pretense. About the same time Father Neyen gave some magnificent presents to Aerssens, the recorder of the States, evidently hoping to bribe him. There was a bill of exchange for fifty thousand ducats, a

[1] "I the King."

superb gold chain, and a diamond of great value for Madame Aerssens. The recorder handed these articles over to the States, and one day, in a full assembly of that body, Barneveld returned them to Verreiken, one of the envoys of the archdukes. "Take them back," said he sternly, "and restore them to their owners; desire the archdukes, if they sincerely intend any treaty of peace, to forbear all such attempts for the future. Think not that here, as in monarchies, we are guided by the will of two or three; our numbers render it impossible to corrupt us, and should any one of us allow himself to be tempted, exemplary chastisement would be immediately inflicted on him."

Verreiken, much embarrassed, protested that Neyen alone was responsible and that the archdukes knew nothing about it; and this very improbable explanation the States allowed to pass.

The unsatisfactory document was sent back to the king, with suggestions as to the changes necessary. By the terms of the armistice, which began in May and was to continue eight months, the king was to ratify it within three months. But it was not till autumn that Neyen and Verreiken returned with the amended ratification. It was found to contain the admission of the States' independence, but with a proviso that this should count for nothing if the peace negotiations failed. The wording was ambiguous, and as before, it was signed "*Yo el Rey.*" The States demurred about accepting it; but the French and English ambassadors advised them to overlook the deficiencies of the paper. It was finally decided to refer the document to the separate provinces, to be considered by their respective legislatures.

At length they agreed that they would enter into negotiations, always insisting upon their independence, and their supreme authority over all their internal affairs, including religious matters. By this time the period of the eight months' armistice had almost expired, but it was prolonged from time to time, through this year and the following one.

There had been a great naval victory won by the Dutch in the Bay of Gibraltar, the news of which arrived just after the beginning of the armistice, in May, 1607. It had spread dismay at the court of Spain, and made it seem more than ever indispensable to put a stop to such disasters in some way or other. Admiral Heemskirk, the same who had previously been distinguished as an explorer in Arctic seas and a bold adventurer in the East Indies, was in command of a fleet of war vessels, sent to cruise along the shores of Spain and Portugal, and do whatever might serve the republic in the protection of its commerce, or otherwise. Learning that a great war fleet, far more powerful than his own, was then cruising in the Straits of Gibraltar in order to pounce upon Dutch merchantmen trading in the Levant, Heemskirk burned to attack it. His officers and men were enkindled by his ardor; they vowed to follow him to the death. It proved that the Spanish fleet, which was commanded by the veteran Don Juan Alvarez d'Avila, a hero of Lepanto, was lying within the bay, under the protecting guns of the Fort of Gibraltar.

When the Spanish admiral perceived the Dutch vessels approaching, he could not at first believe that they could be intending to do anything so ridiculous as to attack his great fleet. With his flagship alone, the Saint Augustine, he was sure he could demolish the whole of them. But before the sun went down on that April afternoon his entire fleet was destroyed, two thousand out of four thousand men killed, including the admiral himself, and the Dutch were triumphant. Heemskirk was killed almost at the first fire; but when his death became known to his men they fought only the more furiously. They found among the papers of the Spanish admiral secret instructions signed by the king, directing the most inhuman treatment of the Netherlanders who should fall into his power. Enraged beyond measure at these cruel orders, they massacred all the wounded or drowning Spaniards on whom they could lay hands as they strove to escape from their disabled and burning vessels. "The barbarous ferocity of the Dutch on this occasion," says Motley, "might have taught a lesson even to the comrades of Alva."

The loss of the Dutch was but small — one hundred killed and sixty wounded. None of their ships were destroyed. The body of their beloved and lamented Admiral Heemskirk was embalmed and carried home to Amsterdam, where there was a magnificent funeral for their hero, at the public expense.

The winter of 1607–1608 was so severe that the rivers and marshes were frozen hard enough for an invading army to march across them without any difficulty. Fortunately such a season had not occurred for several years; and no harm came of it now, except that it delayed somewhat the coming of the ambassadors who were to assemble at The Hague to arrange the terms of the proposed peace. The French and the English courts had already sent envoys to assist in these deliberations. And the States about this time concluded a defensive alliance with the king of France, by which Henry IV engaged to help them obtain an advantageous peace, if possible; and if it should be violated by Spain, to furnish them with ten thousand foot, at his own cost. The States likewise promised to assist him, if necessary. Some time later they succeeded in making a similar agreement with the king of England.

On the last day of January, 1608, the stately train of ambassadors on the part of the archdukes and Spain arrived. It was an imposing spectacle. The Marquis Spinola, and Richardot, president of the privy council of the Spanish Netherlands, were accompanied by Don Juan di Mancidor, secretary of the king of Spain, together with Neyen and Verreiken; and of course there was a long train of attendants and courtiers. At Ryswick, a village not far from The Hague on the road to Delft, they were met by the prince, who saluted them with great courtesy and cordiality of manner. Spinola was invited to sit in the prince's own carriage, at his right hand. Little as Maurice favored the peace, he doubtless enjoyed seeing this great general and the rest of the dignitaries come to ask for it.

Whatever was polite and flattering was doubtless said by each of these great warriors to the other as they rode together into the capital of the United Provinces. Immense crowds almost blocked the streets of The Hague, eager to gaze upon the great personages whose mission was so momentous. For several days the house occupied by Marquis Spinola was thronged with people who had a lively curiosity to see him; and the ambassadors fancied that this indicated their anxiety for peace. The magnificent style in which Spinola lived was so different from the plain republican fashions of the thrifty Dutch that it provoked much comment, and it was not always in a tone of approval.

At the request of the States, ambassadors from Denmark, the duchy of Brunswick, and the Palatinate had been sent by their respective sovereigns to give assistance by their counsels. On the part of the republic, in addition to a deputy from each of the seven provinces there were three to act for the country as a whole: namely, Lewis William of Nassau, Walrave, lord of Brederode, and Barneveld, in whose experienced hands more than in any other the management of the negotiations lay.

The first article of the proposed treaty, which declared the independence and sovereignty of the republic, was allowed to pass more readily than had been expected. President Richardot even remarked rather bluntly that if the Provinces liked to call themselves a kingdom, they were welcome to do so, for aught he cared. Nor was objection made to the usual provision for a general amnesty, and the restoration of confiscated estates. But when it was demanded that the king of Spain and the archdukes should give up the title and arms of the Provinces, there was much complaint. It was urged that the king of England still bore, without objection, the title and arms of king of France; and the archdukes, those of Burgundy, although they owned no dominions there. But the republicans urged that to drop these empty titles would be nothing to the great house of Austria; while its continuing to claim them might prove a real damage to the little republic of the Netherlands. This point was finally conceded; the more readily, doubtless, because there was certain to be a great struggle over the next.

There was of course to be free trade with Spain; but as to commerce with the East Indies, the Spanish ambassadors demanded that it should cease now and forever. The king of Spain considered that the East Indies, as well as the New World, were his private property; no other sovereign or state had any business there. In his treaties with France and England he had not given either of them permission to trade with India; why should he grant it to the Netherlands?

But the English and French ambassadors replied that it was in the nature of the case free; nobody needed to ask leave. This was the ground taken by the States. They had already done far more in the India trade than the Spaniards, or any other one nation. At this time their commerce with the East Indies employed eight or ten thousand men, and amounted annually to forty-three million of guilders, or more than seventeen millions of dollars. To be called independent would be worth very little, if the free navigation of the seas were forbidden. Besides, they had engaged to protect the natives of the countries with whom they had established commercial relations, and they would not abandon these allies.

Prince Maurice sustained these claims — not so much because he cared for the commerce, perhaps, as because he saw a prospect of thus getting the negotiations broken off. The States were implored to concede at least a little; and so they offered to let it be settled that they should continue the India trade for nine years after the conclusion of a peace. In the course of that period some permanent arrangement could doubtless be made.

So Friar Neyen once more went to Spain, to see how the king would like this plan, and Jeannin, the principal French envoy, went home on a similar errand. As this required a good deal of time, the Danish ambassadors, tired of delay, took their leave.

While waiting thus, the States-General heard news from their representatives at the French, English, and German courts, which made them more anxious than ever about the treaty-making. The king of Spain, it was reported, had assured each of these sovereigns that he had no idea of resigning his right to the United Provinces; he had only admitted their independence in order to be able to open negotiations. He should never grant peace, unless they should not only give up the India trade, but should likewise allow the public exercise of the Roman Catholic religion.

Moreover, they learned that Philip had proposed to the king of France a double marriage alliance, offering the crown prince of Spain as the future husband of the princess of France, and his own daughter for the wife of the Dauphin. To be sure, he had also offered his daughter to the English prince of Wales. And this looked as if these conflicting proposals were made just for political effect, especially as the royal children were still in their nurseries.

When Father Neyen returned from Spain, it was found that in return for admitting their independence the king did insist upon the reëstablishment of public worship for the Catholics, as well as the abandonment of the India trade. The French and English ambassadors upheld the States in their resolution not to concede the former. Even Jeannin, who was himself a Catholic, declared that if it were yielded at the dictation of the enemy, it would develop a strong Spanish faction, which would be very dangerous. In itself it would be a good thing to be done, in due time, by the republic unconstrained. But these ambassadors advised to relinquish the India trade rather than break off the negotiations.

It was more than surmised that this last bit of counsel was not altogether disinterested. Henry IV would have liked somehow to secure the India trade for himself; and there was an East India Company in England, whose operations were often more or less interfered with by the Dutch.

The deputies of the republic were stedfast on both of these points. They declared that though they themselves were sincere in beginning the negotiations, they were now convinced that the archdukes and the king of Spain had never meant them to succeed.

So the whole matter seemed to have come to naught. The Spanish ambassadors and those sent by the archdukes took leave, and it looked as if there was nothing else to be done but to renew the war. The French and English envoys now came forward with a proposal to mediate. They were aware that the recent treaties bound their sovereigns to assist the republic, should the war be resumed. In that case Henry would hardly be able to do all that he had promised, while James was neither able nor willing. Jeannin, who was an eminent diplomatist, had long been revolving a plan; and he now ventured to suggest a truce of twelve years, leaving the foreign commerce open, and other things much as they now were.

The States-General looked dubiously at the scheme, and the people were loud in opposing it. Not only did they talk, but they wrote against it. Pamphlets and libels poured from the press. The prince opposed a truce even more than a peace; and he published a letter to the towns of Holland, strongly dissuading them from it. On the other hand, the able Jeannin wrote a spirited and impressive rejoinder to the prince's arguments, which was published in the name of the ambassadors.

Barneveld was chiefly blamed as the author of this plan which was considered so objectionable, and in the intense excitement of the public mind a great deal was said which it was hard for him to bear. One day he made a dignified address in the assembly of the States-General, alluding to these things, which, had they affected himself alone, he would have disregarded. But since it was evident that the dislike borne to himself personally was making the proposed truce still more obnoxious, he begged the States to appoint some one more acceptable to fill his place. He then left the assembly. Almost immediately, five of the members were deputed to follow and entreat him to return. After some hesitation he did return; and then he made a speech in favor of the truce, so convincing that all the deputies except those of Zealand consented to it. At length this province also yielded, and a resolution was passed to enter into negotiations.

Accordingly the deputies on both sides reassembled under the adroit leadership of Jeannin, meeting this time at Antwerp, in the Spanish Netherlands. The States-General came to Bergen-op-Zoom in order to be conveniently near. The articles of truce were proposed by Jeannin; and coming thus as from friendly arbitrators, were more easily accepted. Within a few weeks all was settled. The truce was formally concluded for twelve years, under the guarantees of France and England.

Strange as it may seem, the Netherlanders obtained every one of their three indispensable points. Their independence was conceded; the freedom of their commerce was established; and nothing at all was said about granting the public exercise of the Roman Catholic religion.

Though the India trade was not expressly mentioned, Richardot having objected that, if it were conceded in so many words, they would be forced to say the same in treating with other nations, the liberty was clearly implied. Besides, in a secret article, the king of Spain promised to offer no obstruction to it; and France and England declared that if it were interrupted, they would consider the truce violated.

The ratification by the king of Spain arrived a little before the expiration of the three months allowed. In sending it the king took occasion to recommend kindness toward the Catholics; a suggestion which, coming from that quarter, doubtless made people say to themselves, "Is Saul also among the prophets?"

The States settled handsome incomes upon Prince Maurice and all the Nassau family; which gratitude certainly required, in view of what they had done and suffered for their country.

The truce was proclaimed April 9, 1609. There was immense rejoicing over the event in the Spanish Netherlands, whose inhabitants had suffered far more from the war than had the people of the United Provinces. The satisfaction of the latter was naturally less intense and universal. Foreign nations were unboundedly surprised at the concessions which Spain had made; and now they all began to look upon the sturdy little republic with respectful and admiring eyes.

CHAPTER XXIX.

WHAT HAPPENED DURING THE TRUCE.

LESS than a month after the twelve years' truce was proclaimed, there occurred an incident which, though little noticed at the time, must ever have a special interest to the people of New England. About the first of May, a small body of English Puritans whom persecution had driven from their native country, and who had passed the preceding winter in Amsterdam, settled in Leyden. In that fair and free city, so full of inspiring memories, they established the humble homes from which, eleven years later, they went forth to found a great republic beyond the sea. It might have been said of these, as of the Corinthian believers, that not many mighty, not many noble had been called. Many of them labored with their hands at the trades to which they were accustomed, or learned trades, in order to earn their bread; for Leyden, though the seat of a great university, was also a busy manufacturing city, the Leeds or Manchester of Holland. There were some men of learning among them, like Brewster, who became an instructor in English to German and Danish students, and thus supported his family in comfort; and the pastor, Robinson, who was made a member of the university. Robinson had sufficient means to purchase an estate near the church of Saint Peter, and built upon his grounds cottages for many families of the congregation.

The Dutch were never at a loss for something to do; and now that the war was for a while off their hands they were the more busy in all the arts of peace. Indeed the negotiations were hardly opened before they set about one of those immense undertakings which are possible only to men of indomitable perseverance. This was the draining and diking of the Beemster Lake, in North Holland. It was twenty-four miles in circumference, and the depth was nowhere less than six feet. They began the work in 1608, employing constantly forty mills to pump; the task was finished in 1612, and eighteen thousand acres of fine arable land and pasture, thus redeemed, rewarded those who accomplished the great enterprise. Similar and still more stupendous undertakings have been carried through in later times; the draining of the Harlem Lake, containing about fifty thousand acres, was achieved not very long ago, and possibly the vast Zuyder Zee will yet be transformed into fruitful fields.

The French ambassador, Jeannin, whose influence had done so much in bringing about the truce, soon afterwards ventured to make some observations in regard to defects in the Dutch constitution. "Every resolution," said he, "depends upon a multitude of persons, who mistrust each other, and change their opinions so often that there is the greatest difficulty in keeping them together." This was perfectly true. The constitution of the United Provinces was deficient as to the authority of the central government. It was a loose alliance rather than a well-compacted federation. And during the vicissitudes of the period since it was framed, it had incidentally been modified to its harm. Jeannin proposed a kind of council of state, meeting once a year, with certain judicial and executive functions; it was to have one member from each province, chosen for three years; Prince Maurice, Count Lewis William, and Count Frederic Henry were to be members for life; and Barneveld was to be president. The ambassadors of France and England were also to be members, with power to vote.

But the plan did not find favor with the moderate and cautious Dutch. They were more or less sensible that their constitution was not all that could be desired; yet it had so far worked tolerably well. They had their doubts about the proposed council, on various grounds; perhaps they did not quite see why it should include the ambassadors. But they did not wish to give offense by rejecting Jeannin's advice, and so they politely deferred the question till the following year. Before that time Jeannin returned home loaded with honors and gifts; and then the whole subject — to use their shrewd little phrase — "was noted down in the forget-book."

One very important event of this memorable year, 1609, was the founding of the great Bank of Amsterdam. Up to this date, and indeed for many years longer, there were scarcely more than two or three banks in Europe. People were forced to use coin in most of their transactions, which was of course inconvenient and unsafe. In a foreign country, the gold and silver money one carried was worth no more than so much uncoined metal. The Bank of Venice, established away back in the Middle Ages, was much older than any other; those of Genoa and Barcelona followed centuries later. These received the coins of all nations, and gave the depositors certificates which passed from hand to hand. In less than a hundred years after the founding of the Amsterdam bank its vaults contained in coin one hundred and eighty millions of dollars. It used to issue notes equal in amount to the specie held; and these always bore a premium. The bank also charged a small sum on every account. It was managed, strange to relate, by the city corporation, and they did it honestly and well. Once a year the heads of the corporation examined all the treasure and reported under oath.

The immense importance of the bank to the prosperity of their great commercial city was so strongly felt that this mode of administration worked well. In 1672 it happened that there was a run upon the bank, which was quieted by taking the anxious depositors into the vaults to see what was stored there. When the Bank of England was started, eighty-five years later than that of Amsterdam, it was proposed to have it managed in a similar way by the municipal authorities of London. But it was concluded that as to its understanding of what commercial honor required, London was not yet prepared for so immense a trust. The Bank of Amsterdam, in the opinion of Professor Thorold Rogers, of Oxford, was " the most famous and the most envied institution which Holland contained."

For several years before the truce began, two noted theological professors in the University of Leyden, Francis Gomarus and Jacob Arminius, had been deeply engaged in a controversy about the doctrines of predestination and free will. Each had a body of ardent followers, and the dispute by degrees became so strenuous and the partisans so bitter that both the Church and the State were involved. While each was doubtless sincere in maintaining what he believed to be taught in the Scriptures, it was perhaps not sufficiently kept in mind that no human intellect can fully grasp themes like these. One gazes at the great truth on this side, and the other on that.

Arminius had studied theology at Geneva under Beza, the most extreme of Calvinists; but later his views of predestination had become somewhat modified. After his coming to Leyden, Gomarus bitterly complained of his way of presenting the doctrine, and stirred up most of the clergy of Holland against him. In October, 1609, the mild and gentle Arminius died, in the prime of life, but worn out by anxiety and disease. His followers, though still a minority, gradually became more bold in maintaining their views, and indeed went beyond their leader, as often happens in such a case. At first the discussions were altogether among the learned and were carried on in Latin. But as the contention grew still warmer, it was brought into every pulpit and absorbed even the common people.

In 1610 the Arminians presented to the States-General a paper explaining the positions which they held, on account of which they were so severely censured. They called the document their "Remonstrance," and from that time they were generally spoken of as the "Remonstrants." There were five propositions, since often referred to as the five points of Arminianism. They were in substance as follows:

1. That predestination is only conditional, God having decreed that those should be saved who he foresaw would accept the terms of salvation.
2. That Christ's atonement is sufficient for all, although it avails for those alone who accept it.
3. That no man is able of himself to exercise saving faith, but must be born again of God in Christ, through the Holy Spirit.
4. That without the grace of God man can neither think, will, nor do anything that is good; yet that grace does not act in an irresistible way.
5. That believers are able, by the aid of the Holy Spirit, victoriously to resist sin, but that the question of the possibility of a fall from grace must be determined by further study of the Scriptures.

The next year this last point was decided affirmatively; that is, that to fall from grace is possible.

The followers of Gomarus published a strong "counter remonstrance" in which they asserted absolute and arbitrary predestination and reprobation. So they got the name of "Contra-remonstrants" by which they were almost always called during those days; one needs only to keep in mind that it is equivalent to Gomarists or Calvinists, just as "Remonstrants" means Arminians.

The strife grew more and more bitter year by year. In January, 1614, the States, influenced mainly by the eminent Hugo Grotius and Barneveld, issued an edict of complete mutual toleration, and enjoined it upon both parties that they should cease their strife. But the followers of Gomarus would not obey, and the excitement soon became so violent that the other party felt it necessary in certain towns to have a guard of militiamen — *waardgelders* — appointed for protection in case of a riot.

And now the strife became political no less than theological. Barneveld had always been inclined toward the milder doctrines of the Remonstrants, and indeed toward tolerance in general. He was now decidedly of that party. The prince had been endeavoring to hold a neutral position; but now he came out openly on the side of the Contra-remonstrants, justifying himself by appealing to his oath of office taken in 1586. He had then sworn to defend the Reformed faith, and that meant nothing else than Calvinism in his view. So he used his official power, as well as his personal influence, on that side, even making arbitrary changes in many of the municipal boards for the purpose of strengthening the Contra-remonstrant party. It was a mistake on the part of the Remonstrants to ask for the guards, as it provoked their opponents to still more strenuous opposition, and those cities which had provided waardgelders were forced to disband them, on pain of being treated as rebels.

There had long been talk of convening a great

synod to settle the disputed points, and at length the States-General decided to do so. But it soon appeared that the synod would be made up of Contra-remonstrants alone. In most of the provinces except Holland that party was much more numerous than the other, and Prince Maurice was now controlling affairs so strenuously that even there the Remonstrants had no chance. At Briel, Delft, Hoorn, and other places, attended by troops, he deposed the town councils and appointed only men who would suit his purpose. Even Harlem, Leyden, Rotterdam, and Amsterdam had to submit. So Holland saw its provincial synod, like the rest, appoint Contra-remonstrants only, as delegates to the national synod.

This august body assembled at Dordrecht, commonly called Dort, November 13, 1618. There were in all sixty-three ecclesiastical delegates from the seven provinces, including, besides the pastors, five professors of theology and twenty elders. There were also eighteen deputies from the States-General, and there were twenty-eight foreign members sent by the English, Swiss, and other churches. The sessions were generally attended by a vast number of people, though the speeches and papers were all in Latin.

The Remonstrants naturally wished to be fairly represented, and to have their men share in the discussions on equal footing with the rest. But the political deputies told them that the synod would summon those who were wanted there. And thirteen Remonstrant ministers were accordingly notified to appear within fourteen days, before this tribunal made up exclusively of their declared opponents.

It would fill a volume to tell all that passed in the memorable synod of Dort. It sat until May 9, 1619, not including the sessions held after the foreign members had gone home. The Arminian ministers summoned were from the first treated as an accused party, and did not have the freedom of the floor. They might reply to questions, but were not to comment upon the views of their opponents, and were to hold their peace when the synod had heard enough. This they did not consider fair treatment, nor would they agree to give only brief and categorical answers. Either they would reply in writing after due consultation among themselves, or by the mouth of their ablest man. After a great deal of difficulty they were told not to appear in the synod, yet to remain in Dort. The foreign delegates did not consider these very dignified proceedings on the part of this great assembly, and so the synod after a while permitted the Remonstrants to send written statements within a brief specified time.

At length the synod prepared and adopted — not without much debate on various points — certain canons, refuting the Arminian views and setting forth what they deemed orthodox, in substance as follows:

That God had preordained by an eternal and immutable decree before the creation of the world, upon whom he will bestow the free gift of his grace; that the atonement of Christ, though sufficient for all the world, is efficacious only for the elect; that conversion is not effected by any effort of man, but by the free grace of God given to those only whom he has chosen from all eternity; and that it is impossible for the elect to fall away from this grace.[1]

Then the synod passed judgment on the Remonstrant ministers on trial before them, declaring them innovators and disturbers of the church and nation, teachers of false doctrine, and leaders of faction. They were deprived of all their offices in the church and the university till they should give proofs of repentance. The States-General confirmed this sentence.

After the foreign delegates had left, the Netherland members further decreed that all the Remonstrant clergy, numbering two or three hundred, should be deprived of their office, unless they would renounce their errors. Nor could any person either preach or teach school without having subscribed to the Heidelberg Catechism and the Belgic Confession of Faith, as well as to the canons of the synod.

Now the catechism of Heidelberg, as it is commonly

[1] Davies' History of Holland, 2:509.

called, had long been known and loved in the Netherlands. One would say that it might well find favor with almost any devout Christian. For example, what could be more tender and sweet than the opening question and its glad reply: —

What is thy only comfort in life and death?

That I, with body and soul, both in life and death, am not my own, but belong unto my faithful Saviour, Jesus Christ, who with his precious blood hath fully satisfied for all my sins and delivered me from all the power of the devil; and so preserves me that without the will of my heavenly Father not a hair can fall from my head, yea, that all things must be subservient to my salvation; and therefore by his Holy Spirit he also assures me of eternal life, and makes me sincerely willing and ready henceforth to live unto him.

All through, it seems that those who prepared this catechism were bent, not upon proclaiming cold theological dogmas, but upon setting forth the living Saviour who meets every want of human hearts. Though Calvinistic, indeed, its Calvinism is of the mildest type. All it says on predestination is this: —

That the Son of God, from the beginning to the end of the world, gathers, defends, and preserves to himself, by his Spirit and word, a church chosen to everlasting life, agreeing in true faith.

This is by no means so strongly expressed as in the Westminster Catechism, framed nearly thirty years after the synod. Yet the Contra-remonstrants somehow read " between the lines " enough to bring its meaning up to the stern canons of Dort; and therefore their opponents did not like being forced to subscribe to every jot and tittle of it, as interpreted by the synod. They felt that they ought to be permitted to think a little for themselves as to what the Bible teaches; and because they were so strictly forbidden they persisted the more.

There have been widely differing estimates of this memorable synod. By many it has been profoundly reverenced, and its canons have been their standards of faith. Others have seen in some of its acts rather too much of poor human nature. Doubtless many of its members desired simply to maintain the truth. But a party conscious of having the power in its own hands is ever liable to be overbearing towards opponents, without knowing it. And a party treated with intolerance is quite certain to proceed farther, in the course objected to, than it otherwise would. This was apparent in the subsequent history of the oppressed Remonstrants. Their doctrines diverged more and more widely from the standards which the synod had decreed, and indeed from those of their leader himself. Had they been the majority, perhaps the other party would have been oppressed in their turn.

CHAPTER XXX.

BARNEVELD'S TRIAL AND EXECUTION.

WHILE the synod was sitting at Dort, a very serious matter was in progress at The Hague. The alienation between the prince and Barneveld had now come to such a point that the friends of the great statesman were anxious on his account. Maurice well knew that Barneveld's influence often thwarted his own schemes, as in the matter of the twelve years' truce; and he had been much displeased about the levy of waardgelders to protect the Remonstrants. Having inherited from his elder brother the title and estates of Orange, he was growing more and more arbitrary. And now he was resolved to crush the great statesman who stood so much in his way.

Barneveld's friends privately warned him that he was not safe, but he would not withdraw from The Hague. Come what might, he was determined to remain at his post. On the morning of August 29, 1618, when about to enter the assembly of the States of Holland, he was told that the prince wished to speak with him. On reaching the usual place of conference, an officer of the prince's bodyguard arrested him in the name of the States-General. But the States as a body had not been consulted; besides, Barneveld belonged to the province of Holland, and was under its protection. Grotius, the pensionary of Rotterdam, and Hoogerbeets, pensionary of Leyden, were also arrested the same morning, though they were under the jurisdiction of those cities. The three were separately confined, and neither knew of the arrest of the others.

All this was arbitrary and violent treatment; yet the States-General appeared to acquiesce in it, though the deputies of Holland were dumb with amazement and grief. The States of that province ventured to remonstrate, as did the cities of Rotterdam and Leyden, but it was in vain. The prince sustained himself by referring to the States-General, and refused the petition of Barneveld's sons-in-law, that their aged father might at least have his own house for his place of confinement.

The young king of France, Louis XIII — who had succeeded his father, Henry IV, in 1610 — instructed his ambassador to do his utmost in behalf of the prisoners; but his intercession was unheeded. This displeased the king so much that he would not allow the French delegates to attend the synod of Dort, then shortly to assemble. Barneveld was kept in close confinement at The Hague, and was not allowed to see his wife and children. Even the use of writing materials was at first denied, but his friends secretly communicated with him, and informed him of what was going on.

The membership of the States of the province of Holland had been not a little changed by Prince Maurice's arbitrary reconstruction of many of the municipal boards by whom they were elected; and so they meekly allowed the prince and the States-General to retain their usurped authority over the prisoners. A special commission, made up of persons upon whom the prince could depend, was appointed to try them. The examination of Barneveld occupied twenty-three sessions; he was not permitted to take notes, either of the interrogatories or of his replies, although they covered his whole public career; indeed the questions seemed as if contrived on purpose to confuse and perplex the aged prisoner.

After the examination was finished, the States-General proceeded to appoint twenty-four judges, twelve of whom were of the province of Holland. Now the States-General were perfectly aware that they possessed no jurisdiction in Holland; and they even alluded to this fact, by assuring that province that as a rule they did not propose to proceed thus. And Grotius and Hoogerbeets were amenable only

JOHAN VAN OLDENBARNEVELT,
RIDDER, HEER VANDEN TEMPEL, BERKEL RODENRYS etc.
ADVOCAAT VAN HOLLANDT EN WESTVRIESLANDT etc.

JOHN OF BARNEVELD.
From Bor's History of the Netherlands, 1621.

to their respectives cities of Rotterdam and Leyden, both of which possessed the high jurisdiction. Besides, some of the judges were personal enemies of Barneveld; and most of them had been active in the previous proceedings. It was in vain that the three prisoners denied the competency of the court; it proceeded to condemn them as if it really had the right.

The charges against Barneveld were mostly connected in some way with the theological disputes. One of the chief accusations was that he had maintained " the exorbitant and pernicious maxim " that each province should be sovereign in regard to its own ecclesiastical affairs. Now this had been expressly laid down in the exposition of the thirteenth article of the Union of Utrecht. The levy of waardgelders had been made with the sanction of the States of Holland; if Barneveld had misled them in that instance, it was for them to call their minister to account. The other charges were equally unfounded, and though they were numerous they would not together have amounted to treason had they been proved. The only capital offense charged was that of carrying on correspondence with Spain; and they had no evidence at all for that. But the States-General were cruel enough to send to each province a manifesto stating that many other crimes were laid to his charge; but these could not be proved without "stricter examination"—supposed to mean torture. As the prisoner was so aged, they were not willing to resort to that! One would suppose that for the same reason they would have been unwilling to put him to death without proof.

The verdict of a historian who studied the case with great thoroughness and candor is, that "never statesman more upright, never patriot purer fell a victim to party rage and unprincipled ambition."[1]

On Sunday evening, May 12, 1619—only three days after the foreign delegates had departed from Dort—two of Barneveld's judges came to his prison to tell him that next morning he was to be sentenced to death. He was surprised, as well he might be; but he mildly asked leave to write a farewell letter to his wife. When paper and pen had been brought he began calmly to write. While thus occupied, three ministers came to prepare him for death. He said he had long ago prepared himself to die, but conversed freely with them and desired them to sup with him.

After supper he sent one of the ministers to the prince, asking his forgiveness if he had offended him, and his favor for the children he was about to leave. It is said that Maurice listened with tearful eyes,

[1] Davies, History of Holland.

declaring that he had always loved Barneveld; but that he had been vexed by the advocate's saying that he aimed at sovereignty, and by the personal danger to which the affair at Utrecht exposed him, for which he somehow blamed Barneveld. Still he said he forgave him, and would protect his children as long as they deserved it. When this message was reported to Barneveld he replied that he was not responsible as to the Utrecht affair, but admitted that ever since the year 1600 he had feared the prince was aspiring to the sovereignty.

After this they talked for some time about the doctrine of predestination, which was absorbing all minds; and Barneveld defended the milder view which the Arminians held with arguments so powerful that the ministers were amazed and silenced. Before taking leave they prayed with him; and afterward, as Barneveld found himself unable to sleep, one of them returned and read the prayers for the sick. In the morning they again waited upon him and read prayers, together with some chapters of Isaiah.

The French ambassador, who did not hear of Barneveld's sentence till four o'clock in the morning, sent to ask an immediate interview with the States-General. It was refused on account of the early hour; but he sent a letter earnestly pleading for Barneveld's life. The princess-dowager, widow of

William the Silent, tried in vain to obtain an interview with her stepson, the prince, on the same errand. The intercession of the English ambassador would probably have availed; but James hated Barneveld for various reasons, and his minister did nothing to save the advocate's life.

The sentence was pronounced in a lower room of the courthouse. It contained many accusations not previously made, as the venerable prisoner remarked. His estates were confiscated. "I thought," said he, "that the States-General would have been satisfied with my blood, and would have allowed my wife and children to keep what is their own." To this one of the judges sternly replied: "Your sentence is read; away! away!"

So the old patriot, supporting his steps with a staff and leaning on his servant's arm, calmly went out to die. The scaffold was in the public square in front of the great hall of the courthouse. A crowd of spectators filled the square and gazed from surrounding windows and roofs. Barneveld knelt on the bare planks of the scaffold, while the clergyman read the last prayer. After all was in readiness, he turned to the gazing multitude and with a firm voice exclaimed: "My friends, believe not that I am a traitor. I have lived a good patriot, and as such I die." Then drawing the black cap over his face, he bade the executioner be quick, and bowed his head to the stroke of the flashing sword.

Of the thousands who beheld the scene, many loved the man who had thus been put to death. Crowds pressed to the scaffold and carried away portions of the blood-stained wood and sand as relics. The remains were laid in a rough coffin and interred temporarily at the court church of The Hague. The States of Holland testified their high esteem for their advocate in their record of his death.

The other prisoners were kept in suspense for some time. The scaffold was left standing for fifteen days as if awaiting these other victims. But Grotius, especially, was a man of wonderful abilitiy and learning; it appeared hardly safe to proceed to that length in his case, lest all Europe should cry out. So both were sentenced to perpetual imprisonment in the castle of Louvestein.

Perhaps it is not surprising that in the excitement of the time many severe and unjust things were done by the party in power. It seemed almost as if the old days of persecution had come back. The Remonstrants could hold no meetings, even in private. If any one attended any assembly of theirs, he was fined twenty-five guilders, and required to tell who had gone with him on pain of being fined as much more. Anybody who would arrest a Remonstrant minister was offered a reward of five hundred guilders, and three hundred for catching one of their theological students. Ministers and students who persisted in preaching were sentenced to perpetual imprisonment as disturbers of the peace. At the same time the Lutherans and Anabaptists were allowed to have their public worship as openly as the Calvinists themselves; and even Catholics and Jews might hold private services. This discrimination against the Remonstrants was defended on the ground that the latter were innovators, subverting the established church, while the Lutherans and Anabaptists were sects as old as the Reformation. Had this been a sound argument, it would have been still more serviceable to the Roman Catholics.

Those ministers who had been condemned by the synod of Dort were offered a competent maintenance, provided they would not preach; but only one of the fourteen would promise that. So they were banished from the United Provinces without being allowed to arrange their affairs or take leave of their families. But they were given some money for their journey, and while in exile were treated with much consideration and kindness by many persons whom they met. All the rest of the Remonstrant clergy were deprived of their parishes and silenced; eighty of them, who would not cease preaching, were banished; and matters came to such a pass that for a time the meetings of the oppressed party were hunted up and dispersed by soldiers. Many took refuge in other lands, and — strange to tell — even in the provinces governed by the archdukes.

CHAPTER XXXI.

AFTER THE TRUCE.

THE little community of English Puritans dwelling in Leyden had grown somewhat, during these years of the truce, by the coming of one and another to join them; and they now numbered about three hundred. Captain Myles Standish, who had been serving in the war, was one who joined them in Leyden. They must have found the very air of a city that had such a history a perpetual stimulant to their love of freedom. We can imagine how they listened again and again to stories of the siege, from the lips of old men who bore a part in it all; or from those of men not yet old, who were children then, and well remembered the terrible famine. How often they must have climbed to the summit of the old tower, where the famishing people used to go in those dreadful days of hope deferred, to see if the ships were sailing over the flooded country to their relief! And with what emotion they must have gazed at the burgomaster's house, where the heroic Adrian van der Werf faced the desperate crowd of starving men and told them he would never surrender the town. Well may such scenes and memories have strengthened them for what they must themselves do and endure!

Meanwhile they had doubtless been watching the events in progress around them with anxious eyes. While they had found in Holland a temporary asylum from persecution, and freedom to worship God in their own way, the future seemed all uncertain. The truce would soon close, and none could tell what would follow. Besides, they could not help seeing that the influences surrounding their children were not in all respects what they could desire. They would inevitably forget their English tongue and their English ways if they remained there. Already there was more or less of intermarrying between the young people of Leyden and their own. If they would have their descendants English, they must go and make for themselves a home beyond the sea. And although their Leyden neighbors desired them to stay, declaring that in the whole time of their dwelling among them they had never given the least cause of complaint, the decision was made.

We all remember the story: what difficulties were in the way at the outset; what painful decisions between staying and going had to be made; the sorrowful parting at Delftshaven, the stormy voyage, the wintry landing at Plymouth, and the perils of their wilderness life. Two hundred and seventy-one years after they left Leyden[1] there gathered in that historic city the representatives of the great Independent churches of America and England, to honor the memory of that pilgrim band. A bronze tablet suitably inscribed, which had been placed in the wall of Saint Peter's church, over against the spot where the Puritans used to assemble, was then unveiled.

"That little Leyden church," says an able writer,[2] "is the parent of Independency alike in England and America." In the same article it is stated that in the twenty years following, between 1620 and 1640, upwards of twenty-two thousand emigrants to America sailed from English and Dutch ports — some reckon double that number. "The reasons that compelled their departure determined their quality; they were all men of rigorous consciences, who loved their fatherland much, but religion more. . . . Men so moved, so to act, could hardly be commonplace." He adds: "The growth of the New England States and their independency in religion exercised an extraordinary influence in England. It was the first realization, on a large scale, of the principles of Independency."

[1] The date of the ceremony here referred to was July 24, 1891. A pamphlet containing the addresses was published in the fall of that year at the Congregational House, Boston. See also The Congregationalist of 13 August, 1891, and other denominational papers about the same date.
[2] See article "Independency," in Encyclopædia Britannica.

From time to time, one and another of the banished Arminian ministers ventured back into the United Provinces; but they were as promptly arrested and imprisoned as if they had perpetrated a crime. Sometimes their friends contrived ways for their escape from the jails; and so the States of Holland resolved thenceforth to send all such cases to the castle of Louvestein, where Grotius and Hoogerbeets were confined. It was a remarkably strong fortress, standing on the point of land where the waters of the Meuse and those of the Waal unite. And after this, the party that opposed Prince Maurice used to be called "the Louvestein faction."

The eminent Grotius, who was a prodigy of learning and talent, was busy during his imprisonment in writing commentaries on the Gospels, and a work entitled "The Truth of the Christian Religion." His wife, Maria van Reigersbergen, had obtained permission to share his captivity; and sometimes she got leave to go out to borrow from some of his learned friends the numerous works which he needed to consult, as well as to purchase supplies. The books used to be sent to the castle from time to time in a great box, and when Grotius had done with them they were returned in the same way. At first the governor of the castle used to have the box opened and searched with care every time. But as nothing except books and supplies of linen was ever found, the box at length was suffered to pass without being examined at all.

And now a bright idea occurred to the faithful wife. Would it not be possible for her husband to be concealed in the box and thus make his escape? To be sure it was only a little more than four feet long, but it was broad and deep; and there could be some air-holes bored here and there where they would not be noticed. So she made Grotius get into the chest one day, and she closed the lid to try how long he could endure staying there. After several experiments, lasting two hours at a time, Madame Grotius arranged the details of her plan. She told the governor's wife, whose favor she had been careful to win, that some day before long she wanted the chest of books taken away; her husband pored over them so much that he was wearing himself out. And she confided the great secret to her trusty maid Elsie; for some one must go in charge of the precious box. Elsie was equal to the occasion, though she knew there would be peril to herself.

So one day when the governor of the castle was known to be absent, Grotius, very thinly clad, was locked up in the chest, and the soldiers were summoned to carry it out as usual. Lest they should notice that Grotius was not in the room, Maria had drawn the bed curtains close and left her husband's suit on a chair beside the bed, as if he were ill. When they lifted the chest the men said: —

"How heavy it is! Is the Arminian inside?"

"No," replied Maria, as if enjoying their little joke; "only the Arminian books."

The chest passed through the thirteen locked and barred doors and out of the castle without being overhauled; but there were not a few hairbreadth escapes before it was safe. It was taken across the river in a boat, and then Elsie persuaded the boatmen to carry it to the house of Abraham Datselaer, a flax merchant. One of them declared that there was something alive in the chest. "Oh," replied the quick-witted girl, "Arminian books are always full of life and spirit." When at last the chest was in the house Elsie was in mortal fear lest her master had been smothered by his long confinement, until he was found alive. He was now furnished with the clothes of a mason; and a master mason, John Lambertzoon, took him across the boundary of the United Provinces to Walwyk as one of his hands. Thence Grotius escaped to Antwerp, and at the close of the truce, then at hand, he went to Paris. He was treated with distinguished consideration by Louis XIII, who gave him a pension of three thousand guilders.

The next year Grotius published his book, "The

Justification of the Lawful Government of Holland and West Friesland." The States-General felt themselves aggrieved by it, and went so far as to forbid the book to be published or read in the Provinces. On that account people read it all the more.

The wife of Grotius was detained at Louvestein for a fortnight after his escape; but on petitioning she was set at liberty and praised on all sides for her wifely devotion as well as her brave and well-managed scheme. Hoogerbeets remained a prisoner for ten years.

The truce ended in August, 1621, having been prolonged by special arrangement for four months. The archdukes made proposals to renew it for a longer period, but they involved concessions which the Netherlanders would not make. So the war was resumed.

But the United Provinces were in a less favorable condition as to both their foreign and their domestic affairs than when the truce began. Their internal dissensions had done much harm in various ways, and the synod had cost them a million of guilders. There was no longer at the head of state affairs such a man as Barneveld. His successor, Adrian Duyk, could not compare with him in ability. Indeed, the wisest and best men of the nation, if not banished, had been turned out of office; and though there had been rapid growth in commerce, there seemed not to be money enough at hand to prosecute the war with activity.

The foreign powers that had heretofore been friendly were now cool toward the Netherland Provinces, or had something else to do. The terrible Thirty Years' War was going on in Germany. France had been displeased by the disregard of its intercession for Barneveld; the English king was intimate with Spain; the German Protestant princes dared not offer aid, in view of what had happened to the Count Palatine; nor was Denmark at present able to do so.

During the summer of 1621 the Archduke Albert died, but Isabella continued to govern the Spanish Netherlands, and Spinola was her commander-in-chief. In 1622 he laid siege to Bergen-op-zoom, intending afterwards to carry the war into Zealand. But Prince Maurice succeeded in relieving the city. This was the only gleam of good fortune that came to him after the death of Barneveld. From that time his military talents seemed to dwindle, and he found himself regarded with distrust by men who had been his warm friends.

In this same year one of Barneveld's sons, William, lord of Stoutenberg, formed a plot to assassinate Maurice. At the time of his father's death he had been deprived of the government of Bergen-op-Zoom, as well as of his own estates; and he keenly felt his wrongs. His elder brother, Reguier, lord of Groenveld, who had likewise suffered, was at length prevailed upon to become a party to the plot, along with several others. Stoutenberg, who was a hot-headed young man, urged that if Maurice, who had grown so despotic, were out of the way, the stadtholdership would naturally fall to his brother, Frederic Henry, and matters would then go on smoothly once more.

These young nobles did not intend themselves to strike the blow; but they hired several sailors, not telling them all, however, just what they were to do. It was planned to take place on the sixth of February, 1623, when they expected to surprise the prince riding from The Hague to Ryswick almost alone. But the evening before, the plot was betrayed, and most of the conspirators were arrested. Groenveld, who had been reluctantly drawn into the conspiracy, suffered death; and so did fifteen other persons, some of whom had no real connection with it. But Stoutenberg escaped, and afterwards bore arms against his country, under the standard of Isabella.

People were very sorry for Groenveld, although they could not justify him. Nor did they think it ought to be considered high treason simply to *conspire* against the life of one who was not a sovereign. On the whole, the affair resulted unhappily for the prince. He became more and more sensible that in putting

Barneveld to death he had cut off his own right arm. As time went on, and ill fortune seemed ever to attend his undertakings, he exclaimed bitterly that God had forsaken him. Public affairs, missing the sagacious head and able hand that had so long guided them, fell into confusion. The army was so small and ill equipped that it was unprepared for the service demanded. "As long as the old rascal was alive," exclaimed Maurice with bitterness, "we had counsels and money; now there is no finding either the one or the other!"

In 1624 the States-General did succeed in making a fresh alliance with France; the prime minister, Richelieu, felt that they must be sustained, lest the house of Austria should become too strong. The king promised to loan them a million florins a year, for three years. And as James had not been able to marry his son to the Infanta of Spain, he consented to help the Provinces once more, by making a defensive alliance with them for two years. But almost as soon as it was done there came news of a serious difficulty between the Dutch and the English in the East Indies; so that the old ill feeling between them was revived. Indeed, James was not a comfortable ally at any time, and often made himself disagreeable to his best friends.

Spinola now resolved to besiege Breda, which had

been held by the United Provinces ever since the time when Captain Heraugière captured it by the stratagem of the turf-boat. As it belonged to the house of Nassau, Maurice lost no time in reinforcing its garrison. The marshes surrounding it delayed Spinola's operations not a little; and Maurice took time to capture three less important places in the vicinity, expecting to be on hand by the time Spinola had really begun operations. But it proved that his able antagonist was more than ready, and Maurice was forced to withdraw, leaving Breda to its fate. This disappointment wore upon his health, already impaired by a disease of the liver, and it soon became evident that the great general had not long to live.

He sent for his brother Frederic Henry to come to him from the camp. There had been a coldness between them, for Frederic Henry was inclined to favor the Remonstrant party. As Maurice had never married, his title and estates would belong to his brother; he now urged Frederic Henry to marry the Princess Amelia of Solms. This marriage took place only three weeks before the death of the prince, which occurred April 23, 1625. He was only fifty-seven years of age, though he had been stadtholder for nearly forty years.

To Prince Maurice had been given a grand part to perform in the Netherland struggle for freedom. It is hardly possible to value too highly what he accomplished for his country as a general and commander-in-chief. Under his training the armies of the United Provinces became the best in Europe. They achieved success at last in what had appeared a hopeless strife. The prince's gifts as a statesman, however, were not equally remarkable; it may have been in part because, from the beginning of his career, he could let the able Barneveld manage for him in civil affairs. While his patriotism was sincere and unwavering, what he had to do for his country was not only in the line of his predominant tastes, but it also brought him a large income and abundant honors. Had the contrary been the case, it is not certain that he would or could ever have said, like his noble father: "I have always put my personal interests under my feet; and thus I am resolved to do while life remains." In the latter part of his career he was thought too arbitrary and ambitious; yet perhaps it was only what almost always happens to those who for a long time possess great power. But the blood of Barneveld has left upon the memory of Maurice an indelible stain.

CHAPTER XXXII.

THE CONCLUSION.

AFTER Maurice's death Frederic Henry was immediately appointed to the command of the army and navy of the republic, and before long he became also stadtholder of the two principal provinces, as his brother had been. Being no less able and brave as a general than was the late prince, while he was superior in statesmanship and more disposed to be tolerant, his administration was acceptable and successful. In a few years the theological dissensions subsided, and there was nowhere greater religious liberty than in the United Netherlands. It was not until 1648 that the war was finally ended by the treaty of Westphalia, sometimes also called the peace of Münster. But it was in Germany that the chief part of the conflict was raging, under the name of the Thirty Years' War, which was ended by the same peace. The little Netherland republic was completely triumphant. Spain renounced absolutely and finally all her pretensions to dominion there.

In this great conflict "the creative power of civil

and religious freedom "[1] is strikingly shown. Nature had not lavished her gifts upon the Low Countries; yet the people had somehow turned their disadvantages to excellent account. Even while they were fighting for their freedom, and because they were fighting for it, they were growing prosperous and strong. Before the war was over the republic had won a place in the front rank of nations. In commerce as well as in manufactures it took the lead of them all. It is said by Motley that nowhere was there so large a production in proportion to numbers. Everybody was at work; there were no beggars, and not many paupers. Things beautiful as well as things useful came from those deft and busy hands. There were laces, velvets, brocades, and tapestries, as well as linen, broadcloth, and more common fabrics. Their fisheries and commerce required three thousand ships and nearly one hundred thousand seamen.

In agriculture they gave lessons to the rest of the world. Not only were their cattle the finest in Europe, and their butter and cheese demanded by other countries, but they made discoveries and improvements in the methods of agriculture which were of immense value. It was the Dutch, says a great writer on such matters, who "extended the cultivation of winter roots from the garden to the field, and gradually taught

[1] United Netherlands, v. 4:314.

European nations how to preserve cattle in sound condition through the winter, and to banish scurvy and leprosy by the constant supply of wholesome fresh diet." He adds that the extensive cultivation of the turnip and potato, and similar roots, has made it possible to maintain three times as many persons on the same area of land as could be fed before these methods were known. It should be remembered, too, that success with such crops is much less doubtful than with the various grains. The Netherland farmers also introduced or improved what are called forage plants or artificial grasses — clover, red and white sainfoin, and lucerne, called alfalfa in the United States. It was nearly a hundred years before the English generally adopted these improvements, and still longer before other nations did so. The Dutch had a passion for flower-gardening, particularly for the culture of bulbs. In 1635 and 1636, tulips were all the rage, and bulbs of the most admired species brought fabulous prices. To the present day this seemingly cool and prosaic people are enthusiasts in respect to the culture of flowers.

Learning of all kinds was eagerly cultivated in the Netherlands. More books were printed in Holland than in all the rest of Europe. Its universities were famous the world over. Its learned scholars mastered the languages of the East and gave them to the world.

They were foremost in scientific investigation, and in the healing art they possessed superior skill. Statesmen were there instructed in finance, merchants in banking and credit, soldiers in military engineering, and philosophers in metaphysics. The fine arts had also many devotees. There were already not a few great painters, whose works are the admiration of our own age; and among the middle classes at that day, as well as among the nobles, there was a genuine appreciation of good pictures. There were a great many churches, town halls, and other public buildings whose architecture was admirable.

Motley has declared that "it is impossible to calculate the amount of benefit rendered to civilization by the example of the Dutch republic."[1] The unquenchable longing for freedom was communicated from nation to nation and from age to age. For more than sixty years, English soldiers used to cross over to the Netherlands and fight side by side with the Netherlanders in their battles and sieges, sharing their aspirations no less than their dangers and sufferings. "There was scarcely a man in England," says Markham, "who had not either served himself, or known a relation or neighbor who had been in the wars. . . . The whole generation imbibed and imparted to their posterity a zeal for popular rights. . . . The war of

[1] United Netherlands, 4:550.

independence had a lasting influence on the formation of opinion in England. It thus led to the civil war in defense of the liberties of the old country, and to the founding of colonies in America."[1]

"The Hollanders," says Thorold Rogers, "gave the first precedent for civil and religious liberty. . . . It was before the minds of those who drew up the Declaration of American Independence."[2] It might be added that they likewise furnished, almost unwittingly, a rough outline for a republican union. Imperfect as it was, it has served a good purpose. Their rude model has proved instructive to not a few other nations, who have had occasion to study the subject since. It has been improved, adapted to varying needs, and put to severe tests. Republics have come to be the prevailing form of government in no small portion of the world. Their civil and religious liberty has a powerful influence even where no republics exist. Well may we give thanks for the grand results of that brave fight for freedom in the Netherlands!

[1] From the preface to The Fighting Veres.
[2] Story of Holland, preface.

INDEX.

Albert, Cardinal Archduke. Appointed governor-general, 172; personal traits, 172; takes Calais, 173-175; magnificent style of living, 190, 214; promptness in mustering an army, 221; captures forts, 222; defeats Count Ernest, 228; in the battle of Nieuport, 235, 240; lays siege to Ostend, 249, 252; awaits the surrender, 264; disappointment, 266; denounces mutineers, 274; death, 353.

Amsterdam, bank of. Origin and management, 326; great importance, 327.

Anjou, duke of, 16.

Antwerp. Vast commerce, 19; strategic importance, 20; situation, 22; weak government, 24; quarrels, 26; supplies for siege, 27; bridge begun, 29; river closed, 34; attempt to break the bridge, 37; courage of citizens, 42; attempt on the dike, 44; bitter disappointment, 52; negotiations, 52; famine, 53, 55; surrender, 54; what might have been, 56; consequences, 57.

"Archdukes." *See Albert and Isabella.*

Armada, Spanish. Vessels and equipment, 124; plan for invading England, 126; fatal oversight, 126; disasters off Cape Finisterre, 127; sails from Coruna, 128; uprising of England, 129; Macaulay's poem, 129; disaster in the channel, 131; skirmishes, 132; in Calais roads, 133; the panic and flight, 134; storms and wrecks, 136; Spain in mourning, 136; England's deliverance, 138; Spanish account, 138, *note*.

Armada, the second. Equipment and plan, 183; its fate, 183.

Arminian controversy. Beginning, 327; the "Remonstrance," 328; five points of Arminianism, 329; the "Contra-remonstrance," 329; synod of Dort, 331; delegates all Contra-remonstrants, 331; Arminian ministers summoned, 332; canons adopted, 333; sentence of Remonstrant clergy, 333; results of the synod of Dort, 335; banished clergy, 344, 349; expense, 352.

Arminius, Jacob, professor at Leyden, 327, 328.

Aragon, admiral of. *See Mendoza.*

Barneveld, John of, advocate of Holland. His letter to Leicester, 108; gets hold of letters written by Leicester, 116, 117; ambassador, 198; his scheme for invasion of Flanders, 218; alienation between himself and the prince, 247; is sent to ask aid of James I, 275; favors the peace party, 307; rebukes bribery, 310; in peace commission, 315; tolerance, 330; arrest, 336;

intercessions in his behalf, 337, 341; unfair trial, 338; last hours, 340; sentence and execution, 342.

Barendz, 184, 185.

Beemster lake, 324.

Berlaymont, Count, 289.

Breda. Situation and history, 144; stratagem for taking its castle, 145; delays and perils, 146; citadel seized, 148; capture by Spinola, 355.

Brewster, Elder. At Leyden, 323.

Brussels. Fall of, 34.

Buckhurst, Lord. Sent to the Netherlands, 112; his good influence there, 112; blamed by the queen and Leicester, 113.

Bucquoy, Count. At siege of Ostend, 252, 253, 280.

Burleigh, Lord. His counsel, 64; is berated by the queen, 76, 121.

Buys, Paul, 102.

Cadiz. Sacked by Dutch and English, 177.

Cadzand, 286, 287, 288.

Caron, Dutch envoy to England, 197, 215, 217; brings news of Nieuport victory, 245.

Catherine de Médicis. Advised by her envoy, 23; pretended claim to crown of Portugal, 62.

Ceralbo, marquis of, 163, 164.

Dialyn, Paul, Polish envoy. Pompous orations, 191.

Dort, synod of, 331.

Drake, Sir Francis, admiral. His exploits at Cadiz and Lisbon, 120; comment on the Armada, 136.

Duvenwood, Admiral, 176.

East India Company, *Dutch*. When formed, 271; capital and management, 271; founds trading settlements, 272; wins Amboyna and the Moluccas, 300; ill feeling toward the English company, 301.

East India Company, *English*. Date of charter, 270; original capital, 271.

Edmunds, English envoy. His mysterious visits to the "obedient" provinces, 215.

Elizabeth, queen of England. Encourages the Netherlanders, 63; declines to become their queen, 63; her speech, 66–68; manifesto, 69; proposes to send Leicester, 70; anger at Leicester's disobedience, 76; letter to Leicester, 103; ill-humor toward the Netherlanders, 106, 110, 111; sends Lord Buckhurst, 112; private directions to Leicester, 117; desires peace, 121; sends deputies to confer with Parma, 123; her thanks for help against the Armada, 140; plot by Philip II for her assassination, 167; her proposal regarding Calais, 174; grand pageant to solemnize the alliance against Spain, 180; secret treaty with Henry IV, 181; reply to Polish envoy, 191; invited to desert the States, 216; joy over the Nieuport victory, 245; her death, 274.

England. Population, 58; able queen, 59; small revenue, 79; gallant uprising to repel the Armada, 129; naval expedition of English and Dutch against Lisbon, 141; second expedition a great success, 176–178.

Ernest, Archduke. Made governor of the Netherlands, 166; characteristics, 166; inefficiency, 167; death, 170.

Ernest, Count, of Nassau, *or Ernest Casimir*. With the army invading Flanders, 219; hears of the archduke's approach, 222; sent to hold the bridge of Leffingen, 225; desperate resolve, 226; sudden panic of troops and utter defeat, 227; at siege of Sluys, 286.

Escorial, 203.

Estates-General, or States-General. *See Netherlands.*

Farnese, Alexander, prince of Parma. *See Parma.*

Fleming, Philip, auditor of Ostend, 267, 268, 269.

France. Next in power to Spain, 58; effeminacy of the king, 61; three factions, 142; the League, 143; civil war in France supported by Philip II, 143.

Frederic Henry of Nassau. What occurred at his christening, 19; commands "the new beggars," 215; with the army in Flanders, 219; in the battle of Nieuport, 234; at siege of Sluys, 286; at Mülheim, 300; at Rheinberg, 302; marriage, 356; succeeds Prince Maurice, 358.

Fuentes, Count. Succeeds Archduke Ernest *pro tem*, 170.

Gertruydenberg. Betrayed to Spaniards, 140.

Gianibelli. Why he hated Spain, 35; his floating volcanoes, 36; the explosion, 39; the needless failure, 41; second "hell burner," 43.

Gomarus, Francis, professor at Leyden, 327, 329.

Grave. Besieged by Count Mansfeld, 80; relief attempted, 81; battle, 81; city reinforced, 83; treachery of the commander, 83; his execution, 84; city taken by Prince Maurice, 273.

Groenveld, Regnier, lord of. Involved in conspiracy to kill the prince, 353; his death, 354.

Grotius, Hugo, pensionary of Rotterdam, 329; his arrest, 337; not amenable to the States-General, 339; sentence, 343; works written in prison, 349; his wife contrives his escape, 350; his book interdicted, 351; pension from Louis XIII, 351.

Gwynn, David, galley slave. Captures two galleys of the Armada, 128.

Harlem lake. Draining of, 324.

Haultain, Admiral, 297, 304.

Heemskerk, Admiral, 272; attacks a great Spanish fleet before Gibraltar, 312; wonderful victory, 312; his funeral, 313.

Heidelberg catechism. Quotations, 334.

Hemart, Baron, 80, 83, 84.

Henry III of France. His reception of the Dutch envoys, 61; his costume, 61; duplicity, 63; his assassination, 142.

Henry IV of France and Navarre. Leader of the Huguenots, 142; right to the French crown, 150; besieges Paris, 150; Philip's secret offer of his daughter's hand, 168; war declared by Henry against Spain, 170; he besieges La Fère, 173; anxiety to relieve Calais, 174; insincere in the triple alliance, 182; easily converted to Romanism, 193, 196; makes peace with Spain, 201; is willing to proclaim the decrees of Trent, 217; his delight over the Nieuport victory, 246; real aim, 276; promises to help the States in obtaining peace, 313; private ends,

318; is succeeded by his son, Louis XIII, 337.

Heraugière, Captain. At the Kowenstyn fight, 49; takes Breda, 145-148, 355.

Hohenlo, Count. Recovers Fort Liefkenshoek, 36; at the Antwerp banquet, 51; sent to Grave, 81; lieutenant of Prince Maurice, 110; characteristics, 119; at Turnhout, 188; death, 305.

Hoogerbeets, pensionary of Leyden. Arrested, 337; imprisoned at Louvestein, 343, 349, 352.

Howard, Lord-admiral. Fights with the Armada, 132-135; puts on "a brag countenance," 135; in the expedition against Cadiz, 176.

Isabella Clara Eugenia, Infanta of Spain. Receives the Netherlands as a gift, 202; marries Archduke Albert and comes to Brussels, 212; personal traits, 214; expensive housekeeping, 214; addresses the army, 222; takes defeat serenely, 241; conduct at Ostend, 252, 264, 295; governs after Albert's decease, 353.

Jacobzoon, Jacob. His blunder with the fire ships, 37; fails to send up the signal rocket, 41.

James I of England. His accession, 274; hesitates to aid the Netherlanders, 275; makes peace with the archdukes, 296; results, 297; hates Barneveld, 342.

James, Captain. His remark about the defeat at the Kowenstyn dike, 50.

Jeannin, French envoy to the Netherlands. Aids in arranging the truce, 319, 321; advice about a council of state, 325.

John, Count, of Nassau, 15; his death, 305.

Klauszoon, Vice-admiral. His desperate sea fight, 304; blows up his ship, 305.

"Koppen-Loppen." *See Jacobzoon*.

Kowenstyn dike, 43; first attack upon it, 44; grand assault, 45; almost a victory, 46.

Leicester, Robert Dudley, earl of. His personal traits, 70; what the queen intended him to do in the Netherlands, 71; triumphal progress, 72; admiration of the Low Countries, 73; accepts the governor-generalship, 75; neglects to apprise the queen, 75; sends Davison, 75; professes great penitence, 77; is straitened for funds, 85; invests Zutphen, 86; desperate fight, 90; letter regarding Sidney, 96; visits England, 100-102; the queen's gracious welcome, 103; difficulties occasioned by his bad management, 103; his generosity, 108; returns to the Netherlands, 117; leaves finally, 119.

Lewis Gunther of Nassau. At Nieuport, 231, 234, 237, 238; letter to Lewis William, and reply, 243; generous sacrifice, 244; at siege of Sluys, 286; dies there, 292.

Lewis William of Nassau, stadtholder of Friesland. Improves military tactics, 153; opposes the plan to invade Flanders, 218; at siege of Sluys, 286; encounters Spinola, 291; at The Hague, 315.

Liefkenshoek, Fort. Taken by Spaniards, 28; recovered by Zealanders, 36.

Lillo, Fort, besieged, 29.

Linschoten, 184.
" Little Troy," 283, 292, 293.
Louis XIII, king of France. Intercedes for Barneveld, 337, 341; kindness to Grotius, 351.
Mansfeld, Count Peter Ernest. At council of war, 47; brief word to Count Charles, 49; besieges Grave, 80; battle with English troops, 81, 83; in command after death of Parma, 166.
Marquette, Lord of. At Nieuport, 234; commands at Ostend, 283, 293.
Maurice, Prince of Nassau and Orange. His youth, 13, 52, 144; first military exploit, 86; placed at the head of government, 110; captain-general, 116; recovers Breda, 148; improvements in the army, 153-156; campaigns in Parma's absence, 156-160; plots against his life, 168; brilliant victory at Turnhout, 186-188; successful campaign on the eastern frontier, 195; adroit generalship, 212; disapproves the scheme of invading Flanders, but obeys, 218; arrives at Nieuport to begin a siege, 220; heroic decision, 232; words to his army, 234, 239; thanksgiving for victory, 241; modest account of the battle, 244; takes Rheinberg, 254; takes Grave, 273; besieges Sluys, 286-292; outposts captured, 287-289; defeats relief convoy, 289; town surrendered, 292; at Mülheim, 299; hindrances, 301, 303; not in favor of peace, 307; meets peace commissioners at Ryswick, 314; opposes the truce, 317; provision for the Nassau family made by the States, 322; the prince sides with Contra-remonstrants, 330; arbitrary measures, 331, 338; reply to last message of Barneveld, 341; assassination plotted, 353; unhappy days, 354; fails to save Breda, 356; his death, 356; his character, 357.

Medina Sidonia, Duke of. Commands the Spanish Armada, 124; against his will, 138; burns his vessels at Cadiz, 177.
Mendoza, Francis de, admiral of Aragon. His campaign in the German duchies, 212; at Nieuport, 235, 239, 242; encamped, 273.
Moreo, Commander, 161, 162.
Mutinies of troops, 154, 167, 273, 290, 303.
Nantes, Edict of, 201.
Netherlands, The United. Great principles vindicated by their contest with Spain, 14; the "obedient" provinces, 15; union of the seven northern provinces, 15; small extent of their territory, 16; its dense population, 17; desire protection of France or England, 58; offer made to Henry III, 60-62; sovereignty offered to Queen Elizabeth, 64; she declines, but pledges aid, 66-69; they make Leicester governor-general, 74; alienations and annoyances, 100-104; treasons at Deventer and Zutphen, 104; further treasons, 105; provisional government set up, 109; letters to the queen, 110; naval expeditions against Spain, 120, 141, 176, 185; loss of Hulst, 178; triple alliance against Spain, 181; duplicity of the allies, 181; exploring

Arctic seas, 184; reply to the German emperor's offer of mediation, 190; distrust toward England and France, 196; the States remonstrate with the queen, 197; envoys sent to Henry IV, 198; stormy interviews with Elizabeth, 199, 201; heavy taxation self-imposed, 213; invasion of Flanders planned, 218; great fleet mustered, 219; delayed by headwinds, 220; battle of Nieuport and its results, 236–239, 246; famous siege of Ostend sustained, 248–295; Sluys recovered, 286–292; envoys sent to James I, 275; peace party and opponents, 306; envoys sent by the archdukes, 307, 308; armistice arranged, 309; Neyen's bribes rejected, 309; victory over Spanish fleet at Gibraltar, 312; defensive alliance with Henry IV, 313; with England, 313; peace commissioners received at The Hague, 314; ambassadors from other courts, 315; difficulty about permitting the East India traffic, 316; duplicity of Philip III, 317; his demands, 318; negotiations broken off, 319; French and English envoys propose a long truce, 319; great opposition, 319; feeling against Barneveld, 320; powerful influence of his speech in the assembly, 320; truce concluded, 321; final arrangements, 322; activity in arts of peace, 324; defects of the constitution, 325; edict of mutual toleration in theological views, 329; political strife arises from the Arminian controversy, 330; severe treatment of Remonstrants, 343; close of truce, 352; fresh alliance with France and with England, 355; end of the war, 358; the republic prospers, 359; commercial and industrial activity, 359; agricultural improvements, 359; the tulip mania, 360; effect upon English soldiers of serving in the Netherland war, 361; influence of the Netherlands upon America and the world, 362.

Neyen, John. His diplomatic mission to the States, 308; gifts to Aerssens, 309; returns from Spain, 310, 318.

Nieuport. How situated, 220; a siege impending, 221; approach of the archduke's army, 224; Count Ernest's defeat, 227; dilemma of the besieging forces, 231; the field of battle, 232; the victory won, 239.

Norris, Sir John. In the ambuscade, 89; in command, 103; quarrel with Leicester, 102; brings a message from the queen, 140.

Oldenbarneveldt. *See Barneveld.*

Ostend, 123, 242; beginning of the siege, 248; how situated, and why so important, 248, 250; sum offered by Flanders in aid of the siege, 249; what Dunkirk privateers had been doing, 249; the defenses of the town, 250; the cannonading, 253, 255; talk of abandoning the detached forts, 256; a parley asked and hostages sent, 258; commissioners sent by the archduke, 258; tricks to gain time, 258-265; the conference, 262; besiegers exult too soon, 264; reinforcements arrive, 264; attack on the Sandhill, 268; sluice opened, 269;

heavy loss of the besiegers, 269; outworks lost, 277; Spinola takes command of the besieging army, 279; successive commandants of the town, 280-283; damage done by a gale, 292; capitulation, 293; the garrison welcomed by the prince, 293; what was thought of the siege, 294; immense waste of money and human lives, 294; ultimate result, 295.

Pacchi, Don Pedro. His apparition seen at the head of his legion, 50.

Parma, Alexander Farnese, prince of. His ancestry and characteristics, 21; previous military experience, 21; uses bribery, 23; begins the siege of Antwerp, 29; bridge building, 31; letters to Philip II, 33; his narrow escape, 39; repairs the shattered bridge, 41; letter about the Kowenstyn fight, 50; enters Antwerp in triumph, 54; gets the citadel rebuilt, 55; financial straits, 79; takes Grave and other towns, 84; storms Neusz, 85; quits Rheinberg to relieve Zutphen, 88; besieges Sluys, 114; deceives the queen, 121; cannot assist the Armada, 126; ordered to invade France, 144; chagrin at losing Breda, 149; successes in France, 152; failing health, 161; ill treated by Philip II, 161-163; secret slanders, 162; second campaign in France, 164; sudden death, 165.

Philip II of Spain. His wire-pulling in France, 33; what he would never concede, 53; conquers Portugal, 62; instructions to Parma, 122; meddling in France, 143, 150; insincerity, 162, 163; plots, 167; repudiates his debts, 189; deeds the Netherlands to his daughter, 202; health fails, 202; distressing journey to the Escorial, 203; prepares for death, 205; plans the funeral pageant for himself, 206; last hours, 208; a perplexing question, 209; teachings of Machiavelli, 210; a hypocrite finally self-deceived, 211.

Philip III of Spain, 301, 309, 312, 317.

Pilgrim Fathers. *See Puritans.*

Puritans, English. Settle in Leyden, 323; life there, 324, 346; reasons for going to New England, 347; commemorative tablet set up at Leyden in 1891, 348; Independency originated there, 348.

Rheinberg. Besieged by Parma, 85, 87; by Prince Maurice, 254, 255; captured by Spinola, 302.

Richardot, president of privy council, 314, 315.

Robinson, Pastor. At Leyden, 324.

Sainte-Aldegonde, Philip de Marnix, lord of. Burgomaster of Antwerp, 25, 40; premature rejoicing, 46; capitulates, 52.

"Sausages." Contrivance used in besieging Ostend, 252.

Serrano, Don Matteo. Conference with Vere, 258, 263.

Sidney, Sir Philip. His ancestry, 91; his father's letter, 92; travels on the continent, 93; is sent to Vienna, 93; opposes the French marriage, 94; literary works, 94; governor of Flushing, 95; aids Prince Maurice in taking Axel, 86; wounded at Zutphen, 95;

self-denying act, 95; what Leicester wrote of him, 96; his chaplain's account of his last days, 96-98; universal grief at his death, 98; Spenser's poem, 99.

Sidney, Sir Robert, 174, 175.

Sluys. How situated, 114, 287; besieged by Parma, 114; heroism of its women, 115; desperate daring of the besiegers, 117; surrender, 118; besieged by Prince Maurice, 286-292; extremity of famine, 290; surrenders, 292; ghastly procession passes out, 292; pestilential atmosphere fatal to Count Lewis Gunther, 292; value of Sluys as a seaport, 284, 293.

Spinola, Marquis Ambrose. Put in command of besieging army at Ostend, 279; person and character, 279; makes progress, 281; tries in vain to relieve Sluys, 291; gives banquet to the Ostend officers, 293; reforms abuses in the Spanish army, 298; invades the United Provinces, 298; illness and lack of funds, 301; takes Rheinberg, 302; comes to The Hague with the peace commissioners, 314; magnificent style of living, 314; takes Breda, 356.

States-General. *See Netherlands.*

Stoutenberg, William, lord of. Plot to assassinate Prince Maurice, 353; escapes, 354.

Swint, the, 286.

Treslong, Admiral, 27.

Turnhout, victory of, 186.

Utrecht, union of, 15, 339.

Van den Berg, Count Frederic, 159, 252.

Van den Berg, Count Herman, 158.

Van den Hove, Anna. Buried alive, 194.

Van der Berg, Adrian, 145.

Van der Waecken, Admiral. His privateering, 249.

Varax, Count, 186, 188.

Verdugo, Francis, 88, 159.

Vere, Sir Francis. At Sluys, 115; vice-admiral, 176; at Turnhout, 187; in Flanders, 219; at Nieuport, 224, 231, 235, 237, 245; commands at Ostend, 252; wounded, 255; his stratagem to gain time, 257-264; letter to the States, 265; personal appearance, 261; called to field duty, 269, 272.

Vere, Sir Horace, 267.

Verreiken, envoy of the archdukes, 310.

Vervins, treaty of, 202.

Walsingham, Secretary. Comments on the queen's ill humor, 106, 111.

Wilkes, Councillor, 100, 107.

William the Silent, prince of Orange, 13, 15, 16, 19, 20, 22, 28.

Williams, Sir Roger, 118.

Zapena, 229.

Zutphen. Location and history, 86; invested by Leicester, 86; attempt to relieve it, 88; fight near Warnsfield church, 90; betrayed by York, 104; recaptured by stratagem, 157.

www.ingramcontent.com/pod-product-compliance
Lightning Source LLC
Chambersburg PA
CBHW030358230426
43664CB00007BB/646